IN LOVE
AND IN
BUSINESS

IN LOVE
AND IN
BUSINESS

**How Entrepreneurial
Couples Are Changing
the Rules of Business
and Marriage**

SHARON NELTON

JOHN WILEY & SONS
New York · Chichester · Brisbane · Toronto · Singapore

Copyright © 1986 by Sharon Nelton

Published by John Wiley & Sons, Inc.

All rights reserved. Published simultaneously in Canada.

The author is grateful for permission to use portions of
Chapter 1, Chapter 2, Chapter 11, and Chapter 12, which
previously appeared in *Nation's Business*.

This publication is designed to provide accurate and
authoritative information in regard to the subject
matter covered. It is sold with the understanding that
the publisher is not engaged in rendering legal, accounting,
or other professional service. If legal advice or other
expert assistance is required, the services of a competent
professional person should be sought. *From a Declaration
of Principles jointly adopted by a Committee of the
American Bar Association and a Committee of Publishers.*

Library of Congress Cataloging in Publication Data:

Nelton, Sharon.
  In love and in business.

  Bibliography: p.
  Includes index.
  1. Couple-owned business enterprises—United States—
Management.   2. Work and family—United States.
3. Interpersonal relations.   I. Title.
HD62.27.N45   1986   658.4'09   86-15997
ISBN 0-471-83949-3

Printed in the United States of America

10 9 8 7 6 5 4 3 2 1

To my parents,
W. E. and Mary Forthman,
who are retired
from their business
but still in love

ACKNOWLEDGMENTS

My deepest appreciation goes to the couples and individuals who agreed to be interviewed for this book or to answer questionnaires about being in business with their mates. Time and again I was amazed by—and grateful for—the openness with which they discussed their businesses and their private lives. I was touched by how much they wanted to share their experiences so that others could benefit. How much I learned from all of them! Not just for this project, but for my own life.

Through many conversations, Dr. Marta Vago, a friend and colleague, helped me in the early stages to understand many of the issues I would be dealing with. Her wisdom and professional and personal experience played a very large part in shaping this book.

Many of my colleagues at *Nation's Business* and the Chamber of Commerce of the United States gave me support and encouragement. Let me particularly single out David A. Roe, Robert T. Gray, and Henry Altman, who all recognized that this project was compatible with the goals and spirit of *Nation's Business.*

Thanks go also to fellow journalist Seth Kantor and to my literary agent, Julian Bach, for helping this project become a reality, and to my family and friends, for being so understanding when I had to sacrifice the pleasure of their company in favor of writing.

John B. Mahaney won my heartfelt appreciation for being a firm but gentle and supportive editor. He is the kind of person who makes the hard work of writing seem easier.

And thanks, especially, to Muammer Sagmanligil, my longtime partner in life and my major source of nurturance.

SHARON NELTON

Reston, Virginia
July 1986

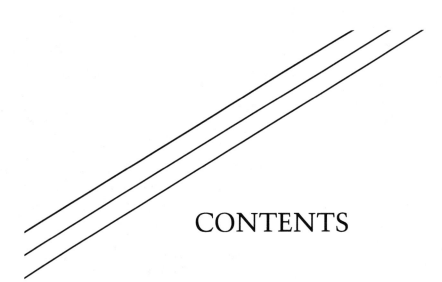

CONTENTS

INTRODUCTION

"Run a Business with *MY* Spouse?"

"I could never run a business with *my* spouse! Together 24 hours a day? You gotta be kidding." Those words reflect the most common reaction I received when people learned I was writing a book on husbands and wives who go into business together.

The second most common reaction seemed to be: "Where do you find all these couples?"

They haven't been difficult to find. The springboard for this project lay in the fact that, as an editor at *Nation's Business* magazine charged primarily with writing about entrepreneurs, I kept running into husband-and-wife business teams—so much so that their frequency took me by surprise. I drew early inspiration from couples like Rebecca and Dan Matthias of Philadelphia, who founded Mothers Work, which produces maternity wear

1

for businesswomen and now has retail stores in 20 major cities; Maureen and Ramon "Gene" Law of R. E. Law Instrument Inc., a Palos Hills, Illinois, high-technology firm that makes and repairs sophisticated temperature control systems; Elizabeth Andrews and Ben Ellison of The Baby Bag in Camden, Maine, whose infant products appear regularly in the catalogs of such outdoors outfitters as L. L. Bean and Eddie Bauer; Joseph and Dorothy Bahnatka, who started Med-Care Convalescent Supply Company, a home health care equipment firm in Rhinebeck, New York, and quickly expanded to nearby communities; Jon and Christel DeHaan of Indianapolis, who played a major role in shaping the time-share industry in the United States by introducing the concept of vacation exchange via their company, Resort Condominiums International; and Lorraine Mecca and Geza Csige of Micro D, one of the country's largest wholesale distributors of microcomputer software, hardware, peripherals, and accessories. Based in Santa Ana, California, Micro D had reached more than $100 million in annual sales before its founders decided to withdraw and move on to other things in 1985.

As my awareness of entrepreneurial couples was sharpened, I began to see that some of our best-known companies are the products of wives and husbands working together: Estée Lauder; Best Products Company, Inc.; the Marriott Corporation; Mrs. Fields Cookies; Häagen-Dazs; and Liz Claiborne Inc., for example.

One thing about these companies seemed markedly different from most of the traditional family-owned enterprises I had encountered. The wives appeared to be as totally involved as the husbands. The businesses were not just "his" businesses. They truly were "his and hers." Ultimately, it seemed to me that there were so many couples running so many interesting, growing companies and having so much fun doing it, they merited closer scrutiny. They were making an impact not only on the way business is done but on how marriage is perceived, helping to make room for women at the top and serving as models for male–female relationships in which equality is more fully realized than in the past.

For couples who are already in business together, this book should offer a useful window into the lives of others who combine business with their personal relationships, showing where such men and women succeed and where they know they fall short. The way they live and work can be a source of knowledge and sometimes inspiration for any couple hoping to improve their own efforts at meshing a business and a relationship.

For couples who are thinking of going into business together, the experiences so generously shared by the women and men in this project can help lead the way to a more sound decision. And for couples who decide to go ahead, this book can be a guide for helping them make their decision work.

While the emphasis here is on growing businesses, start-ups have been included as well. Not only was every large company once a start-up, but the start-up stage is crucial, not only in the life of the business but in the relationship of the entrepreneurial couple. It is a period that frequently requires major adjustments by the man and woman involved, adjustments that if not made can endanger the well-being of the relationship and thwart the potential of the business and even lead to its failure.

Indeed, substantial attention is given to the pitfalls of combining a love relationship with running a business. A business can take its toll on a marriage; likewise, a crisis in the marriage or a couple's personal life can take its toll on the business. We meet divorced and separated people, a woman who had to lay off her husband, men and women who kept businesses going while mates battled psychological traumas or devastating illnesses, and spouses who had to face the death of beloved partners. We encounter fear, jealousy, resentment, rage, guilt, and grief.

Nevertheless, the focus of this book is on success—that is, on the elements that make these relationships work. And so we also encounter respect, trust, caring, and the thrill of personal growth. Most of the people who appear on these pages are involved not only in thriving businesses with their mates but, at least to the eye of an outsider, their marriages appear to be flourishing as well. Some of the couples have been together more than 40 years; Wilbert L. (Bill) and Genevieve W. Gore of W. L. Gore & Associates celebrated their fiftieth wedding anniversary in 1985 and were still in business together when Bill passed away in July 1986.

The findings here are based primarily on the author's personal interviews, conducted especially for this project, with 63 individuals representing 34 businesses and relationships. In nearly all cases, wife and husband were interviewed together. (One exception was a reluctant husband who pleaded that he was too busy. He gave me about 10 minutes of his time, and the rest of the interview was conducted solely with the wife.) Early on, I recognized that the dynamics of talking with a man and a woman together offered far more than interviewing each separately. I could see how the two related to each other—how they interrupted each other, agreed or disagreed with the other's interpretation of events, argued with each other (on one occasion, quite heatedly), laughed together, and teased each other. I could observe body language—a touch on the knee, an exchanged glance whereby one gave the other permission to tell me something. All these nuances would have been missed had they been interviewed separately.

In five cases, the subjects were interviewed without the mate because they were separated, divorced, or widowed. In a most extraordinary interview, I talked with Janet Makrauer and her son, George A. Makrauer, together. Mrs. Makrauer is president of Amko Plastics Inc., a Cincinnati plastic bag manufacturing company that she founded with her husband, Irvin, who died in 1983. George, in his early forties, is the company's executive vice president.

I met with Mrs. Makrauer during Small Business Week in 1985 when she was in Washington to be honored as Ohio's

Small Business Person of the Year. George and his family had accompanied her, and he was helping her get settled in her hotel room. He was most solicitous, straightening his 71-year-old mother's tie, bringing her an ashtray, and getting glasses of ice water for both her and me.

It was a lovely afternoon in May and George intended to take his family to the National Zoo. But something about the beginning of the interview with his mother caught his attention and, thinking to make an observation or two before he left, he began to talk with a passion that belied his quiet courtesy. The success of husband-and-wife businesses, he declared, is "in direct contradiction to what is generally perceived to be the definition of a family business, and that is a business dominated by male members of the family, either brothers and/or cousins who are involved." In his experience, he said, most family businesses fail over the long term because of suspicion and jealousy over who does what and how they are compensated for it. That doesn't happen with couples, he contended, because "there is a team closeness between a husband and a wife that does not exist between brothers and certainly not between cousins." George described himself as a "beneficiary" of the relationship between an entrepreneurial couple and admitted being "a son who misses his father and loves his mother."

I asked him if he could stay and be interviewed with his mother. He laughed and said, "The panda can wait for me." The results of his decision make special contributions to the chapters on the relationships of entrepreneurial couples with their children and the effects of personal crises on businesses.

The second major source of material for this book was found in responses to a questionnaire returned by 60 individuals representing 32 businesses and 33 marriages. (Two couples came from one business.) Candidates for the questionnaire were sought through classified advertisements in *Nation's Business*, *Ms.*, and *Working Woman* magazines; from referrals by people who knew couples in business; from newspaper and magazine clippings;

and from such sources as the U.S. Small Business Administration and the Center for Family Business in Cleveland, Ohio.

It is a lengthy, time-consuming, and personal questionnaire, yet one or both partners of more than a third of the 96 couples invited to participate chose to respond. They patiently and thoughtfully added invaluable information to what I had already gleaned from the personal interviews.

Other sources include interviews with psychologists, accountants, family business consultants, and other authorities; conversations with employees and children of entrepreneurial couples and other "significant others," such as business partners, franchisees, and the like; interviews I had conducted prior to this project for magazine articles; and, of course, newspaper and magazine articles by others, books, and broadcast interviews.

In most instances, the couples are truly entrepreneurial in the sense that they started their own businesses. In several cases, however, the businesses were inherited or purchased; they are included because the couples at the helm are entrepreneurial in their approach to business or simply because their insights make a valuable contribution.

None of the people I interviewed asked not to have their names used, and nearly all were open beyond my expectations, frequently volunteering personal information I did not even seek. Only rarely did they ask that a comment not be used or refuse to answer a question—usually because it involved a company statistic they did not want revealed or something they thought might disturb the privacy of a family member or employee. For the most part, they wanted to tell their stories and to share what they could of their experience with other couples who were weighing the pros and cons of becoming business partners.

The questionnaire responses were infused with the same spirit of sharing. Only 7 of the 60 respondents asked that their names and the identities of their businesses not be revealed. I have honored their requests and have, when necessary, disguised the nature and location of a business to maintain the privacy of a respondent or an interviewee.

It should be emphasized that the author is a journalist, not a scholar. This is not a formal research study; the sample is not a scientific one. What appears here is a journalist's report. It reflects the views and experiences of the participants, along with my own observations, and offers an examination of how many couples blend business with their most intimate relationship. Those who do it well offer proof that bringing a marriage and a business together can enhance both. And for many, doing this provides a challenging and joyous lifetime experience.

1

THE NEW PARTNERSHIPS

Pop Used to Be the
Entrepreneur, Mom the
Bookkeeper. No More.

Back in Poland years ago, Olga Erteszek's parents were in business together. They had a small shop in Krakow where her mother was a corsetiere and her father was the enterprise's "administrator."

Olga followed in her parents' footsteps. In 1940, she and her new husband, Jan, left their war-torn country for California. Having learned the trade from her mother, Olga got a $16-a-week job making brassieres in a Los Angeles sweatshop while Jan, whose credentials as a lawyer in Poland were of no use in the United States, set out to write a book.

But Olga was shocked to see so many otherwise elegantly dressed American women securing their stockings by rolling them up under their knees over a band of elastic. Only the peasant women did that in the old country. It was ugly.

"Somebody should at least make a garter belt to support the hose," she complained to Jan. "Why don't you do it?" he challenged. Hesitantly, she agreed, first making Jan promise that he would go out and try to sell the samples that she made.

Using a nest egg of $10, the Erteszeks bought $5 worth of lace, satin, and decorative flowers and rented a sewing machine with the other $5. Olga designed four samples and, keeping his word, a red-faced Jan went out and made his first sale.

Thus The Olga Company was born. And the entrepreneurial Erteszeks built their famous lingerie firm to annual sales of more than $67 million before they sold it to Warnaco in 1984. Until Jan's death in June 1986, which occurred just as I was completing this book, the Erteszeks continued to preside over the company and its 1,800 employees and 13 factories, Jan as chairman and Olga as vice president of design.

As the Erteszeks demonstrate, Mom and Pop businesses are not what they used to be. Many of today's entrepreneurial couples are reaching beyond the desire just to make a good living for themselves and are creating businesses that not only provide jobs for great numbers of people but that sometimes even change the way business is done or make an impact on society.

There are pioneers like Sydney and Frances A. Lewis, who

shaped the catalog showroom industry with Best Products Company, Inc., which they started with one showroom in Richmond in 1957 and nurtured to $2.5 billion a year in sales and, during the busy Christmas season, over 25,000 employees nationwide. Or Estée Lauder and the late Joseph H. Lauder, who in 1946 founded what is now one of the world's best known cosmetic companies, with estimated sales of more than $1 billion a year. Or Wilbert L. (Bill) and Genevieve W. Gore, who started W. L. Gore & Associates, Inc., in the basement of their Newark, Delaware, home and built it into a multinational company, with Gore-Tex fabric the best known of its many products.

In today's entrepreneurial world, it seems, you can't turn around without bumping into husbands and wives who are in business together. Very successful businesses. Debra J. and Randall K. Fields of Park City, Utah, have opened more than 350 Mrs. Fields Cookies stores in the United States and a half-dozen other countries. Marion O. and Herbert M. Sandler of Oakland, California, acquired a tiny two-branch savings and loan with 25 employees in 1963 and turned it into Golden West Financial Corporation; with more than $12 billion in assets in 1985, it was the sixth largest S&L in the country and a darling of stock analysts. William T. and Sharon (Sheri) Criswell, who own or have under construction more than $600 million in real estate development, are changing the skyline of Dallas with innovative office structures. And Elisabeth Claiborne Ortenberg and Arthur Ortenberg have made fashion and business history at the helm of Liz Claiborne Inc. The firm, noted initially for clothing that appealed to career women, went public in 1981, and in December 1985, *Forbes* ranked it the fourth top-performing new issue of the previous 10 years. Sales in 1984 exceeded $380 million.

It used to be that Pop was the entrepreneur and Mom did the bookkeeping in the back room. If she was out front, she was the receptionist. It was "his" business.

But now, Mom is often an equal partner. Or she's spearheading the company while Pop plays a behind-the-scenes role.

Unfortunately, there are no official statistics on the total number of businesses controlled by husband-and-wife teams or unmarried couples. According to Thomas A. Gray, director of economic research for the U.S. Small Business Administration, nonfarm sole proprietorships operated by married couples are increasing steadily at about 5 percent a year. In 1983, the last year for which figures are available, there were 461,955 sole proprietorships run by couples, up from 440,000 in 1982. If farms are added, the husband–wife business teams jump to well over 900,000.

The trouble is that no figures are kept on corporations and partnerships run by couples, so the statistics available greatly underestimate the numbers of businesses operated by wives and husbands. Of the 66 businesses whose owners participated in interviews or questionnaires for this book, for example, well over half are corporations. Fewer than a dozen are sole proprietorships. Companies like Best, Liz Claiborne, and Gore—and even smaller enterprises, like Century 21 Oasis Realtors, Inc., a Calumet Park, Illinois, company owned by Desi A. and Kay Humphries, or the Akron Women's Clinic, an abortion and birth control center owned by Norma M. and Stephen Goldberger—don't show up as couple-run companies in federal statistics.

Jointly operated businesses are also hidden in the figures on sole proprietorships. In the past, more often than not a husband was listed as the owner of a business, even if his wife put in eight or more hours of sweat every day. And this is still common. Today, the SBA is proclaiming female-owned businesses as the fastest-growing segment of new businesses. An estimated 3 million of the country's 13 million sole proprietorships belong to women. But just as women may have been obscured in ownership records, men may be concealed, deliberately or not, in newer statistics. For example, Karen's Canvas, a small Fort Myers, Florida, manufacturing firm, is a sole proprietorship in Karen Quade's name, although her husband, Dennis, is a co-founder and is as fully involved in the business as Karen is. And Deborah H. J. Livingstone-White of Oak Park, Michigan, is the president

and 100-percent owner of International Consultants, a sole proprietorship of which her husband, William Tyrone White, is
vice president. She started the company, they reason.

SBA's Tom Gray says that not only are husband–wife business
teams increasing in real terms, but women are now being given
more recognition for the contributions they have long made to
family businesses. Where once wives may have played vital but
unrecognized roles in family enterprises, couples are now taking
steps to assure that on paper, a wife is a full and legal partner.

"POETS AND PACKAGERS OF NEW IDEAS"

Craggy-faced and bearing a lion's mane of white hair, Robert
L. Schwartz, a former Time-Life journalist, runs the School for
Entrepreneurs in Tarrytown, New York. He is an entrepreneur
himself—in 1963, he bought the 26-acre Mary Duke Biddle estate
overlooking the Hudson River and turned it into the Tarrytown
House Executive Conference Center, the first such center to be
run on a for-profit basis. The facility attracts meetings of executives from major corporations, and Cornell University calls
Schwartz the "granddaddy of the conference center concept."

Schwartz spent some time in California in the early 1970s
looking at the "human potential" centers. The press, he says,
saw in the centers throngs of people "out for a hedonistic experience in the hot tubs," but Schwartz saw latent entrepreneurs,
people with creativity and energy who marched to a new drum-
beat. Turned off by the notion that entrepreneurs were hustlers
and promoters, they shunned the business world. "But in fact,"
says Schwartz, "they had within them the seeds of a whole
new vision that has marketplace meaning."

To help such potential entrepreneurs overcome their reluctance to get into business, Schwartz launched his school at the
Tarrytown Center in 1977. Since then, it has attracted more
than 1,000 students, who have spent two weekends trying to

determine whether they can turn themselves into entrepreneurs or expand endeavors they have already started.

"Many of these people are exploring new ways to change the world and themselves," says Schwartz. "It's a time for a new kind of society and a new kind of human, and they're very interested in that sort of thing."

Schwartz likes to describe entrepreneurs as "the poets and packagers of new ideas." Victor Kiam of Remington Products, Inc. (he's "the man who bought the company") is less lyrical. "For me," he says in his book, *Going for It!,* "entrepreneurs are those who understand that there is little difference between obstacle and opportunity, and are able to turn both to their advantage. Their willingness to seize initiative sets them apart from their contemporaries. Entrepreneurs don't sit on their haunches, waiting for something to happen. They make things happen."

Entrepreneurs are risk takers, he continues. They are "willing to roll the dice with their money or reputations on the line in support of an idea or enterprise. They willingly assume responsibility for the success or failure and are answerable for all its facets. The buck not only stops at their desks, it starts there, too."

Entrepreneurs may tell you they are after money or power, because those things are easy for others to understand, says Andrew S. Grove, president and one of the founders of Intel Corporation. But he contends that the real force that drives entrepreneurs is the need to prove themselves right. The critical characteristic of an entrepreneur, he says, is the ability to see something that is not there yet. "It's like an artist. He can envision a statue or a painting by staring at nothing. In the same sense, a person who creates a business or product does so by looking at a blank canvas." If the individual trusts that vision enough, Grove continues, he pushes on to convince himself and the rest of the world that "the mirage or image that he sees is really for real."

Venture capitalist A. David Silver of Santa Fe, New Mexico,

also likens entrepreneurs to artists, saying they have "quite a bit in common, not the least of which is the desire to do some one thing really well."

Entrepreneurs who form businesses with their spouses are similar in characteristics and motivations to entrepreneurs who are loners or who go into business with someone other than a mate. And they are just as complicated. Honey bee breeders Susan Cobey and Timothy Lawrence created Vaca Valley Apiaries in Vacaville, California, not because the business would bring them wealth (though that would be nice) but because they are crazy about insects and share an intense desire to keep the North American bee stock free of the aggressive and unpredictable Africanized bee, whose presence, they feel, would be dangerous to American agriculture. Their entomology careers had separated them in the past, and being in business together also serves the purpose of keeping them in the same geographic location. Frustration at not being able to find maternity clothes suitable for herself during her first pregnancy convinced Rebecca Matthias, then the finance director of a small computer company, that there was a market for clothing appropriate for "pregnant executives," and she and husband Dan set out to prove it with their company, Mothers Work.

A passionate belief in natural foods was one of the shared values that first brought Tony and Susan Harnett together, so when they went into business in 1975, they bought a small and faltering natural food shop called Bread & Circus that was doing about $110,000 a year in sales. At first they operated it with Tony and one employee; Susan had just had a baby and was staying at home. Their company, located in Boston, has since grown to four supermarkets and 300 employees. Tony says his mission "is to help the world and society to be a healthier and happier place through nutritious food," a goal Susan wholeheartedly supports. "I have a hard time conceiving of people going into business just to make money," says Tony. "To me, it is wrong. There is nothing wrong with making money, but just to make money, you sell your soul. The business should be one that you are really proud to be part of." When you feel good about the business and you are doing a service to society, he says, "then money comes naturally because you are doing something important and something worthwhile."

When Micro D, the Santa Ana, California, computer distributorship founded by Lorraine Mecca and her husband, Geza Csige, went public in 1983, Mecca, then majority stockholder and chief executive officer, had holdings estimated at $59 million. But when you ask her if money is what drives her, she replies, "No. It's a great scorecard. The bottom line tells you yes, it was a success, or no, it wasn't. But money is not a main motivator."

What pushed her, she says, was the simple desire to be in business for herself. "I had worked for a number of other people and didn't feel that I was always appreciated or got to do many of the things I thought I was capable of doing." (Charlotte Taylor, a Washington, D.C., management consultant who specializes in business start-ups, says the would-be entrepreneur should be able to say yes to the question, "If I had a choice of earning twice as much working for someone else, would I still rather be my own boss?")

In the business relationships formed by entrepreneurial couples, the spirit and vision common to entrepreneurs everywhere are evinced by one or both partners. In many cases, the partners appear to be equally matched in entrepreneurial zest; even without the other, that man or that woman would still be an entrepreneur. In other cases, one partner is clearly more entrepreneurial, inspiring the other to share and support the dream, much as Estée Lauder persuaded Joe to join her in her vision of building a cosmetic empire. This is not to say that the "driver" is more important to the enterprise. Jan Erteszek was chairman of The Olga Company; clearly the leader, he was a much-admired executive, lauded, for example, by University of Southern California management professor James O'Toole in *Vanguard Management*. Even *Who's Who in America* listed Jan and omitted Olga. But could The Olga Company have existed without Olga? Not likely.

Susan Kennedy Stangland readily admits that husband Chris is the driving force in Pepperwood International Corporation, a $3-million-a-year Eugene, Oregon, company that manufactures toys and educational products. "But I'm the navigator," she says. Chris may chart the course but she keeps them on it "by offering inspiration, clarity, and common sense. I'm a terrific partner for Chris and when we veer off course, it's usually because he didn't listen closely enough to me."

Entrepreneurs often take on partners—the potential benefits are many. When the combination is right, partners can complement each other and strengthen a company's management and ability to grow. Many entrepreneurial couples claim their business partnership is no different from any other business partnership. No matter who your partner is, they say, you want to be in business with someone you trust, someone you work well with, and someone who balances your strengths and weaknesses.

Nevertheless, entrepreneurial couples *are* different from other partnerships. A man and a woman involved with each other in an entrepreneurial venture sleep with their business partner on a regular basis, make and rear children together, and go to their partner's parents' home for Thanksgiving dinner. Many, though not all, speak of the added motivations of wanting to enjoy the company of a mate during business hours and even of wanting the bonds of the personal relationship itself to be strengthened by the common interest in the business. In short, entrepreneurial couples are not just business partners, they are intimates. Their business life becomes one with their personal life, and though some complain of not being able to separate the two, many don't try and don't care. They like it that way.

POISON OR PARADISE?

The reaction of many people when they learn a couple is in business together is to say: "And you're still married?" Many of us just can't conceive of a 24-hour-a-day relationship with a spouse.

"For some couples, being together all the time is poison," says psychologist Marta Vago, of Santa Monica, California. "Their personality makeup is not such that they can tolerate that amount of closeness with another person."

But others thrive on the togetherness. Randy Fields of Mrs. Fields Cookies says his relationship with Debbi "is time-dependent. If we don't spend a lot of time together, it doesn't work. We get lonely. We get angry with each other. It's a mess."

Men and women who are successfully meshing business and personal relationships find that blending the two offers some major benefits. *First, it enhances the marriage or personal relationship as well as family life.* The reasons are many, but some of those most frequently suggested by entrepreneurial couples are:

□ Because of the intensified sharing, the bonds between a man and a woman are deepened. I. N. "Skip" Schatz says: "I think our life is more interesting and more whole because we are in business together. We have so much more common ground." He and his wife, Joanne, own a string of Maryland and Virginia Vertech Back & Bed Stores, which sell adjustable beds and other back-related products, as well as the Virginia Adjustable-Bed Manufacturing Corporation.

"We share so many more things now," says real estate developer Bill Criswell, whose wife, Sheri, an attorney, joined the Criswell Company after it was launched. He won't equate being in the same meeting with your spouse when a big tenant agrees to take a lease in your building with being in the delivery room together when your children are born. Still, he says, they are both "mutual relationship experiences rather than *my* experience or *her* experience," and because they are shared, they draw a man and a woman closer together.

"We've experienced the joy of creating, together, something

from scratch and seeing it sold worldwide," says Pepperwood's Susan Stangland. "We've shared the frustrations, long hours, and hard work of building a dream, puzzle piece by puzzle piece. The dream, of course, is still far from being complete, but we're enjoying the wonder and the terror together as we continue to build."

Robert Harnish of the Cortina Inn in Killington, Vermont, points out that a couple can take joint pleasure from the accolades, too, as in 1985 when he and his wife, Breda, were named Innkeepers of the Year for the state and in 1983 when they were named the Vermont Small Business Persons of the Year. The latter experience, which he describes as "incredible," meant a trip to Washington, recognition in their home state, and a variety of speaking engagements. It widened their circle of friends and led to invitations to serve on a number of boards. Says Harnish: "This honor came to the two of us together; we basked in the glow together. Of course, when things go wrong in business, we suffer together."

□ Spouses find they understand each other better because they can see what the other goes through during the day. Jeanette and Howard Shapiro run Howard-Shadim Electronics, Inc., a Crystal Lake, Illinois, firm that repairs television cable converters and other electronic equipment. Jeanette, a former marriage counselor, recalls a period before their business partnership when Howard was an ambitious policeman bucking for police chief. He spent so many nights and weekends working and taking law enforcement courses, she felt neglected. It was a troublesome time for their marriage. Now, as Howard's business partner, she sees how involved he becomes in his work. In the early days of their enterprise, she was working alongside him weekends. "If I hadn't been there, I would never have understood," she says.

"The main advantage of being in this mess together is that it allows complete understanding of what the other person is going through because you are going through the same thing. You have the same concerns," says D. Elisabeth Aymett, co-owner of Cecil's Messenger Service in San Pablo, California. "Someone who was not in the same business might resent the personal sacrifices. Our personal lives must be put on hold at times to take care of business. We have a mutual understanding of the reasons behind that."

□ Depending on the nature of the business, being partners can offer a couple a superbly rewarding lifestyle. Innkeeper Robert Harnish says vacations are a time for "picking up ideas from other resorts and innkeepers around the world." Cookie makers Debbi and Randy Fields spend part of their time in a Hawaiian condominium where, secluded from office life and sheltered somewhat from business telephone calls by the time zone difference, Debbi can work in the kitchen on new recipes. Not only is Hawaii her new product development center, but being there offers her and Randy more time with their children.

When President Gnassingbe Eyadema of the Republic of Togo experienced one of Joanne and Skip Schatz's beds in the presidential suite at Washington's Vista International Hotel, it was, the Washington *Times* reported, a "case of mattress diplomacy, or love at first snooze." The luxurious, oversized bed, complete with massager, had originally been installed for the six-foot-eleven president of Senegal. Eyadema sent the Togo ambassador to find out where it was made. Then, at a cost of more than $20,000, he ordered four of the custom-built beds for his own personal use in his four homes in Togo. The Schatzes were asked to fly to the West African country at Togo's expense and oversee the installation of the beds. They spent a week as guests of the president, who had them accommodated in a five-star hotel on the beach. They were escorted in a chauffeur-driven car and personally looked after by the president's nephew. They had one short visit with the president. And, between sightseeing trips, they did their job and installed the beds. "We were in every one of the president's bedrooms," recalls an ebullient Skip. "I mean, when I was sweating, I would use the president's Kleenex. If I had to go to the bathroom, I would use his toilet."

□ For women, going into business offers some additional advantages. Says Vieve Gore of W. L. Gore & Associates: "A woman who has raised a family, done the shopping, taken care of her husband, taken care of her house, done her decorating, done whatever social things she needs to do—church, women's clubs, whatever—is a very capable individual. And yet, when she goes out into the marketplace, she has a hard time finding a job." That's the point she was at when, on the Gores' twenty-third wedding anniversary on New Year's Day, 1958, she and her husband went down to their basement to start their company. "It was absolutely fantastic for me to have a job to go to—one that we were working on together," says Vieve, now in her seventies and still working.

For younger women, being in business with a spouse offers a way to combine motherhood with a stimulating career. Paula Hamilton and her husband, Raymond "Sugar Bear" Hamilton, a former defensive lineman for the New England Patriots, own and operate Hamilton Printing and Graphics, a $500,000-a-year quick printing company in downtown Boston. Paula, who keeps toys in the office safe, recalls going home and returning with the two Hamilton sons and bedding them down in a sleeping bag once when she and Raymond had to work the night through in order to meet a job deadline. But usually, she says, the business affords her the flexibility she needs to run the children to appointments and events and be there when they need her. Sometimes Raymond takes over the parental duties while she goes to a business meeting.

Frances Lewis, who was in her mid-thirties when she and Sydney started Best Products, was of a generation where it wouldn't have occurred to her to go out and get a job unless she needed the money—which she did not. "I'm wondering what would have happened to our marriage and to me if I hadn't fallen into this," she says. Until then, most of her time, when she was not looking after their three children, was spent in volunteer work. "Yet I realized, after I got into this business, that I was so happy doing this that I wondered what would have happened to my life had I been stuck back there without real work outside the home to do. It made everything much better for me."

The second major benefit of being in partnership with a spouse is that it can result in a more successful business. This can happen for many reasons:

□ It can get off the ground faster. Sydney Lewis says he does not think Best would have been as successful as quickly as it was without Frances. He would not have been able to afford to hire someone to do what Frances was doing. And, he adds, "I think her knowledge of me and my knowledge of her, together with what independent ability we had, made a lot better possibility for success than had there been somebody else." He trusted Frances' judgment, he explains, and he doesn't think he could have placed as much confidence in someone else's judgment. "And trusting that judgment made us move a lot faster."

□ There can be a greater commitment to the business on the part of the partners when they are husband and wife. "You're tremendously more involved and there is absolutely no question about the agreement between you on the objectives," said Bill Gore. "A husband and wife are in it together. They win or lose together. Both of them are trying to make the business a success and whatever it takes to make it successful, that's what they'll do."

Or as Bill Criswell puts it, "We know that our financial and personal interests are entirely compatible, which would not be true of partners—no matter how close they were—if they weren't financially tied to each other through marriage."

□ Business decisions made in the give-and-take between partners are better than they would be if made by one person acting alone. Disagreement can even benefit the process. "It's not uncommon for Howard to start out in right field and me in left field," says Jeanette Shapiro. "The more heated discussions happen when we're really kind of polarized, but we come to an intermediate position, which I often feel is better than either of us started out with."

The ability of partners to serve as a check and balance on each other is also a positive part of the decision-making process. Karen and Dennis Quade of Karen's Canvas disagreed originally over his suggestion to add a line of awnings to what was their major product, boat covers.

"Denny's got ideas coming and going all the time," says Karen. "He always wants to do all these things. I tend to have my feet on the ground a little bit more. I'll say, 'Well, do we really want to do that?' If we both agree on it, after we've talked about it, then we go ahead." They went through that process about the awnings after attending industry meetings on the subject. Now it appears that awnings will be their biggest growth area.

Some spouses—Sydney Lewis, and Debbi Fields among them—deny that there are any disadvantages to working with one's mate. But observers of family businesses, as well as marriage and family therapists and many entrepreneurial couples themselves, know it's not a state of total bliss. There are disadvantages, too.

For one thing, reports Sheri Criswell, there is nobody waiting at home to whom you can say, "Boy, was that guy I work with a pain today!" Says psychologist Marta Vago: "Whether it's fair or not, we do use our spouses for sounding boards and sometimes dumping grounds. You need a safe place in which to express your frustrations or to express whatever is in your heart. But if what you are frustrated about is the business you are sharing with that person across the dinner table, you may have no one to unload on."

Before going into business with each other, many a husband and wife dream about how wonderful it will be to be together all the time. When they learn how difficult it is to separate their business life from their personal life, some couples find their dream begins to resemble a nightmare. "There is no escape!" laments Rebecca Matthias. "You can't unload your problems on your spouse because he's had the same ones." And because Mothers Work is located in the Matthias house, she says, "we can't even change the scenery by going home."

Some couples find that when things go wrong in business during the day, they can go wrong in the bedroom at night. Rocco and Dianne Altobelli, who own the Rocco Altobelli beauty salons in St. Paul-Minneapolis, recall a period of high stress, when the business was beginning its rapid growth to current annual revenues of $5 million.

"We had a lot of arguments, and we brought business home," recalls Rocco. "What would drive me crazy is that we would get ready for bed, and she would bring up some business management things that I hadn't dealt with. That would tee me off, and I'd be up until 4 in the morning thinking about that. And I would yell at her, 'Don't ever tell me anything before I go to bed!' "

There are disadvantages for the business, too, when a husband and wife are at the helm. Not only do couples sometimes take their business arguments home with them, sometimes they also bring their personal arguments to work. And if they haven't sorted out responsibility and authority, employees get confused and production may suffer. A husband-and-wife enterprise, like a family business, is also more vulnerable to a personal crisis than a business where principals are not related to one another.

Some couples learn to adjust their lives to their business and to make room in their business for their personal relationship. When couples don't adjust, marriages fail and businesses frequently go down the tubes with them. At best, such marriages and businesses limp along while the partners carry on an uneasy truce.

COMMON THREADS

The down side of being in business with a spouse and how couples cope with the problems that confront them are discussed at length in the chapters that follow. Most of the couples interviewed for this book appeared to be successful in blending business and marriage, as did a majority of those who returned questionnaires. Because each personality—and therefore each marriage and business—is different, there is no one model for success. But among the couples represented here, some common threads emerged. While they were not all present in every successful couple, they are useful to know.

Marriage and children come first. "Both of us concluded that the most important thing in the world to us was our relationship to each other," says Randy Fields. "Without that, it wouldn't matter whether we had whatever is called business success."

Don and Judy Quine, who run the Professional Karate Association from their Beverly Hills, California, home, each brought three children to their marriage. Don says they decided that if business "got us out of joint with each other, we would ditch the business." They knew the well-being of six children was at stake.

The spouses demonstrate enormous respect for each other. Olga Erteszek says her husband had "great business acumen"; he praised her creativity and inventiveness. Dianne Altobelli says Rocco is excellent at motivating people; he takes pride in her management skills. Debbi Fields calls Randy a "financial genius"; he calls her "a phenomenally good business person."

Respect is the "glue," according to Bill Criswell. "If you respect the other's opinion, even if you're mad as hell about it and you don't like what you're hearing, you have to stop and sit back and think about it and weigh it and consider it when you're finally making a decision."

There is a high degree of close communication. To the Quines, for example, communication about both marriage and business issues is important. If either party is not happy, says Judy, "you really have to talk about it. If you don't confront it, it isn't going to go away. It is going to fester and turn into something that may destroy this unit that you both want to retain." The Quines are highly confrontational, arguing readily both in their business and personal lives, in private and in front of others. Other couples prefer quieter, though not necessarily less intense, modes of communication.

The partners complement each other's talents and attitudes, and they carve up turf accordingly. Howard Shapiro handles sales, production, engineering, and new product development, while Jeanette oversees personnel and administration, which includes relationships with bankers, attorneys, and accountants. Employees in Howard's area answer only to him; those in Jeanette's, only to her.

The partners are supportive of each other. Randy Fields, a successful financial planner in addition to being vice president of Mrs. Fields, loaned Debbi $50,000 to start her first cookie store. Vieve Gore prodded Bill to follow his dream, even though it meant leaving a well-paid and satisfying career with Du Pont.

Bill Criswell says he never would have had the courage to start the Criswell Company if Sheri had not given him advice and support. "She gave me the absolute freedom to fail. She let me know that if the business didn't work out, if I tried it and gave it my best, I would not have a wife who would look on me as a failure."

Entrepreneurial couples have strong family ties. The Fieldses and Altobellis frequently take their children with them on business trips. In many cases, many—sometimes all—of a couple's children join the business. The Gores early on shared a majority of the corporate stock with their children, overriding the advice of lawyers who warned that children don't always turn out the way their parents want them to. Son Robert became president of the company, and all the Gore children are directors.

Spouses compete with the world outside, not with each other. Bill Criswell speaks for most entrepreneurial couples when he suggests that the way they approach their special world recalls the outlook of the determined couple trying to wrest a farm out of the prairie: "We're fighting the weather, we're fighting the pests, we're fighting the bank and everybody else, but we're doing it together."

They like to laugh. Humor helps them keep things in perspective. It eases disagreements. It reminds them that they're in this thing not only because it's their bread and butter but also because they want to have a good time. Many husbands and wives seem to rely on the ability of the other to infuse difficult situations with a sense of comedy or simply to inspire laughter and make the day more fun. Debbi Fields breaks up, for example, when Randy lifts her arm and brags to a visitor about the beautiful bracelet he has purchased for her. She is wearing a rubber band around her wrist. And when Jan Erteszek (who was interviewed with his wife about a year before his death) told the story of selling Olga's first garter belts, his eyes started to twinkle and he began to embellish it, simply to tease Olga: "I didn't know a garter belt from a bale of hay. So when she made them, she said, 'Why don't you go and sell them?' I said I couldn't do it; it was indecent for a man to do this. She said, 'You promised.' And, you know, when a wife tells her husband that 'you promised,' she puts you on your best behavior."

They put their egos in check. While it is typical for the lone entrepreneur to be a person with a tremendous ego, one that often gets in the way of good management, the entrepreneurs who form contemporary business partnerships with their spouses either come into the business with the ability to rein in their egos or, sometimes painfully, they learn how. They make a commitment, spoken or unspoken, to give the partner an adequate voice in the business as well as in the personal relationship. Says Susan Harnett of Bread & Circus: "I respect Tony for what he is, and he respects me for what I am, and we don't ever try to hurt each other, step on each other's toes, call the shots or pull the carpet out from each other." If a wife is not really playing a pivotal role but is, for example, functioning as the receptionist, Tony says, "It is his business, and she just has a job there." It's not really a partnership.

In the final analysis, couples tend to agree that a business has a better chance of succeeding when a couple's relationship is on sound footing before they start. It may simply be too much for a man and a woman to cope with a new business and an unstable relationship at the same time.

Linwood A. "Chip" Lacy, Jr., has worked as an executive for two entrepreneurial couples—Sydney and Frances Lewis at Best and Lorraine Mecca and Geza Csige at Micro D. He became chairman of Micro D when Mecca and Csige left in 1985. One of the first things that strikes Lacy about both situations was the caring he saw between the spouses. "There was obviously a great deal of love and devotion in both cases." He is inclined to believe that the love is what makes the entrepreneurial relationship work.

Mecca also suggests that an entrepreneur's emotional house has to be in order. "You do not have time to exert any mental effort in any direction other than your business," she says. "So if you are trying to build an emotional relationship, you can't do it. One or the other has to fail—either your relationship or the business."

With a laugh, she adds: "You have to be happy with either fidelity or celibacy."

2

GETTING STARTED

Entrepreneurial Couples Are
Team Players

Some people fight tooth and nail to become entrepreneurs. They know, perhaps from childhood, that they are destined to run their own businesses and to bring their dreams to the marketplace.

Others become entrepreneurs in spite of themselves.

A pretty, dark-haired young Philadelphian, Rachel Borish, aspired to a career as a concert pianist in the early 1970s. She enrolled at Conservatoire Rachmaninoff on the Right Bank in Paris, and, for the first time in her life, felt she was blossoming as a student. Then she suffered the first of what would be recurring attacks of tendinitis in her forearms; the devastating pain prevented her from playing the piano and forced her to return home to recuperate and to face an uncertain future.

She finally graduated from Cornell University in 1975 with a degree in French and found herself living with her parents in Philadelphia, depressed and looking for a job. Her sister-in-law suggested that to earn some extra money, Borish might try selling the brownies she was known for among family and friends. Chock full of chocolate chips, they tasted like a cross between fudge and a mousse, with just a touch of cake—Borish today describes them as "voluptuous" and "decadent."

Following her sister-in-law's advice, she began to bake brownies in her parents' kitchen and to sell them, one pan at a time, to a small produce store in the quaint, historic Head House Square area not far from her family's home and near the Philadelphia waterfront. She wrapped the brownies individually in plastic wrap and delivered them herself on a plate of her mother's fine Noritake china. They sold so well that she soon found another outlet, a nearby ice cream store.

In its "Best and Worst of Philly 1976" issue, *Philadelphia* magazine declared Rachel's Brownies as the best in the city, and suddenly Borish's little pastime was on its way to becoming a real business with great potential for growth—definitely not a part of her plan.

An idealist then (and now), Borish saw business as a "dog-eat-dog world that encouraged the basest instincts in human nature and suffocated all that was potentially noble and inspiring in people." Her early success with the brownies posed a troubling conflict for her. In a talk she prepared for students at the request of her alma mater, she said: "Privately, I defined myself as a creative, artistic person who yearned to contribute something beautiful to the world through, if not music, then surely something literary or likewise high-minded. Publicly I had gained an instant identity as a businesswoman—someone trading in cold cash with a product for hire." For her, the agonizing question was how to reconcile the two identities.

"I decided that the only possible compromise was to take the brownies to a couple more stores, ever so slowly, without fanfare, without calling it a business, to keep my dreams on hold for a while, and to see what would happen," she recalls.

Still baking in her parents' kitchen, Borish married photographer Jeffrey Slater in 1978. While Borish felt mortified that she was a college graduate baking brownies for a living and still had a "private loathing for business," enjoyment of her success was creeping up on her. "I was beginning to get a kick out of the fact that something I was doing with my own two hands was pleasing people and making me some money. The brownies were developing into a cult status around the Penn campus; everywhere I delivered the brownies, people acted thrilled when the store owners introduced me as 'the Rachel' of Rachel's Brownies."

The demand for Rachel's Brownies also consistently exceeded the supply, and while Borish was unwilling to give up what she had cultivated thus far, neither did she want to take the plunge and develop it into a full-blown business by herself. The following year, the young couple came to a decision: Slater would give up his fledgling children's photography business and become Borish's 50–50 partner in the brownie enterprise.

Jeff Slater proved to be just the right ingredient for the business. He and his wife were a complementary team from the start. As Borish told the Cornell students:

> I was the perfectionist committed to safeguarding the excellence of the product and all the old-fashioned methods I brought with me from my mother's kitchen, the cautious skeptic who preferred no change at all to the possibility of making a mistake, the ferociously detail-minded maniac concerned about every walnut on every brownie. Jeff was Mr. Outside, a natural salesman, the mover and shaker, the risk-taker, the aggressive tryer of new things who was willing to experiment in all the facets of the business, Mr. Smoothie on the telephone who could handle any kind of difficult conversation with suppliers or salespeople. In a word, Jeff was the accelerator; I, the brake.

Borish asserts that she is not a risk-taker. If she were on her own, she would probably sell just one brownie—but it would be perfect.

Slater provided the drive necessary to move the company forward. In the years since he and Borish joined forces, it has moved three times to ever-larger facilities, and by the mid 1980s, it was making 8 million to 10 million brownies a year for such customers as Giant Food, Inc. (an East Coast supermarket chain), United Air Lines, PEOPLExpress Airlines, Amtrak, and convenience chains like Quick Chek and Wawa. For a surprise party celebrating Henry Fonda's seventy-fifth birthday, his wife Shirlee ordered 30 boxes of the brownies flown from Philadelphia to Los Angeles. The brownies gained added recognition when 25,000 of them were tucked into athletes' lunch boxes during the 1984 Summer Olympic Games in Los Angeles. New lines have been added to the original "Double Chocolate with Walnuts"—"Rachel's Husband's Butterscotch Brownies," which Slater really devised, and "Raisin Spice Breakfast Brownies." Annual revenues for Rachel's Brownies are now around $3 million.

WHY DO THEY DO IT?

Pundits love to probe the entrepreneurial psyche, and theories about why entrepreneurs become entrepreneurs abound. As we have seen, some say entrepreneurs are driven by the desire to prove they are right about something, be it a product or a new way of doing things. Despite evidence to the contrary, others insist entrepreneurs are driven by dreams of wealth. They are said to be risk-takers. Or they are high achievers. Or they are out to outdo their fathers. Most of the studies—hence most of the theories—describe male entrepreneurs, the world not yet having caught up with the growing phenomenon of women entrepreneurs. Lack of opportunity in large corporations or the need to work while raising children are factors that might be motivating forces for women who start businesses, some experts suggest.

Entrepreneurs themselves cite still other reasons: the desire to call the shots for oneself and not be limited by someone else's idea of what is good or right, or to do something one enjoys. "You have to have fun!" Debbi Fields told 3,500 participants at the national conference of the American Woman's Economic Development Corporation in New York in February 1986. She did not start Mrs. Fields Cookies to make money, she said; she did it because she loved what she was doing. Having fun is the most important thing about being an entrepreneur, she counseled. "Otherwise, life is like one long dental appointment."

No one theory of entrepreneurs fits all. Though plausible and certainly applicable to some women, the "female" theories of entrepreneurship, for example, seem not to describe Debbi Fields at all. She did not need to work for a living because her husband was already a resounding success in his own financial management business. There were no children yet when she became an entrepreneur, so she did not have to concern herself at first with a work life that would accommodate youngsters. Nor was she working in a corporation that had put a lid on her ability to rise to the top. She was, after all, only 20 when she started the company with a $50,000 loan from her husband. She says she looked at what she liked to do best and could do best—and that was make and eat chocolate chip cookies.

Nor did Rachel Borish worry about children or corporate plateaus when she started baking brownies. She was too concerned with what to do with her own life. One very important door had closed to her; she had to look for some other open door or open one for herself.

When asked why she and Jan went into business together, Olga Erteszek answers, "Number one, we like to eat." Survival, the simple need to make a living, had to be a top priority for them in their new country.

Over the years, however, Jan took a scholar's interest in the process of entrepreneurship and he spoke of "the element of meaningful coincidence" as being relevant to the entrepreneur. Perhaps, he suggested, people with entrepreneurial spirit are more stimulated and "catapulted" by events to seek ways of directing their lives than people who do not have such spirit.

What if Olga had not responded to the dowdiness of rolled-up stockings? What if she had not been turned down for a $2-a-week raise by a supervisor? ("That got us started!" Olga laughs. "We really owe her that.") What if she had not met Jan's challenge to make the garter belts, or he had not got up the nerve to sell them? Coincidence plays a role in everyone's life, but it's what individuals—or couples—do with coincidence that can turn them into entrepreneurs.

Few couples have capitalized on "meaningful coincidence" better than Diane and Leonard Johnson, the founders of Central Pipe & Supply Company, a Houston firm that distributes steel pipe to the major oil companies. The Johnsons were born and raised in Pueblo, Colorado, and after they were married, Leonard worked for Colorado Fuel & Iron Corporation (now CF&I Steel), selling steel products for nearly 18 years. When CF&I was sold in the early 1970s, Leonard found himself at odds with the management philosophies of his new employers. "It was either accept or quit, and we chose to quit, thanks to Diane's backing and support," says Leonard. "To just junk 17 or 18 years of your life and start all over, you need that kind of support."

Leonard went to Texas to work for a pipe distribution company, and Diane stayed behind with the youngest two of their three children and finished up a degree in accounting that she had started when she was 38 years old. Diane says they had talked about starting a business all their lives, but it was "back porch" talk. Maybe a hobby shop or a book store, nothing as capital-intensive as pipe distribution. They didn't have that kind of money.

Very rapidly, things changed. When Leonard left CF&I, he took a substantial pay cut, but for the first time in his life, an incentive was built into his compensation—a 5 percent bonus on the pipe that was sold. Shortly after he made his job change, the 1973 oil embargo hit, and suddenly, with the push for domestically produced oil, there was not enough pipe to go around. Its price went up dramatically and Leonard's 5 percent became a gold mine. Within an 18-month period, he says, "we put aside a little better than $1 million."

It wasn't just the money. The experience Diane had over the years answering the phone for Leonard, who had worked out of his home when he was with CF&I, now meant something, and so did her new degree in business and Leonard's many years of practical exposure to the business. There was another dimension: in the short time he was with his new company, Leonard felt he learned what the entrepreneurial spirit was all about. And he said to himself, "Hey, I can do that!" Having made some dramatic decisions in their own lives, with Leonard's job change and Diane going back to school, they had a new sense of freedom. As Leonard puts it, the timing and their luck enabled them to utilize the experience they had to go out on their own.

They made one false start in 1975, going into business with another partner. They found they didn't need him, so they sold out to him the following year and started Central Pipe. Five years later, they added a second company, Central Threading, Inc., which threads pipe. The companies do a combined business of nearly $70 million a year.

Leonard says he likes to think he and Diane are entrepreneurs because they enjoy it. They didn't need the money—they could have lived quite well off the $1 million Leonard had made. "I'm convinced that if work didn't exist, humankind would invent it, because it is necessary to the soul," he says.

BLENDING THE MOTIVATIONS

Whatever a couple's reasons for starting a business, one spouse's motivations must be compatible with the motivations of the other. Otherwise, they will find it difficult, if not impossible, to give the equal commitment to the business that will help it succeed and keep the relationship strong. Susan Cobey and Timothy Lawrence of Vaca Valley Apiaries are at one in their motivation: they love working with bees. Money is of lesser importance, except that it enables them to pursue their passion. They feel that even if their marriage didn't survive, they would still want to be in the bee business together because of their joy in the work and their respect for each other's abilities.

Some couples are motivated jointly by the simple but powerful desire to realize their full potential, unfettered by so-called superiors. Patricia and Mel Ziegler met at the *San Francisco Chronicle*, where she was an artist and he was a reporter. Both felt limited by their environment; there was always a middleman between them and the public, determining whether or not their work would be seen.

"I would go out there and write my heart out one day and it would be on page one, and the next day, it would be on the editor's spike and I could never quite figure out why," says Mel. Sometimes, he felt, the story on the spike was better than the one on the front page.

The Zieglers' response was to quit and, with $1,500 and complementary talents, start the Banana Republic Travel & Safari Clothing Co., using surplus military wear from around the world as their first source of merchandise. Their khaki-oriented casual clothing retail and mail order company was purchased by The Gap chain in 1983, but Mel and Patricia retain creative control. By the end of 1985, there were more than 36 Banana Republic stores, with an additional 19 expected to open in 1986.

While Susan and Tony Harnett of Bread & Circus in Boston are united in their desire to promote health food, Susan has additional motives for wanting to be in business with her husband. She has seen too many women from her mother's generation left at the mercy of their lawyers and bankers when their husbands died because they never learned how to deal with the business world. "Some of them didn't even know how to write a check." If something were to happen to Tony, she wants to be prepared. On the other hand, being in business with him gives her the opportunity to be a wife and mother in some very traditional ways. She has the primary responsibility for caring for their three children and, by choice, spends an average of only 20 hours a week on the business so that she has more time for parenting, leaving him free to spend longer hours on the business. Even though she believes she could run the company if she had to, she prefers to let Tony do it and defers to him as the boss in the business. She is skeptical of women who want to "have it all," with their husbands spending as much time minding the children as they do and everything having to be "equal, equal, equal."

"I have never seen anything in life equal," she says. "It just doesn't work that way. I think people are being unrealistic if they think that."

OUTSIDERS AND MISFITS

Despite the complexity and variety of motivations and circumstances that push people into their own businesses, the descriptions and profiles that point up similarities among entrepreneurs do have their uses. They can help the rest of the world understand and nurture entrepreneurship, and they also help entrepreneurs to understand themselves and perhaps feel less alone. In his opening remarks to would-be business owners at his School for Entrepreneurs, Bob Schwartz sets the stage with an inspirational discussion of entrepreneurs and their role in changing society. One of the points he makes is that entrepreneurs tend to feel that they do not fit in. They may be unhappy in a job that everyone else thinks is a plum. They may be fired many times before they go into business for themselves. Says Schwartz: "This course says you are the misfit, Buster. You may be an outsider, you may be a special breed of cat, but there's a socially useful, personally useful pattern to that." He tells budding entrepreneurs that they *are* different, but they should be proud of that difference and use it. "The world needs nuts like you."

In researching an article exploring the psyche of the entrepreneur, *New York Times* writer Daniel Goleman found that the craving for autonomy was the force that propelled an entrepreneur into his "solitary orbit." He quotes Lyle M. Spencer, a psychologist with the Boston-based business consulting firm McBer & Company, as saying, "The entrepreneur is a wild man in an organization. He pushes the rules to the breaking point. He hungers for a free range; he feels stifled in any organization except his own."

Take Chris and Winnie Dickerman. A description of how they met offers some insight into their personalities. Chris was tending bar in a Washington, D.C., restaurant bar that usually closed around 10:30 P.M. Winnie was selling real estate at the time. She wanted to entertain some potential buyers one evening and she stopped by the bar early to find out what time it closed.

"Just as soon as I can get out of here," snarled Chris. He was so nasty, Winnie recalls, that she decided to fix him. She returned with her party just before 10:30, forcing Chris to stay on well past his closing hour.

"I didn't think much of this midget," he says of Winnie,

who is a dwarf. At one point during the evening, Chris recalls, Winnie said her briefcase was missing. "I said, 'Christ, what do you carry in a briefcase anyway?' And she said the magic words: 'Contracts and underwear.' And I knew that I had to have that woman."

The Dickermans are tough-talking, funny, streetwise, and not likely to be found in executive suites. They had to make their own opportunities. Chris, a high-school dropout, says he was booted out of the military with an undesirable discharge because one day, in Vietnam, he stormed into the captain's office and quit. "Throw me in jail," he said. "I don't care. I refuse to work for the Federal government any longer in this capacity." It wasn't that he was a peacenik. Quite the opposite, he says. He wondered why the United States was holding back.

When he came back to the states, he did "this little job and that little job"—trying a small bricklaying business of his own that failed, tending bar, selling cars and encyclopedias, and doing some field surveying. After he and Winnie started living together, he got a job with a civil engineering firm in Reston, Virginia. But after three years, he grew increasingly frustrated watching advancement opportunities disappear for insiders as outside people were hired to fill vacancies. Finally, his own mentor quit. Soon Chris quit, too. The boss, he says, was committed to hiring "brain-dead college types."

Meanwhile, Winnie had her own frustrations. She hoped to convert her real estate background into a property management career. But it was not to be. Because she is so little, she says, "people just didn't have the foresight to see all the things that I could do."

Chris and Winnie had been together five years when Chris' mother died, leaving him $10,000. They decided to get married and then go to the West Coast for a month's break. But when they returned home, the old question was still facing them: What would they do with their lives? They tossed ideas around and finally, says Chris, "based on our *vast* experience in the business," they decided to start an open-air fish market in northern

Virginia. They had realized how much they enjoyed the carnival atmosphere of the Washington wharves, with boat people hawking customers and people from all walks of life shopping in a relaxed way.

Actually, they knew nothing about seafood. Chris says he could not tell one fish from another and, with droll understatement, he adds, "So we had to overcome the product knowledge problem."

He sought out Ben Edwards, who, Chris says, "is a *genius* at cleaning fish. It's majesty to see the man work." He offered Edwards $20 a day to teach him to clean fish. All the men cleaning fish on the wharves were black, including Edwards. "Here I am, a skinny, know-nothin' white boy," says Chris. At first, they thought he was a government plant, looking for tax violators or numbers activity or drugs. But after a few weeks, Edwards was convinced that Chris was who he said he was, and he became the Dickermans' entree into the fish business, teaching Chris how to handle and prepare the products and helping him make the contacts they needed.

That's all history now. The Dickermans' C & W Seafood has grown steadily in the years since and the two "misfits" are toying with the idea of a second location.

In the process of deciding what to do with their lives, however, Chris says they came to the "profound" realization that you do not have to get up and go to work for someone else. Most people think they have to have a job, and, Chris says, that notion is one of the toughest an individual has to rid himself of if he is to cross the line and become an entrepreneur. "You don't have to get a job. Just go make a job. Go do it yourself."

MAKING THE ADJUSTMENTS

The start-up period of any business is both exhilarating and draining, full of the fun of creating something new but burdened by long hours, exhaustion, worry over finances and, sometimes, unexpected challenges.

Television's Beverly Garland, who portrayed Fred MacMurray's wife on "My Three Sons" and currently is Kate Jackson's mother on "Scarecrow and Mrs. King," is also an entrepreneur. Despite more than 200 film and TV roles, she found out long ago that being an actress does not always mean steady work, and she wanted a hedge against down times in her career. She and her husband, Fillmore Crank, a general contractor, decided to go into the hotel business, first building the 262-room Beverly Garland Hotel in North Hollywood, California, in 1973, and later, a 207-room facility in Sacramento.

Their hotels now do more than $9 million worth of business a year and keep 300 people employed. But Garland recalls that when they started out, they envisioned the easy life: they would turn their first hotel over to a manager, and she and Crank would go off to Europe and have a good time the rest of their lives living off the income it brought in.

They realized in short order that a manager working one eight-hour shift couldn't oversee a hotel that is open 365 days a year, 24 hours a day. They also found that he did not have the same commitment to the operation that they had themselves. They fired the manager and decided to run the hotel on their own, despite a complete lack of experience in the hotel business. They learned fast. "We've done everything in this hotel, I can tell you!" says Garland. Once, not long after they opened, the hotel was almost full but the housekeeping staff had been felled by the flu. Crank told his wife she had a choice: she could either make the beds and clean the rooms or she could fold the sheets and do the laundry. She chose the laundry and Crank cleaned the rooms. So much for the life of a glamorous television actress. But, she says, "We're the kind of people that, if something has to be done, we just pitch in and do it."

Despite the demands of starting an enterprise, some couples experience little stress on their personal relationship when they go into business together. A chemical engineer, Bill Gore had been at Du Pont for 17 years when he felt a gnawing desire to go it alone and try two things: first, to figure out how to use Teflon as an insulating material in developing interconnecting systems for transistors, which he was convinced were the key to the manufacture of reliable computers, and second, to develop a highly participative organizational structure based on task forces instead of top-down authority. His wife, Vieve, encouraged him. "If you don't resign from Du Pont and start this new business," she told him, "you will always be sorry. And if you do it and fall on your face, why, you can get up and dust yourself off."

Despite the trauma of Bill leaving a well-paid job and a company and people he enjoyed, and despite the fact that for the next two years, the Gores and their five children lived on the family savings, Bill and Vieve slipped into the rhythm of working together with ease. They couldn't even recall having a discussion about whether they could work together successfully as business partners. "I think that we just knew that we would do what we had to do," says Vieve.

With some frequency, couples "fall" into business together rather than setting out to create something jointly. When Sydney Lewis began testing a mail order catalog, Frances Lewis did the part-time odd jobs that wives often do—typing labels, marking merchandise, and the like. The young company flourished so quickly that in a matter of months, it consumed all the time she had once spent on volunteer activities. More important, she found that she was fully committed to the business. Her joining the company was never a conscious decision. "It just happened," says Sydney. For the Lewises, as for the Gores, working together seemed natural.

The Lewises' personal relationship seemed unaffected by their new business relationship. The biggest adjustment, Frances recalls, was making sure their three children were looked after. But even that adjustment was minimal compared to what many other couples with children faced—the Lewises had always had household help, and Frances, because of her heavy involvement in volunteer work, says, "I was always out of the home anyway."

For other couples, however, starting a business does make an impact on the personal relationship, causing shifts and strains that call for reassessment and adjustment.

Sue Cobey and Tim Lawrence had been together for more than five years when they started Vaca Valley Apiaries. Yet Sue found she had a lot more to learn about Tim. "He became a new person to me, almost," she says. She saw much more determination and conviction in him, sometimes "almost to a point where he was ruthless." She found herself backing off and thinking, "Life can't be that serious." While Tim acknowledges being more intense and frustrated, he feels circumstances changed, not his personality. Nevertheless, Sue realized for the first time how impatient he could be; she found him very short-tempered with her when she got scared, wondering if they could really make a success of their venture.

Friends saw a difference, too. They would tell her Tim had changed and had almost grown cold and callous. He was a real businessman now, they observed. "Where is the old Tim, the fun-loving Tim that we used to know?" Sue felt she had to defend him, because she knew what she and Tim were both going through and how difficult it was.

But there was a positive side, too. She discovered that she was growing more confident—the responses she received, for example, when she wrote a series of articles on instrumental insemination of bees gave her ego a welcome boost. She also found that when she got worried and depressed about the business, Tim had the ability to lift up her spirits within a couple of hours with his own enthusiasm.

Sheri Criswell recalls that when she joined the company Bill had started, "I spent about two years worrying about what other people thought about me and my competence." She had previously carved out her identity as a lawyer; now she was terrified of being seen as "Mrs. Bill Criswell" and living in his shadow. Her fears affected the company. Hiring decisions were influenced, for example, because she was leery of bringing anyone into the business who might challenge her role there.

The Criswells also realized that when you have separate careers, you can edit what you talk about at night, telling your spouse about all your "hits" and leaving out the stupid and embarrassing things you might have done that day. "You try to make your spouse think you're pretty sharp," says Sheri. But when you're in business together, you can't hide your mistakes. "You're exposing yourself to people you love and you want to impress and you want to think well of you," says Sheri.

Bill also found that while he and Sheri had separate careers, he shared certain intimate details of his business with Sheri at home that he did not reveal to colleagues at work. For example, he prided himself on his ability to persuade. "Part of what you do in the process of persuasion is you manipulate other people," he says. "You manipulate them to behave in a way that you get the result you want." Before Sheri joined the company, he would tell her openly just how he would be persuasive, what manipulative skills he planned to use, and the other details of how he was going to achieve a goal. When Sheri joined the business, he found that Sheri expected him to share the same details with her at the office, often with colleagues present, not understanding that Bill still wanted to discuss such details with her only in private.

"For about two years, there was a lot of sorting out, just figuring out how the relationship worked," says Sheri.

JUDGING YOUR CHANCES FOR SUCCESS

How can you determine whether you will be good business partners, able to tough out the start-up period and eventually enjoy the fruits of your labor together? Many couples say a history of mutual respect and trust gave them confidence that they could be successful as business partners as well as marriage partners. While it is dangerous to generalize, couples who have been married longer often seem to make the transition into business with less trauma than other couples experience. Nevertheless, when the personalities are right, a young couple, too, can manage a start-up without threatening their relationship. Jan and Olga Erteszek were newlyweds in their twenties when they started The Olga Company, their relationship apparently unperturbed.

Still, running a company together is not for everyone. Being in love with each other does not necessarily mean you will make good business partners. And, while complementary abilities and temperaments are vital, they are not enough, either.

"For a couple to be an entrepreneurial couple, they've got to be team players," says psychologist Marta Vago. That means they have to feel comfortable sharing the power and sharing the decision making.

A couple needs the opportunity to learn if they can work well together, agrees Tony Harnett, "because the pressure of the business will pull them apart very quickly unless they are a good team." Business is a big test, he points out. "If you haven't been tested before and you're going into business, where you have the dollars on the line, you can lose the business and the marriage at the same time."

To determine whether you and your spouse work well as a team and might make good business partners, Vago suggests looking for clues in projects you have already done together. These can range from something as simple as preparing a meal to creating an elaborate garden—"anything that involves mutual decision making, mutual goal setting, mutual problem solving, and mutual evaluation." Before they started W. L. Gore & Associates, Bill and Vieve Gore had designed and built their house together, right down to pouring the concrete themselves. Prior to getting into the canvas and awning business, Karen and Denny Quade had made a boat cover together; they also made a good team working on household projects.

As you review how you handled such projects as a couple,

ask yourselves such questions as: Do we wrangle over details, or is there an easy flow of views? Do we value each other's opinions? Do we respect and admire each other's skills? Can we freely say to each other, "I would never have thought of that"? Did we have fun doing this project? Was working through the process exciting or drudgery? Were the projects successful? If not, how did we deal with failure? Did we start blaming each other?

"If you cannot plan a vacation together, it is foolish to believe that you can run a business together," says Vago.

Bill and Sheri Criswell say a couple should not go into business together unless they see themselves as peers. They can have very different skills and very different responsibilities, says Sheri, but each must consider the other "equivalently important to the organization."

If one or the other is viewed as superior, she says, "it's not going to be enriching. It's going to be an obstacle that the other learns how to live with."

Like many couples, the Criswells think it is important for both partners to have had some business or professional experience on their own before starting a business together.

"I don't think I would have had the self-confidence to share the limelight if I hadn't had the chance to be a success in my own right," Bill says. Because he already knew "what power tastes like" he explains, he did not feel it was something he was being deprived of when he shared it with his wife.

Tony Harnett urges couples to examine beforehand why they want to go into business with each other. A certain type of business may be right for one because that partner has a particular skill, such as being an artist or an attorney. But it doesn't mean that business would be right for the spouse. "If the other person tags along, they're always going to feel like a passenger." The passenger may feel it is the mate's business, while he or she is the helper.

When a couple starts a business, Harnett says, "it has to be a mutual dream, a shared dream"—something they both fervently want to do.

Try to confront and deal with any foreseeable problems, and set up guidelines for handling unforeseen problems, before you go into business, advises Gail K. Husbands of H & H Research, Inc., in Delta, Alabama, a company that manufactures virtually maintenance-free aquariums. And, she adds, it is important to admit to each other as well as to yourself that there *will* be problems.

Keeping the lines of communication open before you get started will not only help you understand what each of you wants out of the venture but also what each of you expects to put into it. It also gives you the valuable practice you will need in talking out the difficulties, the disappointments, and the nasty surprises that are inevitable in any business.

STRESS POINTS

Successful Couples Use Stress
for Personal and Mutual
Growth

They were only a week or so into starting C & W Seafood, and Chris and Winnie Dickerman were still doing much of the work in their Reston, Virginia, apartment before going over to their roadside market several miles away. On a day when they were particularly tired and strung out, Chris had to leave the apartment to run some errands. He asked Winnie to take care of a major chore while he was gone: put the live crabs into the pots and steam them.

When he returned, he says, "Here's Winnie sitting on top of the kitchen counter—bear in mind, now, that Winnie is three-foot-nine—crying the bejesus and screaming at the crabs that are all over the house."

There were hundreds of them, and they had clawed their panicky way into every nook and cranny. They were in the kitchen, in the living room, in bedroom and bath. Winnie was terrified.

What the Dickermans hadn't realized was that the crabs were hot as a result of their ride from the Washington, D.C., riverfront, and when crabs get hot, they get very active. They had become so jumpy that when Winnie took the lids off their baskets, they scrambled out faster than she could catch them.

Crabs are among the nastiest creatures on earth, in Winnie's view. When they get hold of you, they go right through your fingernails. They draw blood, and they hurt. "And I was just tired and frustrated and angry, and here were these crabs. I just lost it."

When you are in business, it's safe to assume that almost anything that can go wrong, will go wrong. It's also a sure bet that mistakes will be made. Stress comes with the territory, even if you are in business with someone you love.

One day in High Point, North Carolina, Joanne Schatz walked out on her husband, Skip, in the middle of a major furniture show. She had had enough.

Joanne, who had spent most of her adult life as a housewife, decided to start a retail business selling adjustable beds when her second marriage failed. She had used one herself to alleviate some problems with a pregnancy and she knew, because she had bought her handsome model from the mail order branch of the prestigious Hammacher Schlemmer department store, that such beds didn't have to look like hospital beds. She set out to sell them as beautiful pieces of furniture.

She and Skip originally met because they had the same accountant. He had brought them together because he thought they had something in common—Skip was ending a second marriage, too.

Skip and his brother, Kenneth, both Wharton School graduates, had run their own janitorial service, in Alexandria, Virginia, for a dozen years, and on their first date, Skip found himself giving Joanne advice on how to fire a dishonest manager. "I had never done this in my life," says Joanne. "I was really scared."

In the days that followed, Skip called almost daily to see how the dismissal went and how Joanne was. "He was so concerned about me because he knew what stress level it was running a business," Joanne recalls.

They married in 1979, a year after they met. Joanne's business has grown to three Washington-area locations and has now become associated with the Vertech Back and Bed Stores chain. Bored with the janitorial business, Skip and his brother sold it and Skip bought a company that now functions as a complement to Joanne's, manufacturing adjustable beds not only for her business but also for other retailers throughout the country.

They were at their second High Point market when Joanne called it quits.

"She was very uptight about her business," recalls Skip. "She was just beginning to hire and manage, and she felt very let down by people." Their showroom was supposed to have been set up before they arrived. It was not. The beds were still in cartons. Skip's attitude was: "I had 500 laborers working for me when I was in the janitor business, and I know how these people work. It's nothing to get excited about." But Joanne's attitude was: "Whoever was supposed to set it up didn't set it up. These goddamned people didn't do their job!"

Other things were going wrong, too, and Skip, being more experienced, took them in stride. Joanne did not. By her own admission, she got hysterical. "I just couldn't handle it."

She said goodbye, walked out, and took a cab back to the room where they were staying. "I left Skip a note [saying] 'I can't take the pressures of life. I'm leaving. Don't try to find me. Please take care of my children for me.' " She pauses to laugh at herself. "I left him my four kids, you understand."

She packed her bag and, with $85 and her charge cards, she hitchhiked to the bus terminal, deciding that she would stay with her friend Diane in Chicago. But when she got to the bus station, she found she needed $90 in cash for the fare. They wouldn't take credit cards.

On the phone, Diane suggested going to the airport—you could always charge a plane ticket. But Diane also advised Joanne to take a look at the situation before she got on the plane. What was she running from? Was it Skip and the kids?

"I just can't take the pressures of the business," Joanne told her. "I just can't take it."

Skip, meanwhile, had rolled up his sleeves and began selling beds that were still in cartons while at the same time trying to get the showroom set up. When it was ready, he went back to the room where he and Joanne were staying, found her note, took a shower, put on fresh clothes and returned to the show to sell some more.

How the partners cope with stress—from each other, from the business, and from life itself—can make a tremendous impact not only on how the personal relationship functions but also on how smoothly the business operates as well. And perhaps even on its potential for growth. With luck, when one partner is particularly stressed, the other will have enough strength left to serve as a resource or refuge or cheerleader.

Once Chris and Winnie had recaptured their roving crusta-
ceans, Winnie refused to cook them. "I said, 'Well, look, Slim,
this is what we do for a living,' " Chris recalls. " 'You have to
do it. It'll get better. We'll find another place to steam the crabs.
But, now, this is what we have to do.' " And, he adds with
some pride, Winnie came through.

"Winnie and I love each other very much, and we're very
supportive of each other," Chris explains. "We believe in each
other and we trust each other. And we're honest." But he insists
that when things go wrong, he won't take the approach of, " 'Oh,
Honey, it's all right. It's a terrible situation.' Bullshit! She carries
her own weight. I can't sit down in the middle of it and cry
and fall apart." He won't let Winnie do it, either. He will acknowledge that she's tired and say, "Let's get it resolved, and
I'll help." And Winnie is clearly comfortable with that.

Back at the bus terminal, Joanne Schatz was a little surprised
that the police weren't searching for her, nor were the radios
reporting her disappearance. She had expected Skip to be panic-
stricken and trying to find her. "And this was a turning point
for me," she says. Nobody was hysterical, and nobody was looking for her.

She's not quite sure what made her go back, but she got a
cab and returned to the market. Skip was in the showroom talking
to a customer, and when she came in, he said, "Hello, Joanne."
Just like nothing happened. So Joanne started to help.

"You weren't even upset. You weren't even worried," she
said afterward. As she recalls it, he replied, "I don't own you.
If you want to leave, leave. I'll take care of the business. I'll
take care of the kids. If you want to join me, fine. If you don't
want to join me, don't."

Having gone through two divorces, Skip says now, "I realized
that my existence did not depend upon that relationship. And
if she did not choose that relationship, I certainly was not going
to force it. I would just go on; I would do what I had to do.
There's a saying in the Navy: 'When all else fails, carry out

your orders.' And my orders were to man that booth and sell the beds."

THE STRESS PRODUCERS

Any number of things can result in stress for one or both partners in a business. Among the couples who participated in this book, the following emerged as some of the more common areas of friction, frustration, and tension.

"We Have Different Management Styles and Work Habits."

He's a packrat and she throws everything away. She's cavalier but he's a perfectionist. He is a visionary while she gets impatient with his lack of attention to detail and execution. She's impulsive and he's cautious. She's thorough but he's quick. He is organized and she is disorganized. He sees her as hyper, while she says she has a greater energy level, is more aggressive, and gets more work done; he views himself as calm and methodical, but she complains that he procrastinates and questions whether his commitment to the business is as strong as hers.

Frequently the two individuals involved in an entrepreneurial relationship also approach management from different directions, a factor that can be the source of endless arguments. In the extreme, a husband may bring with him an authoritarian style that is more characteristic of the traditional male entrepreneur. He may be dictatorial and have a tendency to look over everyone's shoulder or, out of frustration, do the work himself if he thinks someone else's work is not good enough. By contrast, the wife may push for a more delegatory, participative style, one that may appear to the husband to be "soft." He may think she is mollycoddling the employees.

"We Worry or Disagree about Money."

"Money management has caused us our greatest difficulties," says Susan Kennedy Stangland of Pepperwood International Corporation in Eugene, Oregon. She thinks visionaries like her husband Chris "give more importance to getting the dream launched and are willing to worry about how to keep it flying *after* the fact. I feel more comfortable having a more well-rounded and financially planned course of action."

How or when to spend money can be a sore point. Says Vermont innkeeper Robert Harnish: "I might spend $50,000 on a computer while Breda is convinced that they are of no use whatever. Breda will spend thousands of dollars on an antique table when a reproduction would be much more serviceable." Breda agrees, saying, "It's an ongoing problem which takes a lot of humor on both our parts."

One husband wants to spend more money promoting the business; his wife, less. Another wife reports being particularly distressed because her husband is taking money out of their personal account and pumping it into the business to meet overhead needs resulting from expansion. Jerome and Pauline Berliner of Miami, now retired from an export management business, recall that a major source of friction for them was the establishment of credit terms for their overseas clients. "This is the typical irritant between the sales manager, who wants to make the sale, and the credit manager, who wants to be certain that the invoice is collectable," says Jerome.

For some couples—especially those in the start-up stage or those who haven't hit it big yet—lack of money is unsettling. The fact that she and her husband both depend on their company as their sole source of income creates a sense of insecurity, according to Susan Stangland. When Michael J. Clark and Darnelle M. Knowlton started their Trexlertown, Pennsylvania, firm, K & C Marketing Communications, in 1984, Mike says they wondered if they would have enough business to survive. "What would happen if we didn't make enough to cover our bills?" They coped with their fears, he says, "by pressing onward and getting the clients that we needed to make a success of the initial stages of our operation. Every time we got a new client, our confidence in what we were doing increased."

Ginger Oppenheimer and Tim Boyer, who have a photojournalism business in Bellingham, Washington, have trouble setting priorities, especially since theirs is a new business and money is often in short supply. "When is it more important to buy a gift for a family member instead of office supplies?" asks Ginger. Wilderness buffs who have translated their love of the outdoors into a business, they find that their personal interests compete with their business needs. They may be tempted to buy "outdoor toys" like technical climbing equipment and kayaks when they know they need to put as much money as possible into marketing or to buy a new camera lens.

"We Can't Separate Our Business Life from Our Personal Life."

Rosanne Kranitz, of Pompano Beach, Florida, owns a computer consulting and word processing business, WCK Associates, with her husband, Wesley C. Kranitz. A couple of years ago, she earned an "A" on a talk she gave in a college speech course. It was called "The Husband–Wife Relationship in Business," and in it, she said: "The business is now your life. You will find yourself and your husband eating, sleeping, and making love to the tune of: 'First thing tomorrow morning we have to ship out the Jones' order.' Or, 'I forgot to tell you the bank called and the payroll account is overdrawn.' Just because you leave the business doesn't mean the business leaves you."

"Our feelings of self-worth are totally dependent on the success or failure of the business," laments Tari Vickery of KVTV Carpets, an $8-million-a-year wholesale distributorship in Oklahoma City. "All traveling is business related. We haven't taken a true vacation in the 11 years we've been married. We don't take time to be married people. Our daughter has an 'office' of her own within my office (she's nine) and knows that she comes after the business in our list of priorities. The business consumes our lives."

Diane and Stephen Saliba run Richardson Home Builders, a company owned by Diane's entrepreneurial parents in Lawrenceburg, Tennessee. They not only build homes but also manage some apartments, and Diane puts it this way: "The most constant and difficult problem is not being able to leave work at the office. After the tenth telephone call, numerous deals to follow through on, complaints of leaky faucets, and one kid's supper milk spilled, our personal life is the pits."

In an even more telling statement, one that many couples should identify with, she says: "The stakes are *so* high! Our whole way of life depends upon our keeping our priorities straight. If a desire for success becomes too consuming, patterns of too much work and not enough play start to put a strain on our personal relationship. I feel resentful sometimes that Steve is totally spent after work and has very little left for me. Even though I understand totally his needs and desires, it is difficult for me to be nurturing and loving to our whole family when I feel pretty stressed out, too. It scares me to think about how much we would lose if we lost our love for each other."

The retired Jerome Berliner agrees that the biggest disadvantage of being in partnership with Pauline was the intrusion of their business into family life. "It was not unusual for company activities of the day to be rehashed at the dinner table," he recalls. "We had no reluctance to air our comments, problems, and differences in decision making in front of our sons."

Some couples regret the fact that their total involvement in business isolates them socially. They are always thinking about business, no matter where they are. Others say that because of their immersion in business, they have not developed other interests and there is little else for them to talk about at the end of the day. Some find it hard to make friends. Tari Vickery says that most of their peers, in their mid-thirties, don't understand what she and her husband, Kent, do or what it takes to make it work. She sums it up well when she says: "We sometimes feel like we're on an island. Through the years, we haven't taken time to nurture close friendships, mainly because we don't feel that we 'fit.' At this point in our lives, we're realizing we're going to be lonely old people, and if one of us dies, the other isn't going to have anyone. We are not close to either of our extended families."

"It Hurts When My Spouse Criticizes Me."

It really stings when your spouse is critical of you. Many husbands and wives flare up or become defensive or even lose effectiveness in their work when a spouse finds fault with them. It's not uncommon to feel that criticism means disapproval or loss of respect. Bill Criswell had started the Criswell Company more than a year before Sheri agreed that she would quit her law firm and become his partner. She had done some legal work for him when they were following separate career paths, and they had worked well together. So it was a surprise to both when, soon after she joined the business, they were often fighting. They talked it out and realized that, in their new working relationship, each needed the other's approval so much that they were overreacting to each other. If Sheri expressed a legal judgment that seemed critical of Bill, he would take it hard. She, in turn, was defensive about her work.

"We were both trying to impress each other," Sheri laughs now.

But some couples have a difficult time getting over the hump of learning not to take criticism (or give it) personally. They complain of one second-guessing the other or taking potshots at the other's decisions. They are especially resentful when they feel they have done a good job.

"I take criticism of my efforts very hard when they are successful," says Deborah J. H. Livingston-White of International Consultants, a start-up in Oak Park, Michigan. One husband found fault with his wife's day-to-day decisions so consistently that she now avoids decisions.

"Sometimes I feel nagged because when I'm putting out 100 percent in my opinion, someone wanting a little more is offensive," said one man.

Home builder Diane Saliba says that both she and her husband make bids, but because she makes them faster, he presumes that she has made more mistakes. "But the truth is, mine are usually very good and his questioning only undermines my confidence and makes me feel resentful," she says.

"We Disagree on Business Decisions or Goals."

"I am very growth oriented," reports one wife. "He is more inclined to feel that growth past a certain point involves too many compromises and too much stress."

James Hartman of Electronics Consulting Services, Inc., in Reading, Pennsylvania, identifies defining authority as the biggest problem. "We are basically very different personalities and we make decisions differently. Therefore it is better to define authority than to negotiate."

Early in their business, one couple found themselves at odds over the husband's tendency to hire his friends. They were inexperienced and he paid them too much, his wife said. The friends, as she foresaw, did not work out well as employees.

The worst stress for Norma M. Goldberger of the Akron Women's Clinic in Akron, Ohio, is making up her mind on a major issue and then going against her own feelings and doing what her husband wants instead. She says her husband's philosophy is based on practical considerations, while "I base mine more on emotional considerations."

How couples make decisions and share power with each other

is covered in greater detail in Chapter 4. Most couples do master the art of joint decision making, but even the most successful admit that sometimes, decision making can be troublesome. "Our decisions were frequently shared with difficulty, and not always resolved," says Pauline Berliner. Her husband's view is close: "Most of the differences were resolved by quiet analytical discussions. At other times we screamed at each other, banged desks, called names, until we ran out of steam and settled on a mutually accepted formula. Mutually accepted, but not necessarily enjoyed."

"We Don't Have Enough Time."

Not enough time for oneself, not enough time to be a couple, and not enough time for one's family—all create anxiety. Women, especially younger women with children, are particularly stressed by too much to do and too few hours to do it in. "There is *no* time for *me*!" says Susan Stangland.

Between their innkeeping and civic responsibilities, Robert and Breda Harnish find it hard to take planned time off together. If one is free, often the other has a commitment.

Setting priorities for use of time is as difficult for Ginger Oppenheimer and Tim Boyer as setting priorities for money. "Our major goal in life is to enjoy ourselves, have fun," says Ginger. But, she says, they never seem to have enough time for both the business and the things they like to do for pleasure. "When should we hole up in the office? When should we take a walk on the beach?"

"We Work Too Hard and We're Tired All the Time."

It is easy to work too hard when you are a couple in business, some say, because you don't have to leave work to be together. Putting in long hours is often a response to the demands of a business—a number of couples report bringing the children and sleeping on the office floor some nights in order to meet commitments. But most couples seem to thrive on their work, and long hours and exhaustion are prices they are willing to pay. Nevertheless, some spouses worry about a wife who works too much or a husband "working himself into an early grave." And when it comes to sex, one husband says, sometimes they are "too darn tired."

"We Are Together Too Much."

Those of us who are not in business with our spouses often imagine that being together all the time would be the biggest disadvantage of such an arrangement. Generally this does not seem to be the case. Many entrepreneurial couples genuinely like each other and enjoy being together—or at least nearby—throughout the day. Many even complain that, although they are in business together, they don't see enough of each other; they are so busy with their own separate responsibilities that they may not catch up with each other until the evening, or business travel keeps them apart. In fact, some spouses do not like their partner to be away overnight—sometimes because one mate seems a little insecure about the relationship or is simply more traditional, implying that a wife should be at home at night. Others, like Debbi and Randy Fields of Mrs. Fields Cookies, are uneasy when they are not together. Randy, who says their relationship requires lots of nurturing, calls Debbi three times a day when he is traveling, even if he is gone only 24 hours. "I call her when I get up in the morning, I call her once or twice during the day when I am on the road, and then I call her at night before I go to sleep. I mean, it is really silly, it is childish, but that is how it works." In still other cases, wives with young children experience stress if the husband is away a great deal and isn't available to take on more of the burdens of parenting.

But for the couples who *do* feel the pressures of too much togetherness, the problem is very real.

"Because we are together 24 hours a day, we experience every mood, every need, all anger, disappointment, happiness—every emotion—together," says Tari Vickery. As a result, they see all the good as well as all the bad in each other, and they also depend on each other to fulfill all their needs, she says. "This has put an unrealistic expectation and tremendous burden on each of us." To solve the problem, she and her husband are trying to diversify their interests outside the business.

More often than not, the stress of togetherness is most experienced by couples whose businesses are relatively small or who work out of their homes. Renata von Tscharner and Ronald Lee Fleming, who run the Townscape Institute, an urban planning firm, in their Cambridge, Massachusetts, home. It is von Tscharner's observation that being in business together "forces you to pay more attention to your personal relationship because it affects your daily business life so much and can create such a burden that you have to address it. To be together 24 hours a day suddenly creates a strain. When things are well, they are much better than in couples that do not work together, but when things are difficult, things are much more difficult than if you had two different careers."

"My Spouse Won't Listen to Me."

Put in other words, this means a spouse may not respect the partner's opinion or is just stubborn and won't take advice. While the problem goes both ways, women are more likely to complain about it. Wives, who are often less experienced in business but not necessarily less smart than their husbands, express frustration when they feel their husbands won't take suggestions. Rightly or wrongly, they believe the husband's inability to accept advice from others, particularly themselves, hurts the business.

Rosanne Kranitz found a way to get her husband's attention. While they were still in a business they owned previously, she once quit and got another job. "He now treats me as a professional and not just his wife."

"I Have Two Jobs—Being a Business Partner and Running a Household."

Obviously, it is mostly the women who feel this pinch. Helen G. Deer, a paralegal who runs a law practice with her attorney husband, William, in Bolton, Illinois, says the most difficult part of being in business with her spouse is not the business at all but "keeping the household running as perfectly as I would like." Susan Stangland finds it most difficult "to have full-time responsibilities at the business and then come home to manage our personal business and be a mother."

Judith Kaplan may be president of Action Packets Inc., a $4-million-a-year public company in Ocala, Florida, that distributes novelties and souvenirs to museums, but she speaks of feeling the "usual 'working mother guilt syndrome,' only multiplied due to the intensity of my deep involvement in my business." As for housework, she describes the Kaplans' home as "one step ahead of the sanitation department."

One could assume that the households of entrepreneurial couples are the most liberated in America, with husbands more often than not sharing equally in domestic as well as business responsibilities. And many of them do. But there are still large pockets of women in this group who are doing double duty—and not without resentment and stress.

THE BEAT GOES ON

Mentioned less often but still sources of stress for some couples are the need to compromise or to submerge one's ego; employees who play one against the other or, as one husband put it, "stir up trouble"; competition between the spouses; and lapses in communication.

There are other factors—sometimes more subtle but often crucial—that affect the stress levels of one or both partners and possibly the well-being of the whole family. Operating a women's clinic that includes abortion services, for example, would not be everyone's cup of tea. As Norma and Stephen Goldberger have found, what comes with the territory in this kind of endeavor are protest demonstrations not only at your place of business but around your home. Their children, who are under instructions not to take packages into their house for fear of bombs, have not only been exposed to the hatred of the protestors, says Norma, but have also been teased by classmates at school.

One wife on the West Coast found out the hard way what being in the restaurant and nightclub business could do to her marriage. Her husband fell prey to other women, including one of the waitresses, and to drugs. "Most of the profits went to buy cocaine to support his habit," the wife claims. The marriage ended before the business was two years old, and the wife is still in court trying to wrest from her husband the $60,000 she says she put into the venture.

While not all cases are so dramatic, management consultant Edward Langiotti, of Reading, Pennsylvania, says that a couple going into business must consider ahead of time what kind of impact the nature of the business will have on their relationship. If it is a frantically paced, high-risk business, will one thrive on it while the other falls apart under the pressure? Does one partner love variety while the business requires doing routine tasks every day? The mundane character of the business may be stress-producing for that partner. It could result in the individual not wanting to deal with problems and interfere with his or her ability to be successful at the business.

The stage a company is in and the life stage of an individual or couple play large roles in the amount of stress the couple experiences. Frances Lewis of Best Products says it was much tougher when the business was getting off the ground; she and Sydney not only had to work hard, long hours, but they also had to do many different kinds of jobs because it was mainly just the two of them. It's a lot easier now that Best is a multibillion-dollar company because their hours are shorter and there's always someone to delegate work to.

Conversely, Kathy Keeton, who helps run Penthouse International, Ltd., the New York magazine publishing house, with long-time companion Robert Guccione, says it was simpler in the early days, when they were publishing only *Penthouse.* At first, says Keeton, who joined the company shortly after Guccione founded it in 1965, their goal was to overtake *Playboy,* creating a better and more successful men's magazine. "It's now become a much greater vision than that, and that's to build one of the world's most successful publishing companies." Over the years, they have added *Omni* and other magazines and have become involved in films and video programming. Even though *Forbes* magazine has identified Guccione as one of America's wealthiest men, placing his assets at around $220 million, Keeton says, "We work harder now than we ever did."

Katherine and Ron Harper started what is now Harper Companies International, a string of diversified companies with annual sales of $15 million, in the mudroom of their Charlotte, North Carolina, home in 1971, when they were in their late thirties. Eleven years later, even though their company was a resounding success, Katherine reached a point where, she says, "I didn't care whether I lived or I died." Their five children had all grown up and didn't need their mother the way they used to. The Harpers had hired people to take over many of the responsibilities they had once handled, and Katherine had a hard time finding a new slot for herself. Her self-esteem was slipping away and, she says, "I felt like I didn't know who I was."

Meanwhile, with the business settled into a good growth pattern, Ron grew bored and wanted something different. Against

Katherine's wishes, he took on a heating and air conditioning company, which was quite different from the packaging industry orientation of their other companies. The new venture began having financial difficulties that affected the whole operation.

To make matters worse, Katherine felt that she and Ron were not as close as they once were.

"In the beginning," explains Ron, "our board meeting started about 11:00 o'clock at night when the kids were in bed. Katherine and I were it." As they brought new people on board, however, he tended to discuss situations and ideas with them rather than with his wife. "She began to feel like we perhaps were growing apart."

Their problems were further complicated by the fact that Katherine had put on 50 extra pounds.

Despite feeling that she was "in a void," Katherine clung to the belief that she was still a very vital person. She just had to find out who that person was.

With Ron's blessing, she took time off and went to Sea Pines Behavioral Institute at Hilton Head. The 26-day program there—and the walks on the beach—not only put her on the road to shedding the excess weight but also gave her a new sense of self. It was the first time she had been away from her family in her life, and it was the first time she had done something solely for herself.

When she returned, Ron recalls, "She said to me, 'I have decided I am going to be happy in life with or without you.' "

It was like a burden had been slipped off his shoulders, he recalls. He thought, "Thank God I don't have to worry about spending the rest of my life trying to make her happy."

Katherine describes it as turning one another loose. She had felt like he was smothering and controlling her; he had felt that he had an obligation to make her happy. Now she had taken on the responsibility for her own happiness. Their new understanding was reinforced by visits to a counselor, who also helped them learn to communicate with each other better.

Katherine also learned not to take on Ron's burdens, either. When he became chairman of the Mecklenburg County Democratic party in 1985, party members told Katherine they felt like they were getting a bonus because they were getting her, too. She said she would help, but they had to understand it was his job. "I didn't want to be responsible for his success or failure as a chairman."

They know they have worked through a tough crisis in their relationship, a period when, Ron says, "the love continued, but we just didn't like one another for a variety of reasons." By late 1985, he could say, "Today Katherine is probably the most attractive 52-year-old that I know. And she is one of the most confident 52-year-olds that I know. And she is one of the most successful 52-year-olds that I know, and I am just mighty proud to have her as my wife. I really am."

It goes without saying that the biggest stress producers of all are the out-and-out crises: failure or near failure of a business, and personal disasters, such as a serious problem with a child or the life-threatening illness of a partner.

One couple recalls that the most difficult period they went through was a time when they realized they were personally wiped out financially and their business was about to go under. Until that point, if one partner was down, the other was up and could carry the business and family along. This time, they were both thrown into a depression at the same time, and it took every ounce of discipline they had to pick themselves up and rebuild their company.

Crises may also come in multiples. The day after Norma Goldberger of the Akron Women's Clinic had the Goldbergers' second child, three of the doctors quit in an effort to gain ownership of the facility.

Though it brings financial relief and possibly luxurious lifestyles, success itself results in new kinds of stress. On a number of occasions, for example, successful couples have asked me, as a magazine writer, to please not mention their children in a story. Their wealth has become common knowledge in the media, and the fear of kidnaping or harm to their children runs high.

Sometimes a couple cannot even have their tragedies in private. Lore Harp had gained considerable note as the entrepreneur who started the high-technology firm Vector Graphic Inc. in California in 1976 with $6,000 and a product designed by her husband, Robert. In five years, the company had achieved more than $25 million in annual sales and went public. The national business press speculated that Harp might become the first female founder of a New York Stock Exchange-listed company. But the break up of her marriage to Robert became grist for the media mill, too, as did the downhill slide of Vector, and Harp's eventual ouster as chairman.

THE POSITIVE SIDE OF STRESS

Whatever its source, stress need not break a couple nor destroy their chances of building a viable company. Quite the contrary. Successful couples seem to use stress as a vehicle for individual and mutual growth. Ron and Katherine Harper did so in very personal terms when they were confronted with Katherine's identity crisis. Other couples do so, consciously or unconsciously, not only to strengthen themselves and their personal relationship but also to improve the way they run their business. The stress that results from problems stimulates action to find solutions, and in the process of facing problems and taking constructive action, couples learn and grow.

Every entrepreneur—and every entrepreneurial couple—makes mistakes. Many of them. The Dickermans' disaster with the crabs in their apartment was, to hear them tell it, only one in a very long line of stressful mistakes they made as start-up entrepreneurs. They rented a refrigerated truck for $600 a month and on their very first day, the live crabs they purchased were killed in transit because they were too cold. Eventually, they bought a used truck for $350 and installed a small refrigeration unit to be used for only those purchases that needed to be kept cool. Chris painted a sign filled with words, colors, and different type faces. It didn't take him long to realize that "if I was driving down the road at 50 miles an hour, I wouldn't take time to read all that garbage." So, for signage, they adopted the approach they had already found worked with sales, the KISS method: "Keep It Simple, Stupid." Out of sheer ignorance, they say, they made problems for themselves that they didn't need to make— like not looking under "P" in the Yellow Pages when they needed paper bags. At first, they thought they would have to buy some from a local supermarket.

But they always learned. And in the process of learning from their mistakes, they began to develop policies that would help them through similar situations in the future, not only reducing stress but saving time and helping the operation run more smoothly. They found, for example, that when they came to a heated disagreement over whether an employee should stay or go, they let her go. They had discovered earlier that when the cost—financial or emotional—of keeping an employee exceeded the production of that person, for the good of the organization, that person had to go. In this particular case, they realized that the employee was too disruptive of everyone else in the company.

For the couple in business, it is important to recognize that the personality and skill differences that cause friction, and hence stress, are often the very differences that make the business *and* the relationship function effectively. The visionary versus the detail-oriented. The aggressive versus the laid back. The authoritarian versus the participative. The intuitive versus the rational. These polarities, as irritating as they may be, are frequently what enable partners to say they are successful because they complement each other. Many couples learn that, instead of fighting these differences, it pays to respect and work with them in order to produce both a better relationship and a better business.

Joanne Schatz decided to look at the reason behind her hysteria at the furniture market and concluded that it came from "people not doing their job." In one way, it taught her that she was tougher than Skip: she demanded more of people. She agrees with Skip that she may be overly tough at times, but says he is "underly." Nevertheless, the incident began to make her aware that, because she had had so little previous exposure to the business world, she was naive about it. "I didn't know that people didn't show up on time. I didn't know that people called in sick when they weren't sick." For her, it was a loss of innocence.

Skip, who had been through it all for many years, had already come up with a guiding rule: If a new employee doesn't show up for work on time the first day, that person will not work out—no matter what the excuse. He feels Joanne was looking for infallibility and that he was able to teach her to be more reasonable about her expectations. But he also admits that Joanne has given him a toughness in business that he lacked. "When I fill her in on things, she'll make me look a little harder. She'll have me be a little less tolerant, get pushed around a little bit less. That's been a big plus for me." While he has been Joanne's mentor in the business world, he says, she has been his "mentor in life."

Many couples are convinced that their business life, including all its pressures, has strengthened their personal relationship. For a great number of them, this becomes truer as the years go by and they weather the stresses. Because of the controversy he has stirred up with *Penthouse* and his own flamboyance, Bob Guccione comes across as surprisingly romantic on this issue. He has lived and worked with Kathy Keeton for more than 20 years now, and he says: "As the business grows, so our relationship deepens and becomes more and more complex." The increasing complexity of the business, he contends, "contributes to the success of the relationship in that it gives us more reason to be together, more reason to *want* to be together, more reason to want to talk together, more reason to want to share things, problems, ideas, love."

SHARING THE POWER AND THE REWARDS

We Check and Balance
Each Other

Massimo and Lella Vignelli are co-owners of Vignelli Associates, a prestigious New York design firm with credits ranging from Bloomingdale's shopping bags to church interiors. Massimo is president and Lella is executive vice president. They have a second company, Vignelli Designs, Inc., which does product and furniture design. Massimo is chairman and Lella is president. Both companies are corporations, and this husband and wife get equal salaries. An accountant once suggested that Lella's salary be lower than her husband's; that's one reason why they no longer use that particular accountant. While they are both involved in design, it is Lella who handles all the companies' finances, including, when necessary, securing loans from the bank. The Vignellis have 35 employees, and Lella is generally perceived as the "office boss" while Massimo is seen as the "design boss."

In Houston, Diane and Leonard Johnson are 50–50 owners of $65-million-a-year Central Pipe & Supply, also a corporation. Diane, who is executive vice president, handles accounting and finance, and Leonard, president, is in charge of sales and marketing. But Leonard earns a larger salary. Says Diane: "I never knew of an executive vice president who made the same as the president did."

Robert Guccione and his longtime companion Kathy Keeton run Penthouse International, Ltd., the corporation that publishes *Penthouse, Omni,* and other magazines. Guccione, the chairman, is the creative force behind the company, but Keeton, vice chairman, is its hands-on manager. While Guccione works at home on Manhattan's Upper East Side in what company news releases describe, quite correctly, as their "palatial" townhouse, Keeton spends her days at corporate headquarters on Broadway. Despite her power, she does not have ownership in Penthouse International. The company is in Guccione's name and Keeton, who receives a salary, is, he says, "well paid." She *is* part owner of the renowned art collection housed in their home. The collection includes works by Botticelli, Gaugin, van Gogh, Renoir, Matisse, Picasso, and Modigliani, and Guccione estimates its value at $20 million. If Guccione were to die, the company would continue to be administered by Keeton, and ownership would be shared equally by her and his five children. Guccione describes Keeton as "heavily protected" both financially and in terms of her position in the company. Indeed, Keeton does not seem worried about her future.

Karen's Canvas in Fort Myers, Florida, is a sole proprietorship in Karen Quade's name. "I just work here," jokes husband Dennis, who says the arrangement offered tax advantages. The Quades also thought a company headed by a woman might be a factor in attracting customers. Karen is in charge of manufacturing the company's canvas awnings and boat covers and Dennis handles sales and management. They have six employees (including themselves) and annual revenues of about $200,000. Most of the money has been going back into the business. The Quades don't take any salaries yet; they just draw money out to live on as needed.

In 1985, Lorraine Mecca and her husband, Geza Csige, resigned from Micro D, the Santa Ana computer distributorship that they had started in the late 1970s. Micro D is a public company, and documents show that as of February 18, 1985, then-president Richard Lionetti, at $147,978, had been the highest-paid executive officer for the fiscal year ended October 31, 1984. Mecca, vice chairman and CEO, at $121,215 in direct compensation, was the second highest paid; her husband, who was chairman of the board, does not show up on a list of executives with direct compensation of $60,000 or more. Furthermore, Mecca owned 51 percent of the common stock while Csige owned none. While Mecca was very much the public figure for the company and once told me she was the final decision maker on major issues, such as the decision to go public, some observers characterize Csige as the power behind the throne, though a man who shied away from a public role.

As these examples begin to suggest, the ways in which couples share the responsibilities, the rewards, and, yes, the power of running a business are infinite in their variety. How they make

decisions and the choices they make speak to the satisfaction
each gets from his or her work, to the self-esteem that comes
from both psychic and material rewards, to whether a company
runs smoothly or not, and even to whether it grows in accordance
with its potential. If there is resentment or dissatisfaction on
the part of either, the result can be damaging conflict or a less-
than-optimum performance by one or both partners.

Because the partners are so intimately involved with and invested in each other, all the areas of a business—from the division
of labor, job performance, and decision making to supervision
and remuneration—can be emotionally charged in ways they
would not be if the partners were unrelated. The most difficult
part of being in business with her husband, says Deborah Dodson, a Silver Spring, Maryland, veterinarian, is the "emotions
affecting our business decisions. We are more volatile, more critical, more demanding, and less tolerant of each other than we
would be with someone else. It is difficult to be patient with
your spouse in a business situation—something like trying to
teach him or her to drive a car every day."

Her husband, Raymond Craft, says that when they started
their veterinary practice in 1982, they were engaged to be married
and "too much in love to conceive of any 'difficulties' between
us that the business might cause." Now as he looks back, he
says the greatest disadvantage has been the tension and stress
generated by operating a business, particularly a pioneer business
like theirs—they provide outpatient medical care to pets in a
mobile unit. "The natural reaction is to try to control situations
for favorable outcome," says Craft. "In controlling, all too often
you step on the other person. The end result is damage to your
personal relationship."

GETTING CAUGHT BETWEEN TWO SYSTEMS

It is important to be clear about one thing: conflict and differences are a given.

"Differences and conflict are just a built-in part of our life,"
says Stephen Swartz of Hubler/Swartz and Associates, a Minneapolis consulting firm that specializes in family-owned business.
"It's a question of how do we manage conflict, not how do we
avoid it."

Swartz is an attorney and business consultant and his partner,
Thomas Hubler, is a family therapist and organizational consultant. They view a couple-owned business as one form of family
business, and point out that people in family businesses are operating under two types of human organizations or "systems" with
dramatically different goals and values, and the people involved
can get caught in between.

A family system, say Hubler and Swartz, is emotion-based.
Members are bound together by emotional ties that are both
positive and negative. This system is "oriented inward," toward
the security and nurturing of its members. A family emphasizes
loyalty and protection and, to maintain the equilibrium of the
family, it seeks to minimize change.

In contrast, a business system is based on the accomplishment
of tasks. It is "oriented outward," toward the production of goods
or services. It places high value on the competency and productivity of its members, and, in order to survive, it operates to make
the most of change, not minimize it.

While a couple or a family can never separate the two systems
completely, say Hubler and Swartz, it is possible to treat them
as separate entities. And this is what the couple must do if their
business and their relationship are to thrive. Setting ground rules
and dealing with business issues at the office and marital and
family issues at home is a starting point for a couple to find a
balance between family life and to manage "boundary issues"—
those issues where, unless a couple is vigilant, personal life spills
over into the business or the business spills over into the personal
relationship.

The uses of conflict and differences as a positive force in business are discussed at greater length later in this chapter, and
the separation of business from a couple's personal life is dealt

with in further detail in Chapter 7. But it is important to point out here that how a couple makes decisions and how they structure their company can have a profound effect, positively or negatively, on their intimate relationship. The reverse is also true. As David Bork, a family business consultant based in Frederick, Maryland, points out, the dynamics of a couple's personal relationship gets played out in the business. "Many times, the problems that come out in a business can be explained in the problems that were in the relationship to begin with." The partners' individual personal styles will feed into their individual management styles, which may complement each other or produce conflict. If they are competitive with each other in the personal relationship, they are likely to be competitive in the business relationship as well. And if, in their personal relationship, they have not overcome their reluctance to talk about money, or if the risks they are willing to take with money are at odds, these factors, too, will find their way into the business.

The unaware couple can run into some real problems unless they can arrive at some deep understanding of themselves and their partners and learn to sort out the business and the personal issues. It is possible for them to structure a company and their own behavior in such ways that *damaging* conflict is reduced to a minimum or eliminated and so that the enterprise demands contributions from and rewards each partner fairly.

Swartz and Hubler say that once a business gets beyond the idea or experimental state and is becoming a real business, a couple needs to establish a set of plans in a number of areas. Agreed to and written down, such plans will provide the framework in which a couple can conduct their business. The plans establish rules and clarify issues, enabling a couple to proceed with other decisions without fighting or unnecessary conflict and without power struggles.

The plans that Swartz suggest are fourfold:

1. An ownership plan, which should deal not only with the present but also with the perpetuation of the business.

2. A business plan, setting forth the long-range vision for the company, its objectives, and how the couple is going to accomplish those objectives. Swartz emphasizes that this should be a formal written plan, not something in your head or back pocket. Not having a clear understanding of what the business plan is leaves a couple wide open for conflict.

3. A management plan. With a business plan in place, a couple can discuss management issues in a less explosive way. Once the couple has agreed on the goals and how to reach them, it becomes easier to determine who does what to achieve those goals. Management issues become less of a power struggle and much more based on objective considerations such as skills needed for certain roles, competence, and the like. The management plan should include the following elements: a published organizational structure agreed upon by all members of the business; a description of the management skills your business requires; an assessment of the interests and skills of people currently operating the business; a training and development plan for all the managers; and written job descriptions and performance goals. These plans should take into account the roles of nonfamily members. Hubler and Swartz warn that without a published organizational chart, the family structure tends to superimpose itself on the business, and the distinction between family and business roles becomes blurred. If one person is perceived as the head of the family, for example, that person tends to be responsible for all business decisions, even when those decisions could be better made at other levels in the organization. Other family members may find their careers hampered by feelings and assumptions that have nothing to do with their skills and abilities.

4. An operational systems plan, which should cover the following:

Meetings. Couples may think they don't have to have meetings because they have access to each other whenever they want. But Hubler and Swartz contend that meetings are essential—they help a couple make decisions in a more businesslike fashion, and they help the couple prevent the business from "bleeding" into their personal life. Meetings should include ongoing management meetings held regularly (preferably once a week, away from the office) and planning meetings, such as quarterly all-day sessions to review and revise long-range plans.

Communication. Existing communication patterns have to be looked at so that more effective patterns can be established. For example, are third parties used as a buffer to carry unpleasant news? Does someone withhold information as a way of exercising power?

Decision making. Often in family businesses, there is ambiguity about who makes decisions and on what basis they are made. A couple needs to determine who will make what decisions and to consider not just themselves but others in their company. "A company grows best," say Hubler and Swartz, "when decision making is delegated to appropriate levels. Spreading that responsibility throughout the organization is part of moving from an entrepreneurial to a managerial organization."

Management of differences. When companies acknowledge differences and deal with them, those differences can be turned into an asset.

Compensation. Every business needs an established compensation or salary administration system, and, add Hubler and Swartz, systematic salary reviews will help make decisions about salaries more objective and, if needed, more fair.

Entrepreneurs—indeed, people—are often resistant to formalizing plans and writing them down. But Judy and Don Quine learned how valuable a written plan could be when they were starting the Professional Karate Association in the mid-1970s. The Beverly Hills couple had long been associated with the television and film industry—Judy's father was Barney Balaban, who headed Paramount Pictures for 30 years, and Don, an actor, appeared regularly on television in "Peyton Place" and "The Virginian," and also has written screenplays, produced, and directed. At the last minute, in 1974, a promoter asked them to help publicize a world championship karate program at the Los Angeles Sports Arena for ABC's "Wide World of Entertainment." They did so, producing a live gate of over 12,000 fans and high television ratings.

Soon after, they began to talk about developing the sport, which had not been organized before. It would be somewhat like starting from scratch with football or baseball. Rules and regulations had to be established, a sanctioning body had to be created, and the support of athletic commissions had to be won over. Don began to talk about the kind of "superstructure" that was needed to make such a dream come true. It sounded monstrous to Judy. But one day, he surprised her with a flow chart that he had asked an artist to prepare. His superstructure was, in effect, a business plan, setting his vision to paper and showing how the sport could develop, what entities and divisions would go into it, and what ancillary businesses would grow out of it.

Once she saw it on paper, it began to make sense to Judy and she thought it looked right. Both could see what needed to be done now, and they knew who could do what best. Don, for example, began to work on developing the rules for the sport, and Judy began to negotiate and work with government officials and athletic commissions. Not only did the written plan help them clarify their goals and roles, it made them more committed. If they had ended up as just promoters of karate events three or four times a year, says Judy, they would have lost interest very quickly.

CARVING UP THE TURF

In any family business, says consultant David Bork, "it is impera-
tive that family members have clearly defined areas of responsibility, so that they don't bang into one another in terms of
how they operate in business. If the responsibilities are not delineated, then you'll end up with people stepping on toes and
getting their feelings hurt."

Nearly all the couples in this project would agree with that
observation. They emphasize the importance of each partner having his or her own area of authority and, almost always, responsibilities are divided along the lines of what each can do best
and what each prefers to do. In some cases, responsibility is
defined by sheer talent. Olga Erteszek spearheaded design at The
Olga Company, while husband Jan brought brilliance to the company's management. Artist Jack Pentes of Pentes Design in Charlotte, North Carolina, guides the creative direction of that company while Ruth Pentes, once a social worker, took on the
administration of the business in the early years of their marriage.
(Jack likes to tell people he is "a creative genius and a fiscal
idiot.") Ruth is now exploring new areas and has recently taken
on a role as the company's photographer.

Sometimes the division of labor and responsibility is based
on the knowledge or experience the individuals bring to the
enterprise, or even on what they are willing to learn to do. Diane
Johnson of Central Pipe & Supply says she has been told by
others that her husband, Leonard, is the best pipe salesman
they've ever known. But in addition to his talent, he brought
two decades of sales experience to their company. As for Diane,
at the age of 38, before the Johnsons even knew they were going
to start their own company, she enrolled in college and earned
a business degree in accounting. When they did go into business,
she was ready. The Johnsons do not get involved in each other's
responsibilities. Says Leonard: "She doesn't worry about whether
the sales are going to be there, and I really don't worry about

whether Oklahoma gets its sales tax." It's the "total confidence" that the other will do his or her job, says Leonard, that makes their partnership work for them.

Jeanette and Howard Shapiro of Howard-Shadim Electronics, Inc., in Crystal Lake, Illinois, began working together full time in their electronic equipment repair company in 1982, but it was not until 1984 that a clear division of responsibilities evolved. They had hired an operations manager from a major corporation, thinking he could help their company bridge the gap from a small enterprise to a larger one. It didn't work out. When he left and the Shapiros split up the responsibilities that the operations manager had been charged with, their own division of labor finally seemed to fall into place. Jeanette took over personnel and administration, which meant managing the computer system and dealing with the bank, the attorneys, and the accountants. Howard took over sales, production, engineering, and new product development. Before that, Jeanette says, it was "a very muddled situation," complicated by the fact that they didn't have enough space and were sharing the same desk. Now they have adequate space for carrying on their functions separately. "Every now and again—it still happens—we'll run into each other with great ferocity," Jeanette says. But for the most part, they work together more effectively now because they have created a structure and a division of responsibilities that makes it possible.

Even when a couple carves up turf, they need to monitor the division of labor periodically to find out if it is still satisfactory and rewarding to both parties. For seven years, psychologist Marta Vago was in business with a man she lived with. They ran a psychotherapy training center, and when they first started their enterprise, Vago was in her mid-twenties and her partner was in his forties. He was the visionary, the idea man, the charismatic personality who was an asset in attracting clients. Vago found that she was doing 85 percent of the administrative work, from making sure the checkbook balanced and bills were paid to seeing that the ashtrays were clean and there was toilet paper in the reception area bathroom.

At first, getting the business off the ground was so exciting in itself that Vago didn't resent the role she was playing. She was still so young that, she says now, she truly wasn't as visionary as her partner. Also, it was a second career for her (she once trained to be a musician) and she had not yet developed confidence in herself in her new field. What's more, she recalls, "We were so in love with each other and the business idea that we never really talked about our new 'child.' We never talked about division of labor. We just kind of did it flying by the seat of our pants. And it worked for a while, because there was just so much to do that as long as it got done, we didn't care who did it or why or how we felt about it."

Early on, she noticed the imbalance, but she didn't take it seriously. Her partner would come up with a wonderful idea; she would end up researching and implementing it.

As the years went by, however, the more angry she became at having to do the lion's share of the detail work. She began to experience a need to grow and to do more creative, fun things. She found that the more she tried to grow into new areas, however, the more her partner resented it, undercutting her directions to employees, for example.

"The more I took over the caretaking, the less imagination I had room for," says Vago. "He could afford to be imaginative because he didn't have anything else to worry about. I didn't have any psychic space in my head to be imaginative because I was taking care of all the dirty work. It's very difficult to spend 85 percent of your time taking care of details and still be creative."

If she tried to talk about her needs, he would change the subject. What made matters even worse was that she felt he did not respect the importance of her contribution to the business and placed more value on his own creative role.

Vago finally left. Him *and* the business. Today, she says, "As soon as I stopped working with him, I found that I had a sense of humor. I found that I had a very creative way of putting things together. I found that I was coming up with more ideas and I was amazed at what began to come out of me when I was no longer just doing scutwork. It was a revelation to me."

Clearly, partners have to value each other's role in the business as much as they do their own. Although he and Diane have quite different responsibilities, Leonard Johnson says their input is equal and they respect each other's contributions. That respect has to be there for a husband–wife partnership to work, he suggests. And, he adds with a laugh, "The suffering has to be equal."

But as the case of Marta Vago and her partner indicates, partners also have to give each other room to grow. David Bork adds a third consideration to the interaction of the family system and the business system that Hubler and Swartz talk about, and that is the matter of individual development. "At 49, I am a very different person than I was at 29. The developmental tasks at various ages are different, and so I bring into the decision making not only my family attitudes, not only my understanding of sound business practice, but also where I am at the stage of life I am at."

Linda H. and Kenneth M. Schatz, who own Schatz & Company, a management consulting firm in Alexandria, Virginia, ran into a problem somewhat similar to the one Marta Vago described, but they found they could talk to each other about it and work toward a resolution. Ken started the company in 1979 and Linda worked part-time with him for two years while she also worked as a writer-editor for "Good Morning America" at ABC News in Washington. In 1981, she began working with Ken full time.

"When I first joined the company, I was doing a lot of administrative work—necessary but not very 'high status,' " says Linda. It wasn't a pervasive problem. Nevertheless, she says, "Sometimes I resented Ken for his high-status, high-visibility role, although my capabilities were in fact not equal to his."

Ken (who is Skip Schatz's brother) says, "There were times when Linda felt she needed more work separation to feel fulfilled and keep her individuality. We've worked on the issue together, keeping her contribution unique and providing a chance for growth and challenge. With time, she has also become quite expert in the area of business management and able to be creative at it."

WHO'S IN CHARGE HERE?

Does a business need a boss—someone with the final authority? Some couples think so; others don't. And family business specialists like David Bork say "It depends." The answer is not simple, he contends, and if someone offers a simple answer to that question, "the chances are they don't really understand."

More important than having one boss, he says, is having "one prevailing viewpoint so that the people who control the business are not divided."

Many couples resist the idea that one of the partners is the top boss. Of the 33 couples represented in our questionnaire, 14 indicated that neither was boss, both were boss, or each was boss in his or her own territory. Twelve couples said the man was the boss, and five named the female partner. In two instances, the partners disagreed about who was boss.

Peter Davis, who is director of executive education at the University of Pennsylvania's Wharton School, where he oversees research on family businesses, says it is not uncommon for the wife to be the powerhouse in an organization but to avoid taking a title that would make her appear to be superior, for fear that doing so would "emasculate" the husband.

The issues of power, titles, and who, if anyone, is boss are tricky ones. It would, in fact, seem that couples see the "driving force" in their businesses as often something quite different from "boss." Seven of the couples in the survey agreed that the husband was the driving force in their businesses, but only four of those particular husbands were identified as bosses. Three additional husbands who *did* appear on the boss list named themselves as the driving force, but their wives disagreed or said they were equal. While only five women were seen as boss by both partners, eight were seen by both to be the driving force in the business. There was considerable variation in the answer to the question of who is the driving force. Several couples said they traded off this role; some said they were equal; others said they were each the driving force in their own respective areas of responsibility.

Twelve of the men in the survey held the top title in their companies; eleven couples said they had equal titles (for example, "partner" or "owner"). In eight cases, the women had what appeared to be the top title, and in two instances, the ranking was unclear.

But, in many cases, titles do not reflect what the couples say is the reality of their organization. Bill and Vieve Gore said the titles of their officers don't mean much at all. As we will see in Chapter 13, W. L. Gore & Associates is organized on an egalitarian basis, with no bosses. Decisions are group decisions made by the leaders who emerge in the various endeavors of the company. In 1985, Bill Gore said, "My oldest son Bob is president of the corporation, which is a corporate responsibility and doesn't describe what he does. I am the chairman of the board. Vieve is secretary-treasurer. We have to have these titles by corporate law here in Delaware, and the corporate officers are responsible, in a legal sense, for the corporation."

Then, with a mischievous smile, he added: "If we were ever indicted for an antitrust violation and had to endure a criminal penalty and go to jail, I think the president should go because he is younger than I am." (Bill was born in 1912.)

Similarly, Bob Harnish is shown as chairman of the Cortina Inn while Breda is president. But both agree there is no one boss and that they are equal driving forces in their company.

When they were setting up the original structure of their company, says Jeanette Shapiro, a consultant told them every corporation should have a majority of stock going to one partner or the other and that whoever had controlling stock should also be president.

It didn't make any difference to Howard, Jeanette recalls, but to her it did, even if only symbolically. So Jeanette is president with 51 percent of the stock to Howard's 49 percent. He is vice president. They both laugh, however, and say that Howard's personality is so forceful that he could control the company with only 5 percent. "To draw a symbol for Howard," says Jeanette, "you have to use a battering ram. He just bulldozes his way into things and he keeps going. It's both the thing I respect and the thing that frustrates me at the same time."

Some couples operate comfortably with one or the other perceived as boss. Doing so identifies a final authority not only for employees but also for customers, suppliers, lenders, and other significant outsiders. But many others prefer to be seen as equals, being the final authority in their own sphere of responsibility. How both approaches can work or go awry, particularly as they affect employees, is explored more fully in the following chapter.

What gets sticky is the situation where one partner is playing the role of boss to the other. In some situations, this can work for a while—for example, where the "boss" partner is clearly more experienced than the other, and the other has some catching up to do, or where the "boss" is seen and accepted by both parties as the dominant partner and the spouse is seen as playing a supportive role. The responses to our questionnaires and our interviews with couples suggest that even in these situations, the less experienced person does catch up and the supportive person's role is so vital in making a business function that one spouse playing boss and the other playing subordinate can be very delicate, even dangerous, if it is not done with skill.

One husband responding to the questionnaire said the hardest part of being in business with his spouse was supervising his wife. "It's very easy to produce hurt feelings in trying to reprimand the other partner," he said. We asked David Bork to comment on the man's use of the word "reprimand." While the entrepreneur is the backbone of our economy and the businesses we have today started because there were entrepreneurs, Bork said, "the entrepreneur is not always a sophisticated, knowledgeable manager." The term "reprimand," he observed, is one you use with your children, not a term sophisticated managers think of when they are dealing with the people they work with or supervise.

"I would say this couple is at risk in terms of the scope of experience the husband brings to the transaction," Bork continued. "I think that a healthy dynamic is the ability to work together and to talk openly about performance and the results that come from our efforts."

"When I hear 'reprimand,' " Bork added, "it suggests that that is a person whose resolution of who he is as an individual is not at as high a level as it could be, and this couple will probably have some difficulty in their working relationship."

Still, it *is* possible for one partner to supervise the other in a way that preserves the "subordinate's" self-esteem and protects the relationship. The focus must be on the work itself and not the individual who did it. Instead of saying the equivalent of, "Hey, dummy, you did it this way," Bork suggests, the supervising partner can say, "Let's look at how this got done and how it could be done better so that we achieve this result." If the couple "is truly together in their commitment to the effort at hand," says Bork, they are going to be more willing to engage in the work-focused approach. "But if there's a subtlety of competition between them, they're going to have difficulty doing what I'm describing, and it will get played out in less than positive ways between the two of them."

The very fact that some couples are so entrepreneurial helps them solve the question of "who's in charge?" in a very egalitarian way. They start more than one company so that each is in charge of one endeavor. Veterinarians Ray Craft and Deborah Dodson, for example, started Petvacx, their mobile veterinary service, and Petcorner, which wholesales veterinary pharmaceuticals. Ray is president of Petvacx and Deborah is vice president; Deborah is president of Petcorner and Ray is vice president. Although they say neither is each other's boss in either business, they have learned they must divide responsibilities according to their strengths and weaknesses. Until they delineated responsibility, says Ray, "it was chaotic."

Joanne Schatz owns and plays the leadership role in her Vertech Back & Bed Stores, while husband Skip owns and runs the Virginia Adjustable-Bed Manufacturing Corporation. And while Debbi and Randy Fields own a number of businesses together, she has the final word at Mrs. Fields Cookies and he is the final authority in Fields Investment. Courtney Garton of Annapolis, Maryland, is president of Hats in the Belfry Franchise Corporation, which oversees their franchised stores, while Margie Bryce is president of Hats in the Belfry, Inc., which handles their company-owned stores.

Linda and Ken Schatz have found another way to cope not only with the problem of sharing power but also with Linda's personal growth needs. "Ken was president of the company for the first five years of its existence," says Linda. "I've now taken over the presidency, so I'll have the experience of being responsible for the company and so Ken's sense of responsibility can be lightened so he'll expand his creative energy."

As Ken puts it: "I was the boss for five years. Now Linda is the boss. The company had been my creation and I had the business knowledge. After five years, it's now *ours*, not mine, and Linda has the ability to be the boss. It's better for the company to do it this way now."

STRUCTURING OWNERSHIP OF THE COMPANY—AND THE MONETARY REWARDS

Should a couple's company be a sole proprietorship, a partnership, or a corporation? Should they have equal ownership or is it beneficial to have a majority owner? And who should get what compensation?

Perhaps a quick review of the legal forms a business can take is in order.

A sole proprietorship is a simple form of business usually owned and managed by one person. It is the easiest and least costly form of business to start—in most states, you need only obtain the required local licenses to set up shop. The owner receives all the profits (less taxes, of course). The major disadvantage of a proprietorship is that the owner has unlimited personal liability, meaning that he or she is personally responsible for all the debts of the business. Other drawbacks are limited access to capital and lack of continuity of the business. "When the business is the person, the business ceases to be when the person becomes ill, disabled, or expires," say Norman M. Scarborough and Thomas W. Zimmer in their textbook, *Effective Small Business Management.* The possible lack of continuity and the fact that most proprietorships stay small make it difficult to attract and retain good employees, they say.

A partnership involves two or more people who engage in business as co-owners. They share the assets, the liabilities, and the profits. Like the sole proprietorship, a partnership is easy and inexpensive to establish, but it has the same major drawback: partners listed as general partners (and there must be at least one) are exposed to unlimited personal liability.

A corporation is a legal entity, separate from its owners. It may do business, make contracts, sue and be sued, and pay taxes. Its advantages include the fact that each investor is able to limit his liability to the total amount of his investment; thus personal assets are protected. In addition, corporations are generally more able to attract capital, and their life is not dependent on the health or life of a single individual. However, it takes more time and expense to set up a corporation. And there may be either tax advantages or disadvantages, depending on such factors as the revenues of the company, your personal tax bracket, and whether profits are retained in the company.

Although proprietorships are the most popular form of business ownership in the United States, couples who own *growing* businesses seem to lean toward incorporation instead. Of the 32 businesses represented in our questionnaires, 19 were corporations, 8 were sole proprietorships, 4 were partnerships, and 1 was a Subchapter S corporation. (Frequently used when it is known a company will experience losses, the Subchapter S corporation combines the features of a partnership and a corporation by permitting profits and losses to pass through to the shareholders, but retaining the benefit of limited liability.) Of the 34 businesses represented in the interviews, over 20 were corporations.

"Personally, I believe that incorporating your business is the smart thing to do," says James C. Comiskey in his book *How to Start, Expand and Sell a Business.* "Certainly it's the safest." He thinks the unlimited liability exposure in a sole proprietorship or partnership is just too risky.

Frederic M. (Ric) Zigmond, national director for accounting and business advisory services for Laventhol & Horwath, one of the Big Eight accounting firms, agrees and says that normally L&H reccommends a corporation. But incorporating costs $1,000–$1,500, he notes, and if the business is still very small and the risk of a lawsuit is low, a couple may choose to set up as a sole proprietorship or a partnership. Generally, however, Zigmond suggests that if $50,000 or more is required to get a business off the ground, the couple is in a league where incorporation is the wiser choice.

In community property states, it doesn't much matter in whose name the company is owned because, under law, assets acquired during a marriage belong equally to husband and wife, whether they are in business together or not. However, Zigmond says, if the business was started by one of the partners before the marriage, it makes sense to establish the worth of the business at the time of the marriage. Should a divorce occur, the non-founding spouse would then be entitled only to an equal share of the *growth* that the company had experienced during the marriage.

In most other states, a couple can agree on whatever split they choose. Some advisers counsel against a couple sharing ownership on a 50–50 basis, citing the possibility of an impasse in decision making. But Zigmond disagrees with such advice. "I very rarely have seen people say, 'I own 51 percent; therefore we're going to do it my way.' " Even if the partners aren't married, he points out, a partnership is *like* a marriage. "If anybody starts forcing their will, it's hard to live under it." In theory, if one partner owns 51 percent or more, he or she does have the right to call the shots. "In practice, I just haven't seen it really work that way," says Zigmond. If you continue disagreeing with each other, he says, the reality is that you end up breaking up the business.

Like Jeanette Shapiro, however, a man or a woman may *want* that extra percentage or two for the symbolism it represents. And some couples assign majority ownership to the female partner because doing so helps the enterprise qualify for government contracts in cases where minority and disadvantaged business owners are favored. For that reason, Gayle and Jimmy Sensing of Medical HomeCare Services, Inc., in Nashville have set up their corporation so that Gayle is 75 percent owner and Jimmy owns the other 25 percent.

Fourteen of the businesses in the questionnaires were owned 50–50 by the husband and wife and another two were 100 percent jointly owned. These were followed by an erratic mix of sole proprietorships where either partner was 100-percent owner or corporations where husband or wife retained majority control in varying percentages. Often the spouse who had initiated the company was the one who had majority ownership.

Sometimes if one spouse has ownership of the business, some measure has been taken to equalize the situation for the other partner. In the case of C & W Seafood, for example, the company is a sole proprietorship in Chris Dickerman's name. However, the equipment is in Winnie's name.

When it comes to compensating a husband and wife, accountants have frequently advised couples that one partner be paid a substantial salary while the other (usually the woman) be paid little or nothing. There is a good reason for one spouse taking a very small salary, says L&H's Ric Zigmond: doing so can save a couple a lot of money. When both are paid equal or near equal salaries, it can be very costly in terms of Social Security taxes and sometimes unemployment, disability, and health plans.

Take 1986, for example, a year in which employer and employee each must contribute 7.15 percent of wages to Social Security on incomes up to $42,000. If each spouse is paid $42,000, between them and their company, they have to pay $6,000 in Social Security twice for a total of $12,000. If one spouse is paid $84,000 and the other nothing, they pay Social Security only for the salaried spouse and save $6,000. However, this is the age of Individual Retirement Accounts, and Zigmond says even the lower-paid spouse should receive enough to put $2,000 away in an IRA. A couple must also look at pension plans, their ages, and other factors before making decisions on compensation, and compensation may need to be updated as the situation changes—as, for example, when one spouse retires or one's pension fund becomes fully funded and the couple wants to develop the other's.

However—and this is a big however—Zigmond also points

up the importance of ego and self-esteem in such considerations. While it may cost extra to compensate both spouses equally or according to their contribution to the company, it may be the smart thing to do. "It makes you feel more worthwhile when you're being compensated properly," he says, noting that a check in hand is visible evidence of your worth. If somebody doesn't feel his or her worth, it creates other problems in the company.

Although sometimes tax advisers urge one spouse to take a smaller salary so that the Internal Revenue Service won't question whether that spouse's compensation (including bonuses and perks) is "reasonable," Zigmond says he has never had a client audited on that issue. There might be a problem with a spouse working 20 hours a week and taking a $150,000 salary, but if both spouses are working full time and each is taking $40,000 or even $80,000, he says, "I probably don't see a problem with that."

Whatever legal structure and compensation a couple chooses will need to be determined with the guidance of an attorney and an accountant and must, of course, conform with state and federal law. However, it is important that the partners discuss the issues with each other thoroughly and determine what they want rather than just let themselves be talked into a recommendation that is based on tradition. Make your desires clear to your advisers, listen to the pros and cons, but make your own decision about what is right for your business and for you as a couple. In our interviews and questionnaires, we found that some couples were not sure why ownership and salaries were set up the way they were, and some could not remember, for example, which partner had controlling interest. In some cases, this merely reflected a total trust in and comfort with each other and long years of working together; in others, it suggested that a couple had followed advice without thinking through the issues as thoroughly as they might have.

In many instances, however, couples—like the Vignellis—are

insisting on equal ownership and equal salaries as evidence of the equality of the relationship and the equality of the contribution that each partner is making to the enterprise.

Nevertheless, Hubler and Swartz remind couples that, in their decision making, they should regard ownership and compensation as two separate issues. "We think the compensation system needs to be related to the function that people perform in the company, not to their ownership status," says Hubler. In other words, just because you are 50–50 owners does not necessarily mean you should receive 50–50 compensation.

SHARING RESPONSIBILITIES AT HOME

Since being an entrepreneurial couple usually entails having a wife devote herself 40 or many more hours a week to the business, she is not available to give the time and care to the home and family that she would if she were a full-time homemaker or even had a 9-to-5 job. Help has to come from somewhere, and if the couples who responded to our questionnaires are to be believed, much of that help is coming from the husbands. Still, the larger share of the burden at home is falling to the wife.

Among the 33 couples represented by the questionnaires, 10 of the women said they had most of the domestic housekeeping responsibilities, although two of them said that child care was more evenly split between husband and wife. Eight of the couples said they shared housework equally, and another six said they split domestic responsibilities along traditional lines—the husband took care of the externals, such as the lawn, home maintenance, and the car, while the wife handled cooking and housekeeping. Only half a dozen or so indicated they had some form of part-time help, and Joseph G. King of Florida Azalea Specialists in Ruskin, Florida, said he and Donna had lost their once-a-week housekeeper and were looking for another. "We have to find one soon—that vacuum cleaner is killing me!"

Of the remaining nine, four said housekeepers handled all or most of the housework. Another respondent didn't address the issue of housekeeping, but said her husband shared equally in child care. Another couple reported substantial help from family members.

Sometimes perceptions about who does what differ. In two instances, the husbands said they did most of the housework, but the wives, in their responses, said the work was shared. In fact, one husband said he did 90 percent of the housework, but his wife reported that household duties from cooking to cutting the lawn were shared "but I still tend to try and be the traditional wife!"

One senses, in reading the questionnaires, that even in households where the housework is shared, it is still the woman's *responsibility*. In other words, she is taking the leadership role in getting things done here. Still, these wives seem satisfied with the arrangement, as do the wives where the division was said to be traditional. In the latter, the husband was seen as taking a fair portion of the domestic burden even if it wasn't housework.

There was an occasional expression of resignation, however, as in the case of Breda Harnish of Cortina Inn, who said: "We don't do housekeeping. Our house is kept about 90 percent less than our mothers kept their houses. Bob hauls wood, does dishes. I shop and cook. We each take care of our own clothes. The dust balls form in the corners. We have a beautiful home and I wish I had time to take better care of it." Husband Bob, who points out that he also does much of the laundry and keeps the cars clean, adds, "As Breda says, 'We need a wife,' and we would hire one in a minute if we could find one."

Only among the couples where the wife clearly had the greater household burden was there an edge to some of the comments. Wrote one wife, speaking of herself in the third person: "[She] does all housework and always has. Husband has never felt this was part of the man's job. This poses a problem because wife feels if she works full time in business that husband should share household duties." The husband is not at all apologetic. He writes: "Wife does all the housework and always stays behind. She complains an awful lot."

One husband acknowledged that his wife had more child-care responsibilities because he had longer working hours and more outside activities. But *she* says that although she believes her husband has good intentions and thinks of himself as a good father, he "justifies his being away from [the children] so much by saying that after he reaches this or that illusive goal, then he can afford to stay home more. I feel that he does our family a disservice by being so involved with the future that the burden of raising and caring for our kids *right now* is mainly on my shoulders."

And Susan Stangland of Pepperwood International observes that men don't seem to be able to juggle as many roles as women, do. Asked to fill in her title, she wrote "Businessmom."

But even the overburdened wives are often able to maintain a sense of humor. Says Tari Vickery of KVTV Carpets in Oklahoma City: "We have a housekeeper once a week and the rest of the time it stays a mess. Kent doesn't know which cabinets the dishes belong in, and we've lived in the same house for five years. In other words, I do what little bit gets done. We sometimes will go three months without eating at home." And Rosanne Kranitz of WCK Associates in Pompano Beach, Florida, says her husband is great about sharing the household chores, but if he or their daughter falls down on the job, "I make a sign and go on strike for a day. It works every time."

Couples in the interviews revealed a strong bias for shared domestic responsibility or, at the very least, recognition that a full-time business colleague needs support of some kind on the home front.

Robert and Joan Zimmerman of Charlotte, North Carolina, have been married for 30 years and for the last 27 have been running Southern Shows, Inc., a company that sponsors consumer and trade shows and grosses between $6 million and $7 million a year. As long as 25 years ago, they had a sign in their kitchen that said "Equal Opportunity Kitchen." Robert says that if he got home first, he cooked the evening meal; if Joan arrived first, she did. He did the grocery shopping and pushed the vacuum cleaner right along with her. "Robert is exactly right," says Joan. "He has taken as much of the home burden as I have, and I have taken as much of the business burden as he has." They have an office at home, and when their sons were young, one or the other would often work at home if a child needed attending.

Patricia and Mel Ziegler of the Banana Republic say they share domestic responsibilities the same way they share business responsibilities. They each do what they hate to do least. "He doesn't mind the laundry, but he hates the dishes," says Patricia. They try to find enough help near their home in Marin County, she adds, "to help us feed our cats and sweep the floors."

Bill and Vieve Gore had a housekeeper three days a week. Even so, Bill got breakfast in the morning because he was the early riser. ("I have a hard time getting up in the mornings," said Vieve. "I don't think until a little bit later.") Vieve prepared dinner and, unless they went out, lunch.

At the Tim Lawrence–Susan Cobey household, Tim does 80 percent of the cooking because, says Susan, "He gets hungry before I do, usually." Tim estimates that he also does about 60 percent of the dishwashing, while Susan takes more responsibility for laundry and keeping the house neat. They have no children and do not plan to have any. They both feel that Tim doesn't have the patience for being a father, and he prefers, in any case, to give the fullest possible commitment to their bee business. During pollination season in the spring, Susan adds, the work "gets frantic. It is a struggle just to figure out who is going to cook a meal."

At first it seems surprising that so many of these couples do so much for themselves domestically when the size of their businesses suggests that they would never have to lift a finger at home again if they chose not to. In some of the younger companies, however, the couples are not yet taking out salaries. Even though a business like Mothers Work, formed in 1983, brings in $2.5 million annually and is doubling every year, the Matthiases as of late 1985 had not yet begun to draw any salaries from it. More important, Rebecca says that they once did have a babysitter but found that they prefer not to, the key reason being that when there is no babysitter, she and Dan spend more time with their children. "Since our business is in our home, the children tend to wander in and out of our office all afternoon (they are in nursery school mornings only), and depending on who is busy or on the phone, the other will change a diaper or put a child in for his nap."

Some women do a great deal of their own domestic work because they still experience guilt not doing it themselves, or they are dissatisfied with hired help that does not keep the home as clean as they would like. And some living in small towns or rural areas say they have a hard time finding the household help they need.

However the domestic chores and child care are handled, it benefits the business (and the marriage) if neither partner—and that usually means the wife—is overburdened by having to give full-time work weeks to both home and business. Entrepreneurial couples who recognize this—the Gores, the Fieldses, and the Lewises, for example—have thrived especially well and one suspects that one of the reasons is that the wife has not been totally drained by having to shoulder two awesome and time-consuming responsibilities without support and cooperation from the partner. When a wife is not on overload, she has the mental and physical energy left to contribute to the advancement of the business.

Sometimes this means taking a creative approach. Randy Fields declares himself to be old-fashioned when it comes to the division of labor. "I am not a househusband." He oversees the cars, travel arrangements, and what he calls "the physical universe outside the house." The house and child care, to him, are in Debbi's domain. He will not wash dishes, he will not vacuum, he will not babysit, and he will not change diapers. She accepts that and will not ask him to do those things. They say there is no resentment about the arrangement because they are straight with each other about it and don't have false expectations. Randy doesn't place restrictions on how Debbi handles her responsibilities, insisting, for example, that she do the housework herself. That would put her in an impossible situation, he says. If Debbi chooses not to do certain tasks herself, however, she must find someone to do them or come up with some other alternative. He is not interested in turning Debbi into a subordinate but in finding ways they can accommodate each other.

Says Randy: "I am willing to compromise in terms of paying someone to come wash the dishes, and I am *not* willing to compromise in terms of *doing* the dishes. I will break them first."

Says Debbi: "I just have to think of the solutions."

Says Randy: "What I am saying is I am willing to eat off paper plates."

And with some frequency, they do.

IN PRAISE OF DIFFERENCES—AND CONFLICT

The individuals in any relationship are different from each other. Each looks at the world from a separate perspective, brings different attitudes and a unique set of experiences into the relationship, and has a distinct management style. Each also has a separate set of skills and talents and probably a different mental process or way of organizing knowledge and information. Sometimes partners come from entirely different cultural backgrounds. All these differences can lead to disagreement and conflict. But differences need not tear a couple apart; they can, instead, be used as a tool to benefit the business and perhaps even the couple's relationship.

Differences, according to consultant Steve Swartz, are a big asset to a company. "It's *working* those differences that is going to be the creative spark to do what you need to do." Some family business members keep quiet because they are afraid that if they express themselves, they will create conflict. By holding back, says Swartz, they are cheating not only themselves but also the company, because the company is deprived of the contribution they could make.

Instead of letting disagreements escalate into personally damaging encounters, couples can learn to manage their differences, recognizing that differences can make them complementary partners—with one being strong where the other is weak and vice versa or blending their perspectives to come up with better ideas for products or ways of doing things. Instead of criticizing each *other,* couples can learn to criticize each other's *ideas* or to give feedback on *performance,* and to do so in an atmosphere of trust, without wounding each other. Instead of competing with each other, they can join together and compete against the outside world for their own mutual benefit. In short, they can learn to value and make use of their differences rather than despair over them.

Although he comes from a corporate setting, Richard F. Wright sets an example for making use of differences and conflict that couples might find helpful. Wright is vice president of research and development for Mead Imaging, a division of the Mead Corporation in Dayton, Ohio. Beginning in the early 1980s, Wright built, from the ground up, a team of over 50 people, including 35 scientists and technicians, who have developed a process for dry-developing color images on light-sensitive paper. The process is so advanced that the color images produced are of the quality found in better magazines; ultimately the process will be linked with computer technology.

Wright set out to develop a different "norm" in his organization, one that would result in optimum creativity and productivity. "I wanted a team that worked well together, but at the same time, I wanted people to be free to openly disagree with each other and with me. I wanted people to find ways to develop their own style and yet build a team philosophy which would allow us to find, in a consensual way, what the key issues were, what our primary goals should be, and how we could best resolve these issues and reach our goals."

In a research environment, observes Wright, people must be willing to accept debate, differences, and even argument as part of the game. Very often, however, when people believe their ideas are being challenged, Wright says, "they project this challenge of their ideas onto their self-esteem and become hostile." In order to eliminate defensiveness and the inclination of people to attack each other instead of each other's ideas, Wright found that his job as a manager was to create an atmosphere "which treated conflict and creative conflict resolution as the norm." The effort required constant attention, he says, but he concentrated on fostering a questioning mentality among group members. "I got them used to debate on technical issues. I supported my views tenaciously but accepted being wrong with a smile and with as much lightheartedness as I could muster." By the time his staff grew to 30, this approach had become a part of its "culture." Says Wright: "We were viewed by the rest of the building as a group that constantly disagreed with each other [and] fought in the hallways and in meetings, and yet we always seemed to have fun and we got things done."

Keeping the focus on issues and ideas instead of personalities, Wright found, was the most effective way to create an innovative, productive environment. His approach encouraged disagreement and conflict, but it was structured to minimize the kind of personal attack that so often paralyzes organizations—and couples.

"In a healthy business," asserts David Bork, "conflict is normal and it is productive." The couple that cannot handle conflict that stems from differences of opinion, resolve it, and move on, he warns, "is not going to be as successful in business." Even lack of knowledge on the part of one partner can prove beneficial. Bork says that research shows that if you have five people, all knowledgeable on the subject at hand, working together on a problem, they will come up with a good solution. But if you have four knowledgeable people and one who is not, the second group will produce a better solution because that one person is saying, "I don't understand why you do it that way," or, "This doesn't make sense to me." The second group, explains Bork, "has more healthy debate, which some people call 'conflict.' The questions lead to a more thorough examination of the problem and hence, better solutions."

"If the family cannot manage differences or handle conflict," Bork sums up, "then they are going to be less effective in their business."

Sydney and Frances Lewis of Best Products are among the fortunate couples who seem to have a natural ability to manage their differences and conflicts. When you ask them what the advantages of being in business together are, they dwell first on the way they complement each other.

"I've always believed that two heads are better than one," says Sydney. The Lewises value the opportunity to "run things by each other." When they can both offer their ideas and opinions, it helps them to refine their thinking. They say they also feel free to express their thoughts to each other in ways that they would not with other colleagues. Frances describes herself as blunt and good at being to the point about raising issues that need to be raised, while Sydney is more diplomatic. His diplomacy means that he is better at working with other people. Frances says that she may often see exactly what needs to be done—that, for example, they can get a better price from a vendor or faster delivery. She can raise that issue with her husband and, because of his diplomatic skill, he will "be better at figuring out a way that we could get the other person to do what we want."

While Sydney may be what they describe as more "politic" with others, Frances says he is as direct with her as she is with him. But they describe their relationship as such a good fit and as being so solid that they are able to say things to each other that might cause real difficulty in another couple's relationship but not in theirs. With her, Frances says, Sydney can feel free enough to tell her that her figures are "bum," or to say, "Dummy, you never thought of relating Q to X." With each other—but not with people outside the relationship—she says, "It's much easier to say to each other bluntly, 'that's a damned fool idea.'"

Wouldn't that hurt her feelings?

"No," she answers. "It would make me mad, but I would know there was nothing personal in it."

Few couples can articulate just how it is they learned to have conflict without taking it personally, but Judy and Don Quine of the Professional Karate Association help to offer a picture of how the process works. They recall the early days of their business when they used to have Friday night meetings with others at their office. They would have been working hard and by that time of the week, they would both be tired and short-tempered.

"So Don would say something, and I would say, 'Well, up yours!'" Judy says. It wouldn't really be a vitriolic encounter, "but we'd have a 'partners' argument' about an issue." Judy and Don saw, however, that the others would blanch and eyes would dart around the room. "They were, of course, sure they were witnessing the demise of this marriage," says Judy.

Soon a compromise would be reached or one partner would persuade the other. "The meeting would be over and Don and I would put an arm around each other and say, 'Okay, Sweetie, let's go get something to eat.'" Everyone's mouth would be open, Judy says, because they just couldn't imagine that you could have such a heated interchange and still walk out arm-in-arm.

The Quines make it a point to separate the two entities called "business" and "home." This does not mean they don't discuss business at home—in fact, their office is over the garage of their elegant, rambling Beverly Hills house. But as Judy expresses it: "We were aware of the fact that this was a business we were creating, and then there was the thing called our home, our family, our relationship together as a man and a woman. And the two were not necessarily emotionally linked." Their sense of each other's worth is based not on what happens in the business, say Don and Judy, but in their home and personal life. Business is "an extra."

"The fact that we don't agree with each other in business is not some kind of extension of our home," says Judy. "It's our *business*."

The ability to work out an emotional separation between business and the family—the Quines have six children—did not come quickly. It took a lot of talking out and practice, and they got better at it with time. But Judy says she thinks it has still come more quickly to them than to other couples she knows "who worked together and said they were never able to have a business conflict without it seeming like a marriage battle. Obviously there was some facility in us to be able to do that."

The Quines do recognize their differences. Don points out that Judy is gregarious and comfortable with dealing with all kinds of people while he is an "isolationist"; they have distinct communication styles, with Judy being talkative and very articulate while Don, in conversation, is sparse. Judy likes to cover all the territory, Don says, while he assumes—often correctly, he laughs—that when he talks, people understand what's "between the lines."

"I think part of any marriage finding its legs and keeping its roots solid," says Judy, "is learning to admire those things that are alike and those things that are different, and not needing to have the other person become an image of your own self, in order to validate who you are."

Mel and Patricia Ziegler ponder the thought that if they had not started the Banana Republic, perhaps their marriage might not have lasted. In many ways, their business forced them to learn to interact successfully.

One of the overriding reasons they were drawn together, according to Mel, is that they both look at the world in a creative way and they both question everything. Patricia, however, is more visual in her orientation, while Mel is more conceptual, and they see themselves as opinionated people, each with his or her own vision of how things should be. "Neither of us is the easiest person in the world to get along with," says Patricia.

"It took us years to figure out how to get along in the business, and yet neither of us could have done this without the other," says Mel.

"By going through this business together," adds Patricia, "it made our relationship more powerful, more effective somehow. I feel the power of ourselves as a couple."

One of their biggest struggles was learning to isolate their business problems from their emotional disagreements. "The times we got into the greatest arguments," says Mel, "were when we just didn't argue about the problem but we brought up all the other stuff that we argue about—doing dishes and laundry—as well." He says the best advice he can offer any couple going into business together would be not to mix business problems and personal problems. "Create a moat around the business problems. Do not get personal in discussing business problems. Then, somehow, you preserve the relationship as something sacred; it can't be invaded in the ways that will happen if you don't do this."

Handling disagreements and conflict in the early stages of a business may be tougher because the partners are often still young, unproven, and insecure. Lella Vignelli speaks of the difficult years when you are trying to understand each other and establish yourself, and the competition between you is strong. Later, she says, you are "not so thirsty for recognition." Still, she says, she and Massimo always had the ability to focus their disagreements on the issue and not on each other's personalities.

"We learned to trust each other in the sense that when we make a criticism, even a negative criticism, first of all, we try to be very rational about it," she says. When they are giving criticism or defending a design, they require a well-founded explanation from each other. "It's not just a question of taste," says Lella. Taking this approach keeps them from offering negative criticism out of a feeling of envy that the other partner came up with the idea. "We don't have time for that. We are working for a common goal."

This is not to suggest that theirs are always calm exchanges. Lella describes herself as a person given to outbursts at the office, one who yells and gets mad but who gets over the outburst immediately.

"We might have a really heated discussion about a design and then when that discussion is over, there's no problem," says Massimo. "It doesn't affect our private life." Asked if it doesn't hurt when Lella criticizes one of his designs, Massimo answers, "Well, she might be right. If she doesn't like it, she might see something that I don't see." And when she disagrees with him and offers her reasons, perhaps he can come to see what she sees. The result will be a better design.

Just as the Zieglers believe they are at one on the broader picture, when they speak of looking at the world with a questioning, creative attitude, so do the Vignellis believe their differences fit within a larger, unified framework. Massimo says their basic conception of design and of life is shared. He likes to quote a colleague who says that although Lella and Massimo have their own opinions, "they think together." They have the same goals, Massimo says, but they may have different opinions on how to reach those goals.

ARRIVING AT A DECISION

The way couples manage differences feeds directly into how they make decisions. Couples who respect and value the fact that their differences help them to be a better team are often quick to state that business decisions are better when they can talk things through, hear each other's viewpoint, modify and improve each other's ideas, or offer a consideration that had not occurred to the other. Not that their decisions come easily. Often they are ground in a crucible of thinking, discussing, weighing, disagreeing, reconsidering and finally coming together. It is the spirit in which the process is undertaken and the respect that the partners have for each other that make it work. As Linda Schatz says, "We share decision making by talking things out—we usually have very similar points of view. We resolve differences by looking at the consequences to the *organization,* not to our individual egos."

Rachel Borish and Jeff Slater of Rachel's Brownies say that when they can't agree, they put off making a decision to give themselves more time to think about it. If they feel they need an additional perspective from someone else to help them come to a decision, they'll get it. They frequently use their fathers— Jeff's is a stockbroker and Rachel's is an attorney—as advisers. Often one father or the other can restate an issue in a way that is helpful in enabling the couple to see each other's point of view or in getting them to modify their thinking.

Sometimes, they will turn to a trusted employee for that third perspective. Recently, when Rachel and Jeff were moving their company from its shopping center location to larger facilities in a nearby industrial park, they were faced with the decision about what to do with a small retail outlet they had been operating. They were at an impasse. Jeff had talked with the owner of a cheese shop in the shopping center about having counter space for the brownies in her store, and he wanted to go in that direction because it would save overhead and personnel costs. Rachel wasn't happy with that idea; she thought it would be no different from the way the brownies were sold in other outlets and that they might lose the customers they had built up over a period of time. They turned to their plant manager for her opinion. The plant manager had helped Jeff research the entire corporate move, and she agreed strongly with him that moving the retail operation into the cheese shop would work. Rachel says she trusts the plant manager's judgment "very, very much," so she agreed to try the cheese shop solution. If it doesn't work, she told herself, it doesn't work.

But it did work. "It's done *beautifully,*" Rachel says. "There's a perfect example of where I think my judgment was wrong and I was at first unable to change my point of view." But using their plant manager as a third party to the decision helped them make the right choice, she says.

Some key differences between Jeff and Rachel are pointed up in their decision-making process, but they let those differences work for them instead of against them. "I'm a born procrastinator," Rachel says. "My tendency is to never make a decision unless I've got a gun to my head." Jeff, on the other hand, likes to move quickly. Nevertheless, he says, "Sometimes delaying things helps to crystallize what the real essence of the problems are. Although I hate the idea of delaying things and not taking action right away, I think I've come to see the benefit in not rushing a decision, because it allows us to really, really carefully consider things."

Jeff observes that Rachel does not like to make a decision unless she knows that it is going to be 100 percent right. "She doesn't like the element of risk, and I don't mind the risk. I like to make a decision and move on to the next problem. So together, we end up balancing things out a little bit."

The attitude with which Rachel and Jeff conduct their decision making is certainly one of the keys to their success, perhaps *the* key.

"I think it must be very difficult to be together in a business with someone else if both parties have really, really strong egos and are unwilling to bend and unwilling to learn and grow," says Jeff. "I feel very proud of the fact that Rachel and I are the type of people who admit readily that we don't know all the answers, that we're willing to learn from each other and from other people, and we're flexible enough that we can sort of go with the flow."

Says Rachel: "A lot of people are stuck in real traditional power plays. They derive satisfaction from one-upsmanship or proving that they are right as opposed to the other person being right." Being the one who is right does not give either her or Jeff satisfaction or pride, Rachel says, "because if one of us is right, it means both of us are right. It's a mutual thing."

Couples find many different ways to make decisions. Some divide decision-making responsibilities the way they do labor: the person with authority in a certain area makes the decisions in that area without interference from the other (although one may consult with the other), while major decisions that affect the whole company are discussed and made jointly. Some simply say they defer to the other in his or her area of expertise, or the one most affected by the decision gets to make it. Some couples say the one who feels the most strongly that a decision should go a certain direction may get his or her way.

Not infrequently, couples say that a partner's intuition can influence a decision. Courtney Garton and Margie Bryce made a decision that saved Hats in the Belfry $80,000 once when they heeded Courtney's intuition. Western hats were the craze during the 1980/81 season, and they comprised an incredible 25 percent of their business. The wisdom in the industry was that the trend favoring western hats was getting even stronger, and Courtney and Margie placed orders for close to $100,000 for westerns for the 1981/82 season. Although sales continued strong, Courtney began to see a slight dip in the numbers, and while others in the industry continued to predict the westerns would get better or at least hold steady, Courtney began to fear a decline.

"I can't put my finger on it," he told Margie, "but we've got to cancel $80,000 of the westerns or we are going to get killed." While she did not disagree with Courtney, Margie worried about alienating a hard-won supplier. "And Courtney said, 'It is either our survival or theirs.' He felt that strongly about it." They canceled the orders and soon after, as Courtney predicted, the bottom fell out of the western market. (They were fortunate enough not to lose the supplier. Their competitors had not caught on to the downtrend and the supplier was able to unload the hats elsewhere easily.)

Like Borish and Slater, some couples use third parties to resolve differences or come to a better decision. Linda and Ken Schatz have a board of advisers to which they sometimes turn for help with decisions. Family business consultants, in fact, frequently advise their clients to create a board of directors that includes independent directors (that is, knowledgeable people who are neither members of the family nor financially linked with the company) to be a sounding board and to help the management make key decisions.

Don and Judy Quine say they have had to face critical policy decisions every step of the way in developing the Professional Karate Association. They found it useful to play the devil's advocate with each other as a means of thinking issues through thoroughly. They have a second corporation called Sport Karate, Inc., which handles the marketing and merchandising of rights for PKA. Sometimes, to help themselves understand how a decision in one company might affect the other company, one partner would play the role of PKA and the other would represent SKI, and they would deliberately argue with each other from those points of view.

Consultants Tom Hubler and Steve Swartz encourage entrepreneurial couples to actually decide consciously what kind of decision-making processes they will use.

"Our experience is that when couples have a decision-making system and a managing-differences system that take into consideration the best of what they have to offer, they'll be able to create a business solution that neither one of them could do by themselves and so their differences are an asset rather than a liability," says Hubler.

Besides being a partner with Hubler, Swartz started a business with his wife, Harriet. Called Exploration Travel, the company conducts "exploratory" as opposed to "touristic" tours to such destinations as Eastern Europe and China. It grew out of the fact that Harriet and Steve successfully led a group of 95 people to the Soviet Union several years ago.

He and Harriet found they had many issues to resolve. Since he helped to start the travel company, Steve is very invested in it and feels that it's his "baby," too. Still, he is a full-time partner with Hubler/Swartz, and it is Harriet who runs Exploration Travel on a full-time basis. However, for the first 20 years of their marriage, Harriet had been a homemaker. "She sees me as somebody who's very experienced; I've been out in the business world for 25 years," says Steve. "She wants to develop and emerge, and I want that, too." Their history, however, made it very easy to fall into their traditional personal pattern of relating, even in the business.

"We needed to find different rules for being in business together than we have for our marriage, where we're partners and we're both in charge." What they determined was that, in the business, Steve was the consultant—he would give advice when he was asked for advice, but Harriet was in charge.

They also determined what their decision-making process would be. Steve contends that any decision-making body, even a couple, has to ask three questions: What information do we need to make this decision and do we have it all? What are the considerations that govern this decision? How is the decision going to be made and by whom? (When it comes to who will make the decision, Harriet, because she is in charge, may tell Steve she wants to hear his opinion but that she will decide.) By discussing and answering these questions, Steve says, he and his wife are able to avoid the kind of fighting that so often ensues when there is ambiguity.

Many couples recognize the value of the dialectical process they must often go through to arrive at a decision. "Sometimes one or the other of us has acted unilaterally and the result has often been not satisfactory," says Ronald Fleming of himself and wife Renata von Tscharner. "The phrase I have used is 'becoming prisoners of our own competence,' where because we feel like we know everything about a situation, we act unilaterally and then discover that other information was needed."

Whatever decision-making processes a couple uses, family business specialists urge that they work toward win–win solutions, solutions that both parties feel good about. If they take the attitude that one partner has to win and one has to lose, the "loser" is going to feel dissatisfied. And if one individual feels on the down side more often than not, he or she will stop feeling good about the work and will lose the motivation that is essential to the success of the business.

THE CRUCIAL ART OF COMMUNICATION

Some of the most successful entrepreneurial couples seem to have better-than-average communication skills. In fact, some of them possess a level of communication that is extraordinary.

Debbi and Randy Fields observe that when couples run into trouble, it's often because they haven't made their expectations and feelings clear to each other.

When Randy is doing something that upsets Debbi, she says, "I let him know and I give him the opportunity to fix it." She expresses herself in the first person: "Randy, I need you to understand," or "I feel bad," or "I really need your help." And when she does so, she says, "he is right there and he is on my side. I have not yet found him to say, 'I am not going to help.' "

"When people don't communicate what their frustrations and their feelings are, they blame the other person," says Debbi. The need for communication is constant, in her view, but it must be carried on without blaming. Early in their relationship, Randy would do things that made her mad and she assumed he did them on purpose. "He had not a clue" that some of his habits—like reaching over and eating food off her plate— infuriated her. When she finally was able to tell him how angry some things made her, it opened the way for them to come up with solutions.

So many couples speak of communication as being the key to blending a business and a personal relationship. And yet for a great number communicating is excruciatingly difficult. Bork says that one of the hardest subjects for families in business to talk about is money. "The guts of a business is what you do with the money," he observes, but in our culture, we are discouraged from discussing it.

Some families, Bork continues, cannot give one another negative messages. In one family that he has worked with, he says, "if you had spinach on your lips, someone would look over and say, 'My, what a lovely blouse you're wearing.' They couldn't confront. The result of that is that there were behaviors on the part of some family members that were absolutely unacceptable in business terms or *any* terms." Ultimately, their inability to confront and communicate was harmful to their enterprise.

Some couples have enormous difficulty communicating even positive messages. I was permitted to sit in on a meeting of a group of couples in business who thought they could be helpful to each other if they met on a regular basis to discuss issues and concerns. It turned out to be a lively evening, sometimes heated, sometimes painfully honest. One husband finally said, perhaps for the first time in his wife's hearing: "I don't want to share control with anyone, and my wife has done many things she is not even aware of that have contributed to our success. I often don't seem to come to a conclusion, but the next day, I will do what she said because it made sense—and she doesn't know, because it's a problem of my ability to communicate with her. I'm used to being a take-charge person and not communicating with others." He also added that her contribution had been "the salvation of our marriage." What a pity that for so long, that man had been so afraid of giving up control that he had been unable to praise his wife for what she did for the business and for the marriage.

At the same meeting, a wife said that she and her husband

could appear to be terrific at the office but not speak to each other at night. Or, she might avoid confronting him at the office but "ambush him at home."

One reason couples have so much difficulty communicating, says Tom Hubler, is that they're afraid that if they express their feelings, they will get emotionally hurt. Another obstacle to communication is that, as children, so many of us were taught *not* to express our desires. Hubler, describing an experience common to many of us, says that as a child visiting someone else's home, he was chastised for asking for a piece of candy when he saw a candy dish on the coffee table. He was told it was more polite to wait until it was offered. "And so I waited and I waited, and then I got married and I waited and I waited and I waited. It's like I wasn't getting what I wanted and if she loved me, she would know what I want, and since she wasn't giving it to me, she must not love me. And the fight was on."

A similar dynamic takes place with couples in business. "They don't tell each other what they want for fear that it is going to be a comment on who they are as a person," says Hubler. "It's absolutely critical for people to be able to tell each other what they want and not just *assume* that if their partner loves them, they'll give it to them." At the same time, says Hubler, they have to realize that they're not always going to get what they want, but that does not mean their partner doesn't love them.

Hubler and Swartz periodically teach their clients communication skills that can help them in their business and in their family. The skills consist of speaking for or asserting yourself (saying "I think" or "I believe"); expressing thoughts; documenting those thoughts so your partner understands how you arrived at a conclusion; expressing your feelings; expressing action that you're going to take, and listening.

For couples committed to improving their communication skills, they recommend the book *Straight Talk*, by Sherod Miller, Daniel Wackman, Elam Nunnally, and Carol Saline. It is based on the Minnesota Couple Communication Program developed by Miller, Wackman, and Nunnally.

Communication is essential to a couple as they make decisions that determine how power, responsibility, and remuneration are going to be shared in a company. How well they communicate will govern how appropriate and workable their decisions are. "They need to adopt a style of communication that is not blaming but that is both inquisitive and based on mutual respect," says Tom Hubler. It can't be based on traditional male–female roles where a husband presumes that because he's the man, what he says is better or smarter or more businesslike than what his wife has to offer. "You cannot have a successful business and operate that way."

Chances are that some of you reading this book are now beginning to think your relationship could use some outside help. David Bork says couples might especially want to seek help when they are beginning their business, particularly if they are having difficulty deciding how to separate responsibilities or resolve their attitudes toward money.

Some resources are listed at the end of this book, but it is important to point out that it is still difficult to find specialists who combine all the training that can be most helpful to couples in business. Some couples have indicated that they sought help from a therapist and while that person may have had knowledge about psychology or marriage or family dynamics, he or she was lacking in an essential understanding of business. You will need to keep asking for referrals until you find someone who combines the disciplines of business knowledge, knowledge of family systems, and knowledge of personal development.

How can a couple know for sure that they need help? "When one won't speak to the other," answers David Bork. "When they're not feeling good about each other. When they don't sleep together anymore. When they regularly feel resentment about the things the other party does." But, he cautions, your expectations shouldn't be too high. Things can't go your way 99 percent of the time; in business, it just doesn't work that way. "If you expect 99 percent, you will always be disappointed."

5

MAKING IT WORK FOR OTHERS

With Good Management,
Everyone in Business Can Direct
Energy Toward Making It a
Success

Usually there are relatively few people outside of a marriage who have a stake in the couple's relationship—children, other relatives, and close friends, for example. When a husband and wife or an unmarried couple are in business together, however, the number of "stakeholders" expands. A broad community of people come to have an interest in the dynamics of the couple's relationship because how the couple interacts has an effect on these stakeholders.

That fact came home to Roberta House when she and her husband Jerry first bought a small drive-in restaurant in Watonga, Oklahoma. (It has since grown into the End O' Main Restaurant and Catering Service, with 60 full-time employees.) The first day they took over the drive-in, Roberta recalls, one employee said, "I want to get one thing straight. Who's the boss?"

"That stuck with me right there," says Roberta, "Because nobody can work for two bosses." The Houses decided Jerry would have the honor.

When Dianne and Rocco Altobelli, who run a chain of top-quality beauty salons in Minneapolis-St. Paul, first started working together, employees began to complain that they were confused. Sometimes Rocco would countermand orders Dianne or one of their other managers had given. If an employee protested that she or he had been told to do something one way, Rocco recalls, "I'd say, 'That's too bad. Do it this way.' "

"I ended up causing a lot more problems than I would have if I'd left it alone," he admits. Only by coming to a clear division of responsibility and delegating more authority to others did the Altobellis finally create a more comfortable working environment for their employees.

More than just employees are affected by the business couple's relationship, however. The couple will find that others interested in the stability and workings of their partnership can include suppliers, distributors, customers, lenders, investors, franchisors and franchisees, shareholders, boards of directors, other partners, and even the media (companies such as Mrs. Fields Cookies,

Redken Laboratories, Liz Claiborne, and Micro D have won much desirable publicity as a result of the visible role of the wife). These outsiders are important to the success of the couple and they in turn depend on the couple for some of their own well-being. The husband and wife must find ways to make their blended business and personal relationship work for the benefit of their stakeholders so that the stakeholders, in turn, can perform in ways that benefit the couple and their enterprise.

THE BUSINESS "FAMILY"—OWNERS AND THEIR EMPLOYEES

Employees are, in many respects, the most significant group of stakeholders that a couple must consider. The husband and wife rely on the employees' productivity to make their business work, and the employees depend on the couple's continued success for their livelihood. It is a symbiotic relationship, intensified by daily interaction between the two groups. The influence of the couple's relationship on the working environment cannot be overstated; it sets the pace for the company, and ultimately determines whether the operation is bumpy or functions smoothly.

Family business consultant Tom Hubler says he and partner Steve Swartz have learned that what nonfamily employees find most irritating are couples or family members who "don't have their act together"—that is, families and couples who are openly fighting and bickering. Nonfamily members are usually very loyal to the couple or the family, Hubler says, and so they are often relieved when consultants are brought in to help a family iron out its problems.

"We'll have nonfamily managers who have been in the company for a long time say things like 'I have two families. I have my own family and I'm also a member of this [business] family,'" says Hubler. Their loyalty is so strong, he continues, that "they really feel it directly when the couple or the family is not conducting themselves in a professional way."

This is not to deny the need for disagreement or conflict between family members or spouses. But it does raise some cautions about the kind of conflict couples permit themselves to have in front of employees. As we have seen, some couples—Don and Judy Quine of the Professional Karate Association, for example—feel they can get away with heated arguments in the presence of others as long as they are business arguments. Because Bill and Sheri Criswell regard the Criswell Company as an organization of peers, much like a law firm or any other professional group, they aren't hesitant about arguing with each other over business matters in meetings with employees. Since they feel their relationship is so solid and they can argue "safely" with each other, says Sheri, "sometimes the level will get pretty escalated, and you can look around the room and people who haven't seen this a lot will start squirming." People who are new to the company, she says, go through an adjustment period but eventually become accustomed to her and Bill disagreeing. If two unmarried partners argued, she says, "nobody would think about it." Although they know there's a certain futility in it, the Criswells try to encourage others in the company not to think of them as husband and wife. Sheri says that new people "sometimes will say, 'your husband this' or 'your wife that.' We always say, 'You mean my partner?'"

Some couples, however, are discreet even about airing their business differences in front of others. Linwood A. (Chip) Lacy, Jr., worked closely with Geza Csige and Lorraine Mecca (called "Mecca" by her friends) at Micro D before the couple left the company. "If Mecca disagreed with Geza, she wouldn't publicly challenge him," says Lacy, who is now chairman of the company. "But that would be no different than if I disagreed with Geza on something and there were subordinates in the room. I would tend not to publicly challenge him." Lacy observes that handling disagreements in private is the normal course of procedure in business, whether you are married or not. "I think that if one person is the president and the other is the chairman and they have something they disagree on, they don't air their dirty laundry in front of employees; they resolve it one-on-one, which is the right way to do it."

Whatever a couple's choice is about conducting business disagreements in the hearing of employees, having personal arguments—or letting business disagreements become personal—is quite another matter. Some consultants say they have seen some couples become so angry and ugly and personal with each other in the presence of subordinates that the employees cannot tolerate it. The result can be a very high turnover.

It is not enough, however, for a couple to keep their conflicts from affecting employees. They must also take the more positive measures of making nonfamily managers and employees know they are valued and have an opportunity to grow and progress.

"Our belief is that first of all, it's important to always let the nonfamily person know what their role is in the company," says Hubler. This means, of course, that the couple must be clear about their own roles. Writing in the June 1984 issue of *Minnesota Business,* Hubler and Swartz said: "In any family-owned business, relationships among family members will strongly influence how people operate at work. When family members have unclear perceptions of their roles and responsibilities, and emotions dictate their behavior, ambiguity pervades the business and productivity suffers. With a management plan in place, everyone in the enterprise can direct energy toward making the business succeed."

They advocate open discussion of nonfamily members' roles, including honesty about succession and ownership plans, citing one business founder who told his key personnel, "My son is going to take over the business. But that doesn't mean you'll lose your place in the company. Right now, your job is to train him to be the best manager he can be. If you do it well, there will always be a place for you."

Some of the couples in this book have no children or any other family members who can take over the business. One such couple says that their young but very mature general manager has the capability of running the business, and they have let her know that should both of them be killed, the business would go to her.

Nonfamily employees also need to be given responsibility and adequate freedom to exercise their authority. Chip Lacy recalls with warmth a period in the early 1970s when he was an executive at Best Products and the company had entered its period of rapid expansion. Sydney and Frances Lewis and their son Andrew had surrounded themselves with an especially able and dedicated group of nonfamily managers, according to Lacy. And while the Lewises did not ignore these managers, they were permitted to have "their own turf and their own space and their own independence." It was a hands-off style. "And that," says Lacy, "allowed the company to succeed."

And, of course, if a couple wants to retain their best nonfamily employees, they must be adequately rewarded. Some family businesses offer bonuses to key nonfamily employees. The Criswells chose another way: They make it possible for key employees to have a share in the ownership of the buildings that they help the company to create. "That's the way they can increase their net worth," says Bill.

When a couple is clear about their own division of responsibilities, their goals for the company, and the like, they can minimize problems with employees. Employees will know whom to report to, or which spouse to turn to for a particular decision. Such clarity can also reduce the chance of an employee trying to play one spouse against the other.

In the preceding chapter, consultant David Bork spoke of the necessity of a couple having a prevailing viewpoint about the business. That is, while they may divide responsibilities, they themselves are not divided in their approach to the business. While employees are not children and should not be treated as such, he says, there are some parallels between the entrepreneurial couple and their employees and parents and their children. As with the parents in a family, the couple in a business must present a unified front.

"That means that if I am an employee of a business owned and operated by a man and wife," says Bork, "if I asked one, I know that that's the final answer." The employee should know that one spouse will stand behind the other and that the employee cannot divide them to get the answer he prefers.

Most of the couples who participated in this book spoke appreciatively of their employees, and rarely did they cite an incident where they felt an employee had tried to play one off against the other. Nevertheless, such incidents did occasionally occur. It was just such a situation with their former operations manager that finally forced Jeanette and Howard Shapiro to come up with the division of responsibility described earlier.

When talking with each other in the evening, they would find that the manager had told Howard one thing and Jeanette another. "The most destructive thing that happened was that he became a wedge between us and our people," says Jeanette. He encouraged employees to become dependent on him and discouraged them from making decisions on their own that they were capable of making. As the Shapiros see it, the manager wanted to control the company. When he left, says Jeanette, "we had to mend a lot of fences. There were an awful lot of misunderstandings, because we had allowed him to come between us and a lot of people in our company."

Couples are generally alert to the possibility of divisive behavior on the part of employees. "Generally, it was not a problem since, in difficult situations, Pauline and I personally discussed potential problems, arrived at a consensus, and presented a united front in discussion with the employee," says Jerome Berliner.

Margie Bryce and Courtney Garton of Hats in the Belfry say employees don't play the spouses off against each other because they know Courtney and Margie are always comparing notes and would catch on immediately. Besides, they are not only good employees but they also know that Margie and Courtney think so much alike that asking one is like asking the other. Most of the time, they would get the same answer. "The ones who've worked with us for five, six, seven years have come to understand that it really is an equal partnership," says Courtney.

"Certain employees might have a personality clash with one of us but not with both," writes one questionnaire respondent. "They might try to bypass their correct superior and curry favor with the other. Some felt at times that my orders, coming from my wife, could be ignored or defied. I would have to intervene."

Susan and Tony Harnett say they have never had an incident where an employee tried a divisive technique, but Susan says that sometimes an employee might approach her first about something "in hopes that I will warm up Tony with a little pillow talk." And does she? When she thinks it's justified, yes. For example, she says, "If I think someone should be promoted in the company and they are really talented and maybe Tony hasn't seen them perform in a certain area, I will let him know."

Couples, nonetheless, would do well to look at an employee's motives if he appears to be making an appeal to one partner when he can't get what he wants from the other. If it is an honest appeal, there may be a legitimate business reason behind it.

Sheri Criswell says that she suspects there is some kind of "lore" in existence in the Criswell Company that says, "If you want to accomplish this, Bill's the one to go to. If you want to do something else, Sheri is." If an employee disagrees with either her or Bill, she says, "it gives them a safe avenue to go to somebody else who is equally powerful."

Doesn't she feel that employees are playing her and Bill against each other when they do that?

"Sure!" she answers. "But it's good for the company." The real estate development business is very complicated, she explains, and no one individual, no matter how smart, can think through all the implications of what he or she is doing. "And so you want to have an environment where it's easy—as easy as you can make it—for people to challenge you." Bill, for example, had been handling a very large refinancing deal, but there were some people in the company who were concerned about the direction in which it was going. The transaction was moving very swiftly and Bill hadn't had time to talk with them about what was bothering them. "They started talking to me and got me tuned in to what their concern was so that I could talk to Bill about it," says Sheri. If she hadn't listened to them, "They would have had difficulty slowing down the wheels long enough to get it thought about."

At Micro D, says Chip Lacy, "I would definitely go to Mecca on an issue sometimes and say, 'Mecca, I think Geza's wrong on this. Let me tell you why.'" It would not be done in an undermining fashion but as a way to get things thought through more thoroughly.

The negative side of such a dynamic is that it's time consuming, says Sheri Criswell, who also thinks that sometimes it must be annoying to people in the company if they have to get two people on their side instead of just one. "But on balance, I think you get better decisions."

Psychologist Marta Vago points to one other problem area that couples might experience with employees. Often, one partner—frequently the wife—will be more people-oriented than the other. This spouse may be more empathetic and more emotionally tuned-in to employees. Employees may see a husband who is not very people-oriented as wearing the black hat and a wife who is easier to turn to as wearing the white hat. "The wife in this instance would have to be very careful not to polarize the staff," says Vago, suggesting, for example, that she should avoid saying things like, "If you've got a problem, you just come to me because he doesn't understand." Even though the wife may legitimately handle personnel issues because of her talent with people, she must make it clear to employees that there is a division of responsibilities, with the husband in charge of certain areas while she is in charge of others. Employees should understand that when a matter falls in the husband's realm, they must go to him.

THE OTHER STAKEHOLDERS

There is a variety of situations in which the fact that business partners are married to each other is of more than passing interest to others besides employees, and couples may find that they need to take others' concerns, right or wrong, into consideration in the way they do business. In some cases, stakeholders may be concerned about the stability of the marriage—in effect, the stability of the business partnership. In other cases, the stakeholders may have prejudices about women that have to be circumvented or overcome.

Sometimes, there is even concern that the husband and wife will band together to form a power base. For example, Don and Judy Quine took a third partner with them in the Professional Karate Association—Joe Corley, an Atlanta karate promoter and retired middleweight. Corley said that his lawyer and friends cautioned him that if he went into business with a married couple, they would solidify their position on decision making and outvote him. To resolve that concern and make the partnership work for Corley as well as for the Quines, it was set up so that each individual owns one-third of the shares but Corley has 50 percent of the voting rights and Judy and Don each have 25 percent. They were always able to arrive at a compromise, Corley said in 1985. However, if they were not able to do so, their partnership agreement called for them to go to arbitration. Despite their precautions, as this book was being completed, Don Quine said that Corley and the Quines had decided it would be best if they went their separate ways. The partnership was to be dissolved, with the Quines staying with PKA.

Steven and Valerie Bursten of Decorating Den Systems, Inc., took James S. Bugg, formerly of Century 21, as their partner in 1984 in a split that is close to 50–50 between the couple and Bugg. But Steve says, "I don't think that the stock ownership would ever be a basis upon which a final decision would be made." So far, he says, they have always been able to reach a consensus on decisions. If they were not, says Steve, they would put the issue before their executive committee.

As developers, the Criswells work with a variety of partners in the different projects in which they are involved. They hold their ownership of the properties in Bill's name, says Sheri, "simply because I've never felt that it was appropriate to have our lenders or partners worrying about the possibility of a domestic problem affecting the ownership of a building." Logically, she says, theirs is not any different from any other partnership. Other partners could squabble with each other, too. But because they're married, she says, "it is unusual, and it's something you don't need to have people sitting around and wondering about."

Investors are likely to look at a husband-and-wife team with an especially sharp eye. Cyril W. Draffin, Jr., vice president of Greater Washington Investors, Inc., a Chevy Chase, Maryland, venture capital firm, says that a husband-and-wife combination can reflect a lack of resources. It's fine for one spouse to be put on the payroll to help out the other during the early start-up period, he observes, but when a company seeks venture capital, it needs to be at a stage where it has technical, financial, management and marketing capabilities. That usually means four key people "as a bare minimum," he says. If a spouse cannot ably fill one of those roles, he suggests, it is time for that spouse to "slip away" and for a more appropriate person to be hired.

Another problem Draffin has found as a venture capitalist is that when a husband and wife are among the principles, they tend to team up and control the company, to the detriment of the business. He recalls a husband and wife who were principles of a software company that had an excellent chance of success.

They were trying to bring in a new chief executive officer, but the company was structured so that they could outvote him. Draffin pushed for a different structure. "They responded that my comments were very helpful and insightful, but they didn't act on them. The net result is that they hired someone, it didn't work out, and the company went into Chapter 11 bankruptcy."

With so many husbands and wives going into business together as franchisees of every kind of business, from fast food restaurants to regional direct mail advertising, parent companies are naturally eager to see that they are sound teams that can bring a small business along. That is true of Decorating Den, but in addition, since its founders are a couple themselves, they know that they are role models for many of their franchise owners. And because they have been through the process of starting a business together, the Burstens also know how to help other couples handle some of the stresses that plague a husband and wife as they try to sort out the roles between themselves.

If a couple needs professional counseling, the Burstens will recommend counseling. But sometimes it's a matter of a husband who serves as the installer getting mad because his wife or the manufacturer got a customer's drapery measurements wrong. "We try to help him understand that that's the way this business is," says Steve. The husband will be reminded that every individual and every company makes mistakes sometimes. Steve might tell him, "If your wife makes a mistake, remember she just sold a $2,000 order and put $500 or $1,000 in your pocket. Be a little patient." The Burstens try to help the wife understand that she's not a bad person just because she made a measuring mistake.

Occasionally, a marriage will go down the tubes and that will hurt a franchise. But the Burstens say a marriage failure can work the other way, too. The wives are usually the most involved in a Decorating Den franchise, and Steve finds that some women unconsciously use their franchises to develop strength and independence so that they can get divorced. And sometimes when an unsatisfactory marriage is ended, the business improves.

When husbands and wives give support to each other and seriously address the concerns—real or imagined—of their various stakeholders, they can usually gain the cooperation they need to move their businesses forward. On occasion, this takes some real creativity. Chris and Winnie Dickerman of C & W Seafood had to confront not only the fears and superstitions that fishermen and crabbers have about dwarves and women, they also had to deal with the prejudices of the seafood industry itself. "Shippers, wholesalers—they're not going to talk to some broad," comments Chris. The Dickermans presented a united front. If a situation called for it, each would remind a customer or a supplier (or an employee!) that the other partner was equal in the business and insist that the stakeholder deal with that partner if it was the other's area. Winnie also developed some coping techniques of her own. To deal with a particularly reluctant supplier, she began to play "I'm just a dumb girl" and to pick his brain.

"Look," she would say, "I'm new at this. You have to explain things to me."

It was flattery, but it worked. The supplier became quite grandfatherly. He took Winnie under his wing and did indeed begin to teach her what she needed to know. Winnie still turns to him when she has a problem or needs some information and now, the Dickermans say, the supplier would rather deal with Winnie than with Chris any day.

6

"WOMEN'S ISSUES" THAT MEN SHOULD THINK ABOUT, TOO

Giving Her Room to Be a
Full Partner

Because we are just beginning to shake off the traditional male and female roles that have defined us for so long and to recognize women as equals in society, a woman frequently has more issues to consider than her husband when it comes to determining whether she should join him in business. This is not to say that *he* doesn't have some things to think about, too. Will he be able to share power that has heretofore been a male prerogative? If she is smarter than he is in some ways, can he celebrate her intelligence rather than feel emasculated by it? Can he give her credit? It is true that a man going into partnership with his wife may find that if the business and the relationship are to function effectively, he may have to let go of some traditional male powers and to develop himself in ways that permit him to curb his ego. In return, he may gain the best business partner he could imagine.

Still, what I have found in dozens of conversations with entrepreneurial couples is that among the women, there is often an underlying or overt current of frustration—either present or *remembered*—about how they are viewed or about roles they feel forced to play, as *women*, in business. Although some men are able to admit that they are uncomfortable about giving up some of the control to their wives, I have never heard them express resentment about what it means to be a *man* in business.

Because of our society's expectations of women in the domestic sphere as homemakers and mothers, roles that tend to be poorly regarded except in sentimental ways, women business partners often find themselves patronized—sometimes by the husbands themselves as well as by the world outside the relationship. A woman may also find herself playing the same role in business that she does at home.

Here are a half dozen common situations that can breed frustration and anger for women. They are issues that husbands and wives who are thinking about going into business together—or who are reassessing their roles in business—need to discuss openly and to resolve. If a couple cannot come to a resolution, the wife may be resentful, and a resentful partner is certainly not going to turn in a top performance in the business. Her negative feelings will put the personal relationship at risk as well.

Resolving these issues does not depend totally on a husband's willingness to share power or to support his wife's growth or status—although Chapter 8 looks at how a number of husbands are doing those very things with excellent results. A wife, too, must come to grips with her own development and who she wants to be. Is she willing, for example, to assert herself? To risk confronting and communicating with her spouse in ways she may not have done in the past? To increase her knowledge and skills so that she becomes more confident about her participation in the business?

RECOGNITION

Women have a tough time gaining recognition for their contribution. This is by far the key issue for women, and almost all the other sex-related issues feed into it. Because women are so often viewed as the "wife of" or the "mother of," they find it difficult to get credit in their own right. They have trouble getting recognition outside the business and often they have trouble getting it inside the business as well, particularly when the husband is not comfortable about a wife who has status. Things *are* changing. One woman said, "It was unheard of 20 years ago for a man to say publicly, 'My wife did it, not me.'" Now, many men can say, "My wife did it." Nevertheless, another woman who has been married nearly 30 years and who helped her husband start their family business years ago and has worked in it ever since, says, "It drives him up a wall to have anyone tell him the business wouldn't be what it is without me." When that happens, he gives her the cold shoulder all evening.

More frequently, however, women speak of the attitude that

the world outside the business displays toward them. All too often, the assumption is that it is the man's business or that he is the final authority. Not infrequently, the husband gets credit for the wife's achievements. At a family business seminar not long ago, the leader of a session, a man, asked the attendees to introduce themselves. One woman, a widow, said she and her late husband had founded the business, and now she was beginning to plan for succession. "Your husband started the business and you're carrying on his work?" the leader fed back to her. "I was a co-founder of the business," the woman corrected. "You're carrying on his work," the leader repeated. The woman finally gave up.

Women who have been in business a long time, such as Lella Vignelli of Vignelli Associates, say they do have recognition from their peers, their suppliers, their customers, and the like—but it was not always the case. The year 1973 was a turning point for the Vignellis, when Lella and Massimo jointly received a major award, the Industrial Arts Medal of the American Institute of Architects. Before then, Massimo says, "people were always trying to identify our teamwork with me." The award solidified their peers' recognition of Lella as an equal contributor. Since then, the Vignellis have won a number of awards jointly, including honorary doctorates from the Parsons School of Design and the Gold Medal of the American Institute of Graphic Arts.

Susan Stangland of Pepperwood International says she handles a full load at the business, takes care of the family's personal business, and is a mother besides. She speaks for many women when she says, "When I feel resentment, it's usually because those handing out praise (bankers, business community, media) usually give it to Chris and his brother (who is not an owner), and if I'm included, it's usually backhanded. When I'm holding down three jobs and getting less salary, this is the final blow to my self-esteem. There are times I'm slighted, and I know it's because I'm viewed as 'the wife' instead of the more reputable 'partner.' This angers me because my signature is required on all the legal documents, loan agreements, and guarantees. If I were male, there's no doubt in my mind I'd be thought praiseworthy on an equal level with Chris and *I'd* be invited to lunch by the banker, too!"

One disadvantage of being in business with your husband, echoes Renata von Tscharner of the Townscape Institute, "is that most people still assume that it's the husband's business and that the woman is basically his assistant." The idea of a husband and wife being equal partners, she adds, is difficult for most people to grasp. She thinks people's attitudes toward her would be different if she were in business for herself.

The beekeeping business is a very old-fashioned business, says Sue Cobey of Vaca Valley Apiaries, and she has often found herself annoyed when she is at industry meetings and it is assumed that she is the beekeeper's wife and not the beekeeper. "I am always the only woman at the table in these meetings," she says, and many of the men wonder why she doesn't go off to the women's auxiliary.

Often the worst offenders are other women. Even though Joanne Schatz runs her own Vertech Bed & Back Stores and is the one who signs the leases for retail space, one female rental agent made it clear she preferred to deal with Skip. ("The agent was even pregnant," Skip says with wonderment.) And once a female customer insisted on talking with Joanne's boss. In exasperation, she finally got Skip on the phone and told him to tell the customer he was in charge. (But Skip also notes that for the first four years that Joanne was in business, it was almost impossible for her to admit she was the boss. She comes from a generation where women were supposed to grow up and become housewives. "My mother, to this day, has never told me she's proud that I'm working," says Joanne. "She thinks it's horrible that I work.")

Often, women partners learn to deal with such situations with life's indispensable ally: a sense of humor. Central Pipe & Supply once got a call from a woman who insisted on talking with the owner. When she was put through to Diane Johnson, the irritated caller said, "I was holding for the owner of the company."

"Well, Sweetie, you got her," Johnson answered.

THE CARETAKING ROLE

Some women find themselves locked into an undesirable role. They may discover they are subservient both at home and at business, or are subtly expected to be the nurturer. Because of the expectations that society has for them as wives and mothers, women often are thrust into what Marta Vago calls the "caretaking" role, which is, of course, the position in which she found herself when she was in business with the man she lived with. But it is a phenomenon she has seen in other couples as well.

Caretakers are the supporters and the ones who do the detail work that makes the creative work possible. They may indeed be skilled managers and administrators, but often neither the husband nor the world views them that way. They are "helping" him. Occasionally, a man may be a caretaker, but Vago says that women are the more likely ones to be found in this role. "Women—especially women age 30 and up—are socialized to be caretakers, to be detail-oriented, to be the support system." The caretaking woman, Vago continues, is "the person who sets things up, the person who follows through, and the person who supports behind the scenes what goes on."

Women, Vago advises, really have to take a hard look at whether or not they want to fulfill a caretaking role. "Now some love it, thrive on it, and think it's great, and that's terrific," she says. "If you don't, then watch out." In the extreme, the caretaker may discover that she has become a nag, or the relationship takes on a parent–child structure, with the caretaker as the parent. Neither development is very good for the intimate side of a husband–wife relationship.

We described one caretaking situation to family business consultant Tom Hubler. The husband and his caretaking spouse argued frequently about money in the business—he wanted to spend it and she, because she was the bookkeeper, knew they didn't have it to spend. What happens in situations like that, says Hubler, amounts to "an emotional division of labor between the couple—he is the one who gets to pretend that he's worry-free, and she does all the worrying. Essentially, they balance each other, and that's how they maintain the status quo." The problem, he says, is a structural one, but it becomes experienced as an interpersonal relationship issue, where the spouses begin to blame each other. One way to break the deadlock, he says, is for them to start scheduling business meetings and talk about their concerns about the financial side of the business. Then it no longer is just the woman's responsibility to worry about money but a joint responsibility.

In some situations, the wife—or the husband—becomes the heavy. One woman said that she realizes she's "a bitch" in the business. Her husband comes off as the nice, pleasant one, but, she says, "I became what he needed me to be."

PROTECTING HIS EGO

Some women feel they must protect their husbands' egos. As you will recall, Peter Davis of the Wharton School said that with some frequency women may be the real powerhouse in a business but are reluctant to take on the trappings of power—such as titles—for fear their husbands will feel emasculated. One wife commented, "The spouse who is smart enough to control without wearing the control hat is the one who gets the job done."

Susan and Tony Harnett of Bread & Circus have observed other couples who are business partners and find that sometimes the women are more assertive and talented than their husbands. In one case, the husband accepted that and became the secondary person in the company; in another instance, the husband couldn't accept it and the marriage failed. Susan says she knows of still another situation where the woman is clearly the stronger one. "But she is very clever and lets him feel that he is the boss." And that, says Susan, has worked out very well. Tony adds: "I think the husband can accept it, knowing in his heart that she runs the business, but he gets the limelight." (But it is also true, adds Tony, "that businesses that are very successful are the ones where it does not matter who gets the credit.")

Some wives say they are quite content to see their husbands in the top role, and it appears that many such women aren't taking a secondary role just to make their husbands feel manly. Frances Lewis, for example, says that it's fine with her that husband Sydney became president and then chairman of Best Products while she stopped at executive vice president. While she knows of many women "who want to make all the decisions," Frances says she is not one of them. "I am very happy to give all my opinions and not have to make the decision," she laughs. Sydney likes making hard decisions, but Frances says, "I sweat." Both she and Sydney agree, however, that in the earlier years, Frances could have taken the company over and run it if necessary—as indeed she did for a while in 1962 when Sydney was recuperating from a heart attack. Whether she could have made the company grow to its present size, she's not so sure.

PLAYING CATCH-UP

A woman may have to play catch-up. Although more and more women are starting businesses that their husbands eventually join, the reverse is more often true: the husband starts the business and the wife follows him. For a variety of reasons, the wife may find herself somewhat behind him in her ability to make a contribution at first. Not only has she not had the same intimate involvement as he has had for as long a period, but, if she has been a homemaker, she is likely to be less experienced in the business world than he is.

It may take a while, but most spouses catch up and *do* make an equal contribution. As one wife puts it, "Now that I have been in the business long enough, I have got my own opinions." The trouble is that sometimes husbands fail to see how far their wives have come and continue to treat them as less experienced people; under such circumstances, they resist letting the wife become an equal partner. Other couples, like Linda and Ken Schatz, actually plan for the wife's development and see to it that she gets the experience necessary that will pave the way for her to make an equal contribution.

Katherine Harper had five children and a part-time job as a bank teller when she and Ron started Harper Companies International in 1971. Ron already had 19 years of experience in the industry under his belt. He admits now that it has been only in the last five or six years that he has come to fully respect Katherine as a businessperson as well as a wife and mother. He can look back and see how often she was right and he was wrong. Katherine, meanwhile, has gained so much self-confidence as Ron's business partner that in 1986 she made a bid for the Democratic nomination to run as candidate for the U.S. Senate.

MOTHERHOOD

It's difficult to keep in touch when you're home having babies— and hard to find your niche when you return to the business. Although we will deal with this subject more in Chapter 9, it bears mentioning here because it *is* an issue husbands and wives must address. Having children does affect the business, and particularly a wife's role in it. Not only will a husband miss the day-to-day involvement of his partner but, if they decide she is going to spend some child-rearing years at home and come back to the business when the children are older, she may have some reentry problems, perhaps even having to prove herself all over again to those employees who joined the business in her absence.

When Jack and Ruth Pentes of Pentes Design began their family, Ruth decided she wanted to stay home and enjoy the children while they were small. When, some years later, she finally returned, only a few employees remained who knew of her previous contribution as the business manager of the organization. In addition, she was no longer needed for her old tasks—someone else had been hired to handle finances and administration. "I didn't quite know where I belonged," she says. That's when she took up a camera and began to carve out a new niche for herself as the company's photographer.

ATTITUDE

Age and cultural background of a husband may place limitations on the wife's role. When Grace (an American) and Jere Shafir (a Polish immigrant) married in 1972, she was 24 and he was 50. Grace, now a widow, had already enjoyed a brief but successful career as a sales representative for a New York fabric company. Her new husband wanted her to stay at home and be a housewife. "I lasted about two weeks," says Grace. "I have never had the ability to be a housewife. Many people do it very well, but I was not one of those people."

Jere said that if Grace wanted to work, she should come to work for him at Kingshead Corporation, a company he owned in Hackensack, New Jersey. It was a suggestion that the company's accountant viewed as nepotism of the worst kind; as a result, Grace received no pay for the first year. She dabbled in advertising and public relations for a year or so, and then began to edge into sales. It was a move her husband resisted at first. "I was extremely protected," says Grace. "It was almost like I was in a cocoon. Nobody was allowed to come near me or hurt me or anything like that. I guess that's why he didn't want me to go into sales—because it wouldn't be within his ability to protect me from anything. He always worried about men giving me problems, and I always told him that if one conducts oneself in a certain manner, it's not a problem. And it never was."

Grace set out to create a niche for herself in her husband's company and he gradually began to let her make her way. It was, in the long run, fortuitous; he died after a lingering illness in January 1984, leaving Grace with four young daughters and a company to run. Had she not been able to make room for herself in the business, she might not have been ready to take over when she had to.

While these kinds of issues are still very much with us, their impact may diminish, perhaps even disappear, in future years. David Bork says that women traditionally have been the compromisers. "The prototype of couples in business is the case where the woman takes a not necessarily subservient role but a lower profile." However, relationships have changed dramatically in the last 50 years, with some of the greatest changes coming for women in the last decade. Until recently, Bork observes, women have been deterred from developing the characteristics of the entrepreneur—being demanding, visionary, doggedly determined, pushy, and single-purposed. While there have been exceptions, women in generations born before 1950 "simply were discouraged from pursuing that entrepreneurial style of behavior because it was not 'womanly,' " says Bork. "Men could do that, but not women."

Younger women now are not discouraged from developing such behavior patterns and, as a result, they are becoming more entrepreneurial. And what we can expect to see, says Bork, are more family businesses in which there will be more bona fide equality between husband and wife than we have seen before.

While there may always be some men who fear a loss of masculinity as women emerge, Bork feels that the more liberated that women become, the more liberated men will become. "I would focus on the couples that can come to this transaction as equals and not be diminished by each other in any way. And that to me is a real partnership, rather than one being the passenger."

7
MANAGING TO
BE A COUPLE

"We Do Fine in the Romance
Line, If I Can Catch Her"

Steven and Valerie Bursten recall a weekend in New York when the city was besieged by a hurricane. They holed up in the Marriott overlooking a nearly empty Times Square and, Steve says, "We lay in bed all day Friday and watched it hit." They were still able to take in three shows. As Steve recalls, "That was a great, exciting, romantic weekend for us."

The travel required of them as founders of Decorating Den Systems, Inc., an interior design company with 300 franchises nationwide, means opportunities for romantic getaways that nourish their personal relationship. Just the same, they occasionally make time to relax together at home. "We've gone Saturday to Sunday and we've never gotten out of bed, not from the standpoint of sex so much, just watching old movies on TV," says Steve. They'll go into the kitchen and raid the refrigerator and return to bed. "It is so nice not to be on the road and not to have to be at dinners and not to have to be with people, and not to have reports due. My God, it's just a refuge to be able to stay home and do nothing." Valerie, who says it's hard trying to look her best all the time on the job, adds, "I love it, you know, with my hair sticking out all over the place and not having to wear makeup. It's good."

One of the toughest issues facing any couple in business is finding the right balance between their business life and their personal life.

For some couples, their business life *is* their personal life. The two facets are woven inextricably together and the man and woman involved are so entranced by what they do, they have little desire to make a separation. "Why would you separate it?" Steve Bursten asks, despite his joy in rare do-nothing weekends with his wife. "If you can't tell your work from your play, why would you stop?" Valerie adds: "We're workaholics, and we love it."

Designers Lella and Massimo Vignelli say that most of their friendships are built on their professional relationships. And although there is a business side to what they do, they spend more time concentrating on the creative aspects of their enterprise. It's not so much a business as a vocation, Lella observes, and Massimo speaks of the "critical eye that never goes to sleep." When he goes to a restaurant, he is thinking not just about the food but also the design of the flatware and the plates. When he walks down Madison Avenue, he is continuously checking to see what is going on in the jewelry stores or the clothing shops. Doesn't he ever feel the need to get away from design? "It's like a fish," he responds. "Does it get tired of swimming?"

For many entrepreneurial couples, however, the need to separate their business from their private life is a serious, sometimes crucial, concern. Unless stringent measures are taken, they find that too much togetherness and interaction erode their relationship instead of bringing them the joy they anticipated. The demands of their business may be so overwhelming that they become exhausted and lose interest in sex. Or the arguments they have over business matters during the day sneak in under the covers with them at night, destroying the desire for intimacy. Or, being with a spouse all day, one partner discovers that the other makes mistakes, uses bad judgment, doesn't work hard enough, or neglects to return important phone calls—all of which tests one's tolerance and may result not only in the loss of desire for sex but loss of respect and trust as well.

In still other cases, the partners in the relationship have differing needs. One thrives on business all the time and is happy to bring it home and discuss it through the night and on weekends, while the other wants a complete separation, with absolutely no references to the business after office hours.

While being in business together offers a tremendous potential to a couple for cementing their personal relationship, it also carries with it an enormous power to destroy. Each couple must find the equilibrium that works for them, an equilibrium that usually encompasses two major efforts: (1) shielding the relationship from business intrusion, and (2) taking deliberate steps to nourish the relationship, both on and off the job.

PROTECTING YOUR PERSONAL LIFE

When they started their small-business consulting firm, Creative Management Concepts, Patricia and Edward Langiotti, of Reading, Pennsylvania, found that as much as they loved it, it infested their private life. It joined them at the dinner table, it threatened their relationships with their children, and it went to bed with them at night.

It is a second marriage for the Langiottis, and both have children from their previous marriages. They married each other in January 1983, the same month Pat launched the business, with the plan that Ed, who was a manager for U-Haul, would quit his job and join CMC when it could support them both. This he did 11 months later. Because they couldn't afford to have a separate location for their company at first, they opened shop at home, with an office in the basement.

Pat says that because she and Ed "are relative newlyweds and people who treasure a personal relationship," they perhaps place more value on their private time together than other couples their age, who, they often find, are tired of each other. "We have a personal relationship that I think rivals any that I've ever seen. I mean, we really love each other. He's my best friend and my most fun person."

So they tried to keep their business separate from their personal life. But entrepreneuring, they found—not only from their own experience but also from the experiences of the entrepreneurs who are their clients—can be all-consuming. "And when you have two people with that level of commitment together in a family, it monopolizes the whole family," says Ed. "That becomes their life. It becomes their social life. Every bit of their energy and their money is spent on thinking of how they can make it bigger and better or make it succeed."

The Langiottis were not immune, and work quickly became the focus of their lives. "What we found happening," recalls Ed, "was that we felt very, very free to extend the business time. If we got up early, we started to work early because we were at work already. And if it was 5 o'clock and we just wanted to work a little bit longer to get this one project done, we'd keep at it—7 o'clock, 8 o'clock, 9 o'clock." Personal time and time to relax kept on shrinking. And when you are husband and wife and you let business time slip over into personal time, Ed says, "that mix is very volatile."

Pat's son, then 16, lived with the Langiottis when they were getting CMC under way. He hated the business. If a client was in the basement office, he had to be quiet; he couldn't behave like a normal, noisy teenage boy.

"All you ever talk about is CMC," he complained to Ed and Pat. "Can't you talk about anything else? I feel like that's all there is." He was miserable, reflects Pat, because she and Ed had a shared interest in developing the business and her son had no role in it. Sometimes his attitude was, "If I have to hear five more minutes of this, I'm going to scream."

The business also affected the Langiottis' relationship with each other. Says Pat: "I would go to bed and lie there at night and be clicking off about this client and this client, and Ed would be talking about this one and this one. It was like, 'Hey, why don't you invite them in?' "

They both had successful management careers before they went into business for themselves, and they were brought up short when they realized that CMC was taking over their lives. "We said, you know, we just had 18 years of this," recalls Pat. Some changes were in order. Moving the business out of the home and into a separate location eased some of the problem of encroachment, but it was not a complete answer. They began to abide by some rules, such as never allowing business discussions to cross the threshhold of their bedroom.

But a more unusual step—and one they now often suggest to clients—was to adopt separate identities for work and for home.

At work, Pat is a powerhouse. An outgoing person, she takes leadership with the clients and is perceived by them as "the boss." Ed may challenge Pat and argue with her and not infrequently get her to change her mind when they disagree. But when it comes to handling clients' problems, Ed will ultimately defer to Pat's judgment. Not only does he respect her judgment but he also explains that Pat is on the front line with clients and it is important to them to believe that she stands 100 percent behind any solutions that CMC offers them. A quieter person, Ed plays the behind-the-scenes role that makes Pat's up-front role possible.

But at home, they switch roles and Ed becomes boss.

Says Pat: "When I leave that office, I become somebody's little girl. And he is wonderful to allow me to have those different personalities. At work, I am gung ho, in charge and very strong. At home, I'm soft as they come and he takes complete care of me."

Is that how Ed perceives it? "Absolutely," he says.

Ed takes the lead in protecting the privacy of the Langiotti home life. And when they're at home, he says, "It's just a household, and we just try to do what we can to relax and have fun and enjoy each other."

FIGHTING SMART

Ed also plays the major role in doing something that many couples find hard to do: keeping business disagreements from becoming personal. Pat will avoid conflict, but if Ed thinks it's important for the business, he will push an issue to confrontation.

He'll get her into what he calls "a fighting mode" and what she calls "ready to kill."

"I have so much confidence that no matter what amount of conflict there will be at work, it won't carry over at home, and I feel very free just to set anything on the table I want to and say, 'Okay, let's hash this out,'" says Ed. He then sees to it that they go nose to nose on it until it is finished.

She gets angry; he doesn't. He has the ability not to take a business argument personally, no matter how hard Pat may attack, and when they get home, "It doesn't count any more. It's fresh turf."

But, he says, "I think I'm also good at the other end"—that is, doing the things and saying the things that make it "very, very incompatible to continue to argue" once they leave work.

"He'll want to hug or have some tenderness between us," laughs Pat. "And I will not want him to touch me, because I am mad. And he won't stop." He may take her to a romantic place for a drink or shopping for something she wants but hasn't taken the time to shop for. "He'll be so persistently nice that I get mad because I can't stay mad at him." Sometimes, Pat says, she resents "having to fight with him at work and then having to come home and love him and like him."

It is important, say the Langiottis, that one member of the duo be the person who will take charge of the transition. That doesn't happen very often with their clients. In many entrepreneurial relationships, both partners get angry and stay that way, and the battles escalate to the point where the couple is torn apart.

If you are not married to or living with someone you work with, you may see that person as a whiz at detail work. You probably don't know he's a pig in the kitchen or a disaster at golf. But husbands and wives have access to a great deal of information about each other and if they choose to, the Langiottis point out, they can use that information to hurt each other and gain an advantage at the office. If, for example, a wife feels unsure about her development as a business manager and is taking courses to try to catch up, the husband may use her lack of self-confidence against her. No matter that she has done a super job. Pat explains: "If he wants to buy something that she knows they don't have the money for because she's learned how to budget and manage cash flow, he'll get mad at her and say, 'You're no good at that. You know you're not. You're just trying to pretend you know what's going on.' And she crumbles." The husband has chosen to fight dirty, playing on his wife's insecurities instead of addressing the issue of whether or not they have the money.

When the Langiottis disagree over a business issue, they try to use facts and figures to support their views and persuade each other.

"But," says Pat, turning to Ed, "you never take advantage of my personal vulnerable spots to get something at work, nor do I of you." Yet, she adds, if she wanted to, "I could hurt him very easily." And that's what she sees other business couples doing to each other "over and over and over."

THE ALL-INTRUSIVE HOME-BASED BUSINESS

While Pat and Ed operated CMC from their home, they learned firsthand what myriads of couples who run home-based businesses know: any business is consuming, but when it is at home, it's even harder to keep it out of your private life.

When they got married in 1966, Eric and Jean Flaxenburg bought six sheep and a lovely eighteenth-century stone farmhouse on 40 acres near the village of Elverson in the rolling Pennsylvania Dutch country. They settled down to what they hoped would be a life of pastoral serenity, despite the fact that Eric still had to drive 50 miles daily to Philadelphia where he was vice president of his father's industrial packaging company.

Seth, their first child, was a colicky baby, and they discovered that when he lay on a sheepskin, he was quiet. So Jean, who had been a theatrical costume designer, made him a sheepskin baby bunting to sleep in. That worked, too. "He was our first customer," she says.

She made some more buntings, and Bloomingdale's in New York bought a dozen at $20 apiece from Eric and sold them for $75 each. And when Seth grew a little, Jean made him a sheepskin coat. When others admired it, she said, "Why don't we make them for adults?"

That was the beginning of French Creek Sheep & Wool Company, which makes top-quality coats, sweaters, and other garments of shearling, leather, cotton, silk, suede, and wool. The Flaxenburgs call it "America's most elegant cottage industry."

Years ago, the business was moved from the farmhouse basement down the lane to the ever-expanding stone barn, which now houses cutting, sewing, and knitting rooms, a computer operation, and a retail shop. But most of their sales, which top $5 million annually, come from mail order, and they count such luminaries as Tom Selleck, Kenny Rogers, Burt Reynolds, and Ginger Rogers among their customers. They have had as many as 70 employees, about half of whom have worked at home in cottage industries of their own.

The Flaxenburgs have paid a price for their success, however. The setting, bordered on three sides by French Creek State Park, is as beautiful and unspoiled as ever. And they are proud of the fact that the kids, five of them now, have never come home to an empty house (or barn, Jean amends, because that's where she and Eric usually are). And they are pleased that their children have a chance to see, firsthand, how the family living is made. In some families, Eric observes, "the kids spend all the money without any knowledge of what it takes to get it."

There was a time when Eric would have said the advantages of living where their business is outweighed the disadvantages. "I think today I would say the opposite."

The most difficult problem is that they can never get away from the stress of their enterprise. "The only way I can feel free is by leaving here physically," says Eric. He turns to Jean to tease her, suggesting that she must feel the same way because "you are always going shopping."

Leaving the barn and going up to the house is not enough. If there is a problem or a phone call, employees call them there. "And on weekends when the shop is open, people are always coming around," says Eric. They finally resorted to leaving word with the employees that they are not at home.

"And then when you go out socially, people say, 'Oh, you're the people who own French Creek Sheep & Wool,'" Jean says. "'Tell us *all* about your business.'"

"I hate it. I hate it," Eric mutters.

They used to comply with such requests, but now, Jean reports, "Eric has gotten very rude. He says, 'If you don't mind, I'd rather not talk about it. I talk about it five days a week.'"

Another problem that the Flaxenburgs face—and one that worries many other couples who work at home—is employees. For the Flaxenburgs, it's getting too close to their people. (Pat Langiotti said the one employee they had when they were working out of their home was like a member of the family. A young, single woman, she ate with the Langiottis often and went to social events with them. "It was kind of like having a big kid.")

Eric says: "We are all on a first-name basis, and some have been here for a very long time. You develop a personal relationship which at times is very good for the company, but at other times can inhibit it."

"We live here, you see, and so these aren't merely employees," he continues. "These are people coming to your house every day, and your attitude toward them tends to be somewhat different than it would be, I would think, if you met on a neutral ground."

It is not merely the matter of disciplining that becomes more difficult. "If you have to fire somebody, it becomes impossible."

Another disadvantage, Jean says, is that employees know so much about your personal life. "They know exactly what you're doing every weekend because you're making arrangements while they're sitting there. They know if you're having people over for dinner. They know if you're going away because you have to leave them a phone number where you can be reached." (One wife recalls being ill with the flu and getting up from her sickbed and sitting on the stairs in her bathrobe, feeling weak and nauseated, as she tried to give her secretary instructions for the day. And Renata von Tscharner and Ronald Lee Fleming, urban planners whose nonprofit public interest firm, the Townscape Institute, is located on the first floor of their Cambridge, Massachusetts, home, are committed to improving the environment and try to instill that commitment in their employees. But their work also requires a heavy social life, and they worry that employees get mixed messages when they see the couple readying themselves for formal functions in Boston society.)

Couples who combine their home and business do find ways to relieve the stress or protect their private lives, however.

The Flaxenburgs did not want to give up the closeness they enjoyed with their employees, but they solved some of the problems inherent in that closeness by turning all hiring and firing over to their general manager. To escape the stress, they make it a point to get away a couple of times a year, which may mean skiing in New England or a trip to the shore with the whole family or an ocean cruise by themselves. Some couples, to get a respite from 24-hour togetherness, take separate vacations.

While their business was still at home, the Langiottis adopted some rules, rules that they now suggest to clients with home-based businesses:

☐ Designate some rooms as personal rooms and do not permit any discussion of the business in those rooms. "There have to be parts of your home that can't be invaded by your business, ever, under any circumstances," insists Ed. For them, the bedroom was an obvious choice, and sometimes it meant they had to get up out of bed and go stand in the hallway to talk about a client. They felt that, psychologically, the rule was a good first step.

☐ Don't let the telephone intrude. "We stopped answering the work phone at 5 o'clock, even when we knew big things were going on, because it became important to us to say, 'This has to stop,'" says Pat. She and Ed recommend having a telephone line that is not a business line and using it only for personal calls. If necessary, it can be an unlisted number, given only to friends.

☐ If possible, have an entrance that is a normal residential entrance into your home, not a business entrance. For example, a business located in the basement can use the basement door for its entrance, while the front door is reserved for family and friends.

Such measures, explains Ed, provide you with some "evidence of normality so that you can mentally make a transition from work to home," even though your home and your business occupy the same physical space.

THE TYRANNY OF THE CAR

The transition to and from work can help or hinder the way a couple makes a separation between their business and personal lives and the way they protect their relationship. Some couples say that even the *way* they get to work counts.

Sitting side by side in chairs in an office overlooking North Dallas and peering straight ahead, Bill and Sheri Criswell of the Criswell Company run through a little drama. They are demonstrating their daily half-hour ride to work. Bill's hands grasp an imaginary steering wheel.

Sheri (playing the role): "Bill, you've got a lot of stuff to get done today."

Bill begins to explain, and Sheri starts giggling because she knows exactly what her husband is going to say. From Sheri's point of view, he says, "We have arrived at the office the minute we get in the car. *I* don't think the business day begins until I arrive at the office."

If you count the return trip, Sheri has extended the workday for Bill by a whole hour.

They can laugh about it, but Bill suggests that if they really needed to take formal steps to protect their personal relationship from the business, he might begin with the automobile.

When Dennis Quade leaves for work in the morning, he kisses his wife, Karen, goodbye. He goes off to breakfast at a local restaurant and then heads on to Karen's Canvas, the Fort Myers business that he and Karen own.

Meanwhile, Karen gets herself ready for work. When she arrives, she greets the employees and says good morning to her husband as if she were seeing him for the first time that day.

For the Quades, the ritual is one way of separating the two facets of their life.

Chris and Winnie Dickerman of C & W Seafood in Herndon, Virginia, have also found it useful to drive to work separately.

"Once we get in the car," says Winnie, "it's like somebody turned on a switch that says, 'Now the questions have to start. You have to get on a roll. You have to produce. You have to do this, you have to do that.' I can't get the questions out fast enough for him to answer and it's the same with him."

They get along a little better at work, she says, if they don't ride in together. They like to have breakfast at a nearby restaurant and it's even better there if they drive separately and meet each other.

Winnie wakes up very slowly in the mornings while Chris says he is ready to roll. "I like to get up, shower, look at the paper, complain about the government, and get out. I'm not frustrated sitting around waiting for her. And she's not hurried by Mr. Ass jumping around, going crazy."

WHAT ABOUT ROMANCE?

Does being in business with one's spouse ruin a couple's love life?

"Nope. Quite the contrary," answers attorney William H. Deer, who is in his mid-fifties. "We do fine in the romance line if I can catch her."

It should be encouraging news that many couples find that being business partners is good for the intimate part of their relationship. "It enhances our romance," said one wife. "After a hard day's work, I think we have more respect for one another. We see what each other has accomplished. I personally am very proud when I watch my husband at work. With most couples, one can come home from work and say they're too tired, but the other doesn't really know if they're tired or if it's just an excuse. We know."

Couples like Joanne and Skip Schatz say that their business problems in no way harm their sex life. If anything, says Joanne, their love life offers a means for reaching out to each other when problems occur.

Other couples say being in business together has no effect on bedroom activities, one way or the other. Still others insist that sex is no different for them than for couples who are not in business together—even then, a bad day can be a detriment to romance while a good day can augment it.

But many couples do admit that the rhythm of their enterprise does hold sway in the bedroom. A deal that falls through, a financial crunch, or a disagreement can leave one or both partners depressed and uninterested in sex or just too angry. But just as a bad day can forestall the pleasures of romance, a check in the mail or a new client or contract can put a couple in the right spirits. Some say sex is better when business is good and they are freer from financial pressures.

For many, the business partnership increases the opportunities for romance. Michael T. and D. Elisabeth Aymett run Cecil's Messenger Service out of their San Pablo, California, home, and, time permitting, Michael says, "We can spend our lunch hour together in bed if we want." She and her husband have more than 60 employees, but one wife spoke of locking the office door in the middle of the day and making love on the sofa. When you are in business together, say some, it is easier to plan for love making than if you have separate careers.

In some instances, the nature of the business creates a lifestyle that reinforces romance. Ronald Lee Fleming says: "Being perceived as a business couple gives us a certain romantic aura, I believe, in some people's minds, because we do have a certain style which is perhaps different from the average American." That "style," he explains, enables him and his Swiss-born wife to combine a conference in Europe preceded or followed by a weekend in London or Paris. They were able to organize a four-day social event surrounding the christening of their daughter in Cathedral Bern, where they were married, and combine it with information-gathering for a book and interviews with business associates. "Often, we stay with friends when we are on business trips and tend to have candlelight dinners with our associates in a particular city while still pursuing some business-related goals during the day."

On home ground, nevertheless, he admits that he and Renata are "exhausted at night and Renata tends to go to bed earlier than I do. As a result, our romantic time together is usually in the morning. But this is somewhat complicated with two children of small age."

Exhaustion is just one of many complaints that entrepreneurial couples make about their love life. Gayle H. Sensing of Medical HomeCare Services, Inc., in Nashville, says, "It is difficult to be romantic at night after you've been together all day. This is a real problem." Another wife complains not about lack of quality but lack of quantity.

When resentments over the business creep into the bedroom, some couples can find themselves in serious trouble; their anger may become so deep-seated that they have no intimate relationship left. In some cases, going into business together throws preexisting problems into sharp relief as the couple's relationship is put to new, sometimes insurmountable, tests.

Consider, for example, the wife who has been relegated to the "caretaking" role, handling the details and remembering to do the things her creative, visionary husband forgets or avoids, and perhaps even telling him what to do. The wife will begin to perceive the husband as, in many ways, a child who needs looking after. She becomes the "parent."

While this may not happen on a conscious level, psychologist Marta Vago says, "To the extent that a relationship turns into this parent–child structure, to that extent it can really undermine the romantic, sexual aspects of the relationship."

In another case, a husband, by virtue of being older and more experienced, might take on the parent role. No matter who plays which part, if this kind of unequal role differentiation is going on, Vago warns, you have to look at whether you "really feel like making love to your mother or whether you really feel like making love to your father or whether you really feel like making love to your daughter or son, because, on some level, that's what it can turn into." One partner may still respect the other's work, but if the interaction between them is like a parent and child, says Vago, "It's very bad for sex."

Disagreements become detrimental to sex in part because men and women have different capacities for turning emotions on and off. Says Wesley Kranitz: "Rosanne especially had a hard time leaving business disagreements at work. I seem to have a lot less problem doing this. Once the disagreement is over, it's over. Rosanne tended to hold a grudge. Sometimes it would be a couple of days before she could allow herself to not be mad."

The Kranitzes are not unusual. "I think men are socialized to have their feelings in little, neat compartments so they can be mad as hell at their wife, but when they walk in the bedroom and turn off the lights, it's like—poof!—'Let's get it on, honey!'" observes Vago. Women, at least those over 30, she says, have been socialized to have their feelings "more of an integral part of their entire experience." A woman is more likely than a man to say, "I can't turn my feelings on and off like a faucet." If she is angry with him for something he did at the office, whether it was failing to return a phone call to a client or making a $500 mistake in the checkbook, she is less able to turn the anger off and get amorous.

This difference can be a constant source of tension. The man can shut *his* angry feelings off and wonder, "How come you can't?" He in turn may take it personally and feel threatened that his mate does not feel loving, because he does not understand that her feelings are more integrated with the rest of her consciousness. She may not be able to become aroused sexually until she resolves whatever made her angry and disappointed. "It had nothing to do with him *personally*," Vago continues. "It had to do with him in that situation—his behavior, his choices, and so on."

Negativity can start seeping in at very subtle levels in a business, and if the couple discounts it, they may begin to play out games in the sexual area. "People do all kinds of things unconsciously," Vago says. "They can unconsciously punish each other in their sexual life, either by withholding sexually from the other person or making unreasonable demands of the other person."

She likens the process to toxic waste that begins to infiltrate the water supply. "There is a little stream, a contaminated stream, that starts to go into the well that supplies the water. And you can't taste it, you can't smell it, but things begin to turn. It can make you sick, eventually, if there is enough of it."

Couples who find themselves perpetually unhappy about what

their business is doing to their personal relationship, including their sex life, are wise to seek professional counseling. But when the negative impact is only occasional or seen as temporary, couples often are able to work it through.

Pauline Berliner recalls that an "argumentative" day would dampen desire, but, she says, "we would make a conscious effort to separate the aggravations of the day by maintaining our relationship 'from the neck down.'" She and Jerome worked at both their business and personal lives instead of walking away from problems, she says, "since we were convinced that basically we had something to offer to each other as well as to our sons." With two strong-minded people, Jerome comments, there are going to be situations "fraught with animosity." And when those occurrences spoil romance, there may be no way to "handle" it except to give it time: "There is a family to be concerned about, a business to be operated in the morning, and a thousand and one things to attend to. Thus, tensions hang high for a couple of days, and gradually, emotions cool and the parties just have to revert to important matters. If there is a mutual desire to declare an armistice, a kiss, a pat on the fanny, some flowers should help to 'handle' a delicate situation."

"The business has put a dent in our love life," acknowledges Elisabeth Aymett. "Yes, a mistake made in business can definitely affect bedroom activities. It's hard to make love if you are feeling resentful. We try to handle it by talking about it. This seems to work."

No question about it, agrees Chris Dickerman, a bad day can hurt your sex life. How do he and Winnie cope? "Go to bed, get up the next morning and start over again."

"Even if we're angry," adds Winnie, "we sleep very close to each other." Somehow, that helps.

With patience and caring and a commitment to their relationship, couples survive not only the bad days but the bad nights as well. They may well find the reward that Diane Saliba speaks of when she says "making love can be a celebration of work done well and [that] happens sometimes when we feel good about ourselves and what we've accomplished."

NURTURING THE RELATIONSHIP

No matter how much they love their business or how much time they devote to it, an entrepreneurial couple must give attention to their personal relationship if it, too, is to thrive. The kinds and amounts of care and feeding a relationship needs varies from couple to couple, as do the ways couples fulfill those needs. However, psychologist Marta Vago has found that many couples engage in "intimacy rituals"—predictable and regular activities that provide nourishment to a relationship. They may be as simple as going to a particular restaurant every Friday night or taking a drive on Sunday afternoons.

"These little patterns of closeness emerge fairly early in the relationship," she says, noting that couples often start them spontaneously during courtship.

Entrepreneurial couples, however, face the risk of putting so much of their energies into their businesses that these rituals fall by the wayside. "It is very unfortunate when that happens because often these rituals are the only predictable source of nourishment to the relationship that the couple has," says Vago. She views a relationship as a separate entity from the individuals who are in it, and because it is separate, it needs to be cultivated and taken care of "as one would a plant or a child or anything outside of oneself." By engaging in intimacy rituals, she says, a couple is taking time out "to pay attention to the business of their relationship rather than the business of their business."

There is considerable evidence that entrepreneurial couples do fall into patterns of habits and rituals that support their emotional closeness. When Lorraine Mecca and Geza Csige were heading up Micro D, for example, they still tried to get away to the movies on Sunday evenings. Some couples look for ways to make each other feel special; one pair said they try to create an atmosphere of "dating" each other and often give each other little gifts to show appreciation. Another reported that when possible, one partner leaves the office early, goes home, lights the fire, and, in general, makes the house cozy to welcome the other home.

Some develop rituals that function as a healing process and as a means of communication. Pat Langiotti says that for a time, one of the children would say, "I love you seven," because to her, that was the biggest number that existed. Now when Ed knows Pat is really angry with him, he will ask, "How much do you love me?" And Pat will answer, "Six and three-quarters."

Says Pat: "We do that humorously, but that gives us a vehicle for communicating 'I am not okay with you' in a way that's not 'I hate your guts, you son of a bitch.' It's a way for me to say to him, 'I'm irritated with you right now; leave me alone.' But it gives us something maybe warm and tender to relate it to, or something humorous that softens the blow."

Nonverbal communication is important to Chris and Winnie Dickerman. They rely on a lot of touching, and they encourage other couples to do the same. For them, physical contact is part of the daily routine, just as easily practiced on the job as at home. Winnie says she might walk by Chris "and pinch him on the butt" or give him a little pat on the leg.

"I have no idea how many times a day we touch each other," she says. "That says everything. It gets rid of hostility. It gets rid of tension and frustration. It says, 'I love you,' or, 'Boy, I'm really pissed at you.' And when you go home at night, you have a tendency to want to sit together."

But predictable behaviors are not the only things that enable a man and a woman to nurture a treasured relationship. Most couples find that simply taking time out from the daily grind and spending it with each other in a different way is important. Some deliberately plan romantic vacations; others say they try to get away together on a fairly regular basis, such as a weekend a month, or several vacations a year.

Vago says it's preferable if partners can plan time away from work that gives them a chance to be separate from each other as well as together. One formula that worked very well for one couple in a publishing business involved their going away for two or three weeks perhaps twice a year. They would spend the first three to five days separately. "Each would go off by themselves just for their own enjoyment, private reflection, and self-renewal. She would go off to a spa; he would go off to a tennis clinic." For the second part of their vacation, they would meet somewhere and go on a trip together, to a resort, perhaps, or on a cruise. "Symbolically, they separated themselves out first and took care of their individual, personal renewal," says Vago. "Then they came together, apart from business."

Inherent in the various devices that couples use to keep their love for each other alive is good communication, and many couples say communication is one of the most vital factors in making a combined business–personal relationship work. Fight fair, get disagreements on the table, and settle arguments quickly. And somehow demonstrate love and appreciation to your partner.

For many couples, the business itself provides the vehicle for shared interests, communication, stimulation, and mutual commitment, and more than a few say their relationship, instead of being torn asunder by the business, is made better by it. It has, some say, given them a chance to strengthen their positive feelings for each other by increasing their respect for what the other can do, and by giving each the opportunity for personal growth as well as the chance to grow together and to achieve together.

Valerie Bursten says she thinks she and Steve had been married 10 years before they really fell in love. She was 24 when they married and had been a nurse and a flight attendant. Steve agrees that she really didn't love him at the time. She lacked other options, he says, and he was the "least worst alternative for her." And she says, "I knew he was going to be a success, and successful men attract me like flies to honey."

What perhaps she didn't count on was that she would be a

success right along with him. Both she and Steve have grown with the business and Valerie, particularly, is doing things she never imagined possible—including making big sales and speaking in public. The realities of life and of business have changed her attitude not only toward herself but also toward her husband.

She apologizes for sounding corny when she tells you that a couple of years ago, she finally arrived at the point where she really wanted Steve to be happy. She can now say, with genuine caring, "How are you?" Or, "Is anything bothering you?"

"I never used to say that," she says.

SUPPORTIVE
HUSBANDS

"He Moved so I Could Go to the
Law School I Wanted to Go To"

I couldn't sit back in the shadow and feel like I had pumped somebody else up and have that vicarious sense of pride and pleasure. Ed can. And so it's a perfect pairing in that sense. If he gives me an opportunity to have the limelight and run, I love it. That's my nature.

PATRICIA LEE LANGIOTTI, PRESIDENT
CREATIVE MANAGEMENT CONCEPTS
READING, PENNSYLVANIA

She is intuitively a phenomenally good business person. She understands what consumers want. She understands what people who work for her want. She understands that if you make the consumer happy, if you make the people who come to your counter or your business feel good, they will help the people who work for you feel good, and that is what is most important to business success. . . . Debbi is obsessed with the process of business—not the goal of business, the process of business. And it is a talent. It is an extraordinary talent. So to be in the shadow or not mentioned in relation to someone who I think in this century will leave her mark on American business, it is terrific.

RANDALL K. FIELDS, VICE PRESIDENT
MRS. FIELDS CHOCOLATE CHIPPERY
PARK CITY, UTAH

He had the bright idea I should go to law school at night as a hobby. And I went and took the LSAT test and my grades were really excellent. I'll never forget this: I called Bill at 3 o'clock and told him. He came home at 6. He had gone and talked to some attorneys in his company, and he said, "Well, they said you can probably get in most anywhere, so you go apply at law schools in the East and on the West Coast and I'll look for jobs and we'll just move." So he moved so I could go to the law school that I wanted to go to.

SHARON CRISWELL, PRESIDENT
CRISWELL COMPANY
DALLAS, TEXAS

The supportive wife is the accepted thing. When an entrepreneur, usually male, starts a business, the wife is expected to play a helping, enabling, nurturing role. When a man climbs the corporate ladder, the wife in the traditional household is there to help him make that climb.

In the last two decades, women in the United States have cried out for supportive husbands, men who would not seek the limelight just for themselves but who would also recognize the wife's need to grow and achieve and to fulfill her potential. To be somebody.

Many of the men who are part of an entrepreneurial-marital team give new meaning to the phrase "supportive husband." These particular men encourage the aspirations of their wives and enable the wives to realize their goals. They don't patronize ("She's really superior to me"). They enjoy their wives' company and respect their intelligence and abilities. They insist that their wives share equally in the recognition and rewards that come with owning a business together. More than other men, they have learned to temper their egos in ways that not only surely benefit their marriages but also their businesses.

This is not to say that all men in business with their wives are supportive husbands; it is still true that many of them are of the old school, being paternalistic, authoritarian men whose spouses have to fight to be heard and to struggle for every piece of recognition that they get. Nor do we wish to deny that supportive husbands are sometimes ambivalent about the pioneering role they have chosen. Some research suggests that some men in dual-career marriages, though ostensibly supportive, secretly resent their wives' success. Research on entrepreneurial couples might well turn up a similar phenomenon.

Nevertheless, in the environment of the contemporary entrepreneurial marriage, the supportive husband is found to flourish. Here, in larger numbers it seems, are husbands who will put their wives forward, live in their shadow if necessary, play behind-the-scenes roles, acknowledge—indeed, celebrate—the wife's equal contribution, and joyfully share equal credit with her for building a business. Without the emergence of such supportive husbands, in fact, the new entrepreneurial couples would not exist. We would have the same old business of the past, with the man in charge and the woman, if she is part of the business at all, as the helper.

IN HIS OWN INTEREST

For some men, being a supportive husband goes so far back it seems second nature. When Bill Criswell suggested that Sheri go to law school, they were living in St. Louis. Her decision to go to Stanford meant more than just Bill changing jobs and moving with her to California. They had two children who Sheri describes as "little *bitty* things" at the time—in fact, their daughter was born when Sheri was a law student. The Criswells had a deal: Sheri would study only between 9 and 11 at night and one whole day of the weekend. Frequently, Bill would pop the baby into a backpack, put their two-year-old son on a bicycle, and pedal off to a football game or a park so that Sheri could study all day undisturbed.

Other fathers might resent being the babysitter. But Bill says: "I'm really a very lucky father, because many, many fathers don't get to share that much *alone* time with children, particularly when they're very young."

The Criswells believed that Stanford had one of the best— and therefore one of the toughest—law schools in the country. But part of their agreement was that if Sheri couldn't "hack" law school with those restrictions on her hours, "then," says Bill, "too bad. Law school was just going to have to give."

"And it turns out that she wound up second in her class," Bill chuckles. "So clearly, she was able to hack it just fine."

Bill's pattern of supporting Sheri would continue when they were in business together. Despite her fears that she would lose her identity and end up in his shadow, that did not happen. "Bill has always pushed me out in front and he's been very generous about sharing the leadership of the company with me," says Sheri. "I really have to credit him a lot with making that possible, so that I wasn't threatened. He made it possible for me not to have to run around and demonstrate to everyone in the company what I contributed."

But Bill says that if he pushed his wife forward, it was "self-serving."

"I knew how sharp she was and it is not in my interest to have the perception of her not match with the reality," he says. "It was important to me that other people understand what I already knew."

He also says that he had learned a long time ago, from being involved in sports, that self-confidence builds on itself. "The more Sheri saw that others recognized her for the competent businesswoman that she is, the more self-confident she got about conducting herself that way and acting in more of a leadership capacity."

But it worked both ways. Sheri is as much a supportive wife as Bill is a supportive husband. She had finished law school and was practicing law in San Francisco when, one day, Bill asked, "How would you like to move to Dallas?" He had an opportunity to work for a real estate company there. Sheri at first did not want to move, but she recognized that it was her turn. They went to Dallas in 1974, and two years later, Bill saw the opportunity to start his own business.

"I've told many, many people I would never have had the courage to start the company and go out on my own and try to make a go of this business if it weren't for the advice and support Sheri gave me early on." She boosted him up and reminded him of the things he was good at and, he says, "she gave me the absolute freedom to fail. She let me know that if the business didn't work out, if I tried it, gave it my best, that I would not have a wife who would look on me as a failure."

What she thought was what mattered the most to him, he says, and she let him know that not trying would be more of a failure than trying and failing. "That's all the support that I needed to get going."

"SHE IS THE BEST"

Debbi Fields was only 20 years old when Randy loaned her the $50,000 that enabled her to open the first Mrs. Fields Cookies store. She had had two years of community college, but Randy, an economist, had earned a B.A. and an M.A. at Stanford and had already established himself as a successful financial consultant. He may have had the academic credentials and the experience, but she showed him that a business could be an extraordinary winner even if it didn't go by the books.

It is a temptation to come to the conclusion that Randy Fields is the brains behind Mrs. Fields Cookies; in fact, according to *Inc.* magazine, competitor David Liederman of David's Cookies has made that charge. In its July 1984 cover story, *Inc.* says that Liederman refers to Debbi as "that airhead."

But Randy is a staunch defender of her intelligence and her achievements. Slim as a model and blessed with long, luxurious blond hair, flawless skin, and a smile that never quits, Debbi is, Randy says, "by almost anybody's standard an attractive woman." People don't believe attractive women can be successful, he observes. "I know it bothers Debbi, but there really is this assumption in the world that this whole thing must be Randy. It is not because Debbi is a woman; it is because Debbi is a *pretty* woman."

Mrs. Fields Cookies, he says, is *clearly* a woman's company. He gets the laugh he is angling for when he adds that if it were *his* company, he would immediately rip out the butter and substitute margarine. (Debbi has insisted that she will *never* use a butter substitute or sacrifice the quality of the recipes in any way.)

Randy is still a flourishing financial consultant, and he and Debbi are co-owners of a number of businesses. Besides the financial company (The Fields Investment Group) and Mrs. Fields Cookies, they have joint interests in real estate development, oil, and venture capital—what Randy calls "miscellaneous odds and ends." He spends about half his time on Mrs. Fields Cookies, where, he says, Debbi is not only the president—she is the boss. "This is her company. Like the people who work for her, I work for Debbi. We are joint owners in terms of the ownership, but power does not flow from the ownership. She is the heart and soul of the business. So if she says, 'This is how we are going to do it,' that is how we do it."

She listens to his ideas. Sometimes he can change her mind on something; other times, she may proceed with a decision that he disagrees with. When she does, he still gives her his support. "I am a classic subordinate," he says. Once the decision is made, he follows along.

Though he has always encouraged Debbi, she appears to enjoy even deeper support from him now than she did at the beginning. When the first store was opened, he thought she had bought herself a job, not a company that would grow to more than 3,500 employees in eight years. Watching what she did changed his perspective. He used to be a "by-the-numbers, management-by-objectives" kind of person, he says. You ran a company the way the business schools at Harvard and Stanford told you to run it.

Debbi, however, was intuitive in her management style. If a cookie needed one more macadamia nut to make it right, it didn't matter what that nut cost. She believed that if she could make people smile, that was what was important.

According to Randy, they made most of their mistakes when they went by his by-the-books approach or relied on the advice of professionals "rather than following Debbi's intuitive sense of what is appropriate." When Debbi suggested something, it worked; when the professionals wanted to do it their way, it didn't.

"So you do what works," Randy says. "Her ideas have been incredibly successful." One result is that they have stopped using marketing professionals. "The marketing of the company now belongs to every person who works for the company," says Debbi.

Randy says Mrs. Fields Cookies is going in the opposite direction of what a growing company should be doing. "As a company gets larger, it ought to become more professional, more thinking, less feeling." Instead, he finds, Mrs. Fields Cookies is less intellectual, less professional, and more spontaneous, and there is more encouragement of people who are "feelie" types as opposed to thinking types. While the Fieldses are tightlipped about company revenues, Randy says, "The results are staggering, absolutely staggering."

Debbi's approach has been not to sell the cookies but to give people a taste and let the cookies sell themselves. As for employees, Randy describes her style as one of "empowering" people, giving them the sense that they can achieve anything they want to. She is also big on people having fun at work.

Debbi herself says that she believes it is her responsibility to create the philosophy of the company and "to create opportunity so that people will continue to grow and develop and be challenged on to greatness." Her greatest joy, she says, is watching people grow.

Debbi traces her management style back to the days when she and Randy were first married. Randy, the hot young financial consultant, was getting a fair amount of attention in the national press, including *Forbes* and *Time*, and Debbi was just regarded as "Mrs. Randy Fields." She was treated like a nobody, and that experience taught her that everyone hungers for recognition. "When you get positive strokes, that makes you feel good. When you feel good, then you feel successful." It works for employees, and it works for customers. (These days, they jokingly refer to Randy as "Mr. Debbi Fields.")

Randy says he is paid to be brutally objective. Having said that, he adds that Debbi "is the best business person that I

have ever met, without question." And he believes there will
be other businesses in the future with Debbi's name on them.
"Watch out, General Mills."

EACH OTHER'S BEST CRITIC

Because they sit at the top of a franchise corporation in which
the vast majority of franchisees are women, Valerie and Steve
Bursten of Decorating Den Systems have a special perspective
on the importance of the supportive husband. In at least 80
percent of their franchises, they say, the husband has some level
of involvement, with many even spending five to ten hours a
week helping with the installation of interior design products
or doing bookkeeping.

   The Burstens look carefully at the husband of an applicant
for a franchise. Will he go to franchise meetings with her? If
she has to make a sales call at night, can he handle things at
home or will he be screaming because she didn't have a hot
meal on the table for him? Or is he a highly paid executive or
professional who is buying the franchise for his wife to get her
out of his hair?

   If they aren't reasonably sure the husband will be supportive,
the Burstens nearly always disqualify the applicant. Their experience tells them that if the husband isn't going to be a source
of encouragement to the wife—if he puts her down, for example,
or tells her the franchise is a stupid idea, or doesn't treat it
seriously—then the franchise will have a hard time of it.

   Assessing his own abilities as a supportive husband, Steve,
who is nearing 50 years old, says that he is still in a transition
stage—becoming better at being supportive, but not as far along
as some of the younger husbands of Decorating Den franchise
owners. In 20 percent to 30 percent of the cases, he finds, the
woman is the dominant partner in the marriage; in other cases,
but more rare, the husband and wife seem nearly equal in their

dominance. In both types of marriages, he has seen very supportive husbands—men who are willing to do the laundry and look after children so their wives can do what is necessary to run the franchise.

Because of the nature of the Burstens' business, Steve has learned to be a more supportive husband himself, despite his tendency to dominate. The success of his company has depended on his ability to help "literally hundreds of women" emerge, he says, and he has nurtured many of them from a total lack of self-confidence to the point where they have become sales leaders and savvy managers. He speaks proudly of a Texas woman who was so fearful that she brought her mother along to the initial Decorating Den meeting. She was a slow starter, and, at first, Steve thought she would fall by the wayside as a franchisee. But little by little, she built up her clientele. She took good care of her customers and she drew inspiration from other women franchisees who won sales awards. As her business grew, her husband, also a quiet person, joined her full time. Now the franchise is doing nearly half a million dollars a year in sales and has about 20 employees. Steve knows that Decorating Den helped that woman achieve her potential, and as he developed his ability to nurture the women in his business, he found he could transfer it to his marriage.

Valerie, who never dreamed she would be helping to run a multimillion-dollar company, give speeches, or become an extraordinary salesperson, says that whenever she faced a challenge, Steve would say, "You can do it." And because of his belief in her, she did it.

Because he is in the same business, Steve says he understands the pressures Valerie is under and can empathize with her. Even when she goes on a business trip, he knows what her days are like. Visualizing a day on a recent trip she made to the West Coast, he says: "She started early in the morning. She had plane connections." He saw her going from little town to little town in Washington, giving seminars, helping people with management problems, and talking with someone who is trying to build sales. The days on such a trip are long and tiring, and, says Steve, "I know when she gets off that airplane and she comes home that I want to give her all the support I can. I want to be sure the house is clean. I want to be sure that the dog is shampooed and the kids are in good shape and almost meet her at the door with a martini because I know what she's been through for that week she's been out traveling."

As with many other couples, that support is a two-way street. Over the years, Steve and Valerie have learned to be what he calls "top level, loving critics" of each other. They agreed first that they wanted each to bring out the best in the other. Without that kind of foundation, Steve says, being each other's critic could never have worked. "But there was a fundamental spoken and unspoken agreement between us that we both wanted to be the very best that we could. We wanted to live up to our potential the very best that we could. And we invited the other person, within reason, to try to help us achieve that."

How is one a "loving critic"? You take the attitude that you want the other person to blossom, Valerie answers. If your spouse writes something and wants you to read it, instead of saying, "It's a bunch of garbage," you can say, "What do you feel your readers want to read?" and offer guidance from there.

They never take the criticism personally, says Steve. "There's no way that one of us feels the other one is trying to tear something down or take away from anything—only that we're challenging each other to do the very best job we can."

Valerie has helped him improve the quality of his management, his writing and speaking, and his ability to work with people, says Steve. "She has helped me to gain stature about myself and to enhance myself." He believes he has done the same for her, and she would agree.

Valerie is a woman of quiet reserve, while Steve is immediately friendly and talkative. Nevertheless, he carefully defers to her in conversation, often inviting her to speak first or making sure her opinion is heard. He seems to truly want to know what she thinks and, just as much, to want others to know what she thinks.

It was not always so. In the first years of their marriage, before they founded Decorating Den, he was running his own business and he was quite successful. "I tended to think of myself as pretty much God—you know, the typical small entrepreneur—and everyone around me was my servant to do things at my behest. And I treated Valerie exactly that way."

Valerie made it clear that she would not continue the marriage on those terms. "She was going to refuse to bow," says Steve. In what was probably the most significant crisis in their marriage, they sought professional counseling. Out of that experience, Steve learned that sometimes he would have to be the follower; he couldn't always be the leader, or he would find that he was leading only himself.

GIVING HER ROOM

If Steve Bursten had trouble curbing his dominant personality and turning himself into a supportive husband, it was perhaps even more difficult for Rocco Altobelli, who did not have franchisees to learn from or to reinforce the process. As his name suggests, he is of Italian ancestry and, by his own admission, he is "very Latin, or very Italian, in my emotions." In other words, volatile. Dianne Altobelli's ancestors were Norwegian-German; hers is a much more controlled personality, given to calm at times when a calm response drives Rocco nuts.

Rocco grew up in a hairdressing family, and finally, in 1972, he started a quality salon—called, appropriately, Rocco Altobelli—with the dream of someday creating a large business, one with the strength and staying power of a major corporation. It was his hope to sustain the quality of his original salon and still grow. If he succeeded, it would be a most unusual achievement in the industry, where, he says, it is difficult to sustain top quality past two salons.

The answer turned out to be Dianne. For the first several years, Rocco ran one salon, then two. He became a local celebrity, appearing often on television in Minneapolis-St. Paul. Dianne, who has a degree in health, physical education, and recreation, was working in a community center part-time, rearing the two Altobelli sons, and keeping books for Rocco.

After Rocco took on the second salon, Dianne became more involved, taking on more responsibilities. Rocco soon suggested that Dianne run the business end of things while he oversaw the artistic and creative side. With that decision came a period of rapid growth, with the company increasing to eight salons by 1986 and more than $5 million in annual revenues.

In effect, Dianne turned out to be exactly what many entre-preneurs need: a professional manager who can shepherd the growth of a company once the initial start-up period is over. The transition was a tough one, rife with fights. While he was glad to be freed of the minutiae of management and to have the opportunity to devote more time to the creative areas of the business, Rocco also had a hard time letting go. "I wanted Dianne to do it all, but I wanted Dianne to do it all exactly like I would have done it."

Rocco describes himself as "a very dominant and very intimi-dating type of person." He would blow up at Dianne—"vio-lently," he recalls—and she, not being a vocal person, would sit down and write Rocco "violent letters."

"I must have resigned four or five times," she says.

It came to a point where they knew they had to resolve the problems in their business relationship or they would have to separate as a couple. They ruled out the latter—they still loved each other and they loved their family.

"What I did was just back off," says Rocco. He stopped going to management meetings and started praying that his business would still be there when he went to work.

It was. Perhaps still amazed, he says, "I let her alone and, behold, she did a fantastic job and did things better than I could do."

When the company was smaller, Rocco could hire hairdressers who were eager to work with him and learn from him. As the business grew, that one-on-one system of motivation and transferring knowledge didn't work anymore. Dianne devised a middle management system, with trained managers who could keep each location running smoothly and oversee quality. Where Rocco had been authoritarian, Dianne set up quality circles. Rocco is still not comfortable with them—they come up with ideas he discarded long ago, he complains. But he still admits that Dianne's way is better.

For Rocco, being supportive meant backing away and giving Dianne the room to do what she could do. It meant a shift in the relationship and in the home life; the more she became involved in the business, the less he could expect that old family style, like the one in which he was reared, where "everything is kind of built around [the man's] way of life."

Sometimes Dianne feels a tinge of resentment that Rocco, because of his celebrity (which she acknowledges is good for the business), gets credit for things she has done. But he counters that she has come to be recognized as the manager of the company. And he takes pride in that fact. "I was the first one to promote her and give her that authority," he says. "I'm very happy for her."

THE MANY FACES OF SUPPORT

Support takes many forms. When Mel and Patricia Ziegler sold the Banana Republic to The Gap, Inc., in 1983, they agreed to stay on and run their creation. It was suggested to Mel that his salary, as president, should be larger than that of Patricia, who is executive vice president.

But Mel refused. "We never let The Gap think of us as individuals," he says. "We're the founders, and whatever we make, we share. Our value is absolutely equal, and it would be totally inappropriate to do it any other way. I'm not worth a penny more than Patricia and she's not worth a penny more than I am—because we're each worthless without the other."

Ed Langiotti started out in a supportive role. Long before he and Pat fell in love, married, and started their management consulting business she was his boss in another company. Because Pat started the company nearly a year before Ed could join in, she got a head start. As far as the clients were concerned, she *was* the company. She had the visibility; she also had a nonintimidating personality, and clients felt comfortable opening up to her. They could tell her their problems and admit it to her when they didn't understand something.

When Ed joined, he carved out a role for himself as the secondary person. It wasn't by design; the Langiottis more or less fell into it. But it worked. With Ed behind the scenes, the clients' perception of the company was not disrupted. With a background in administration, Ed had skills that Pat didn't have but which were valuable to the company's growth. Furthermore, he was comfortable with a low profile.

Says Pat: "He lets me think I'm the boss, and he gets me to do exactly what he wants me to do." He does not feel resentful being in Pat's shadow because, she says, he has set her up. He is, in effect, the director of Pat's performance.

Ed acknowledges that he manipulates Pat, but says he does so in the best interests of the company. With Pat in the forefront, he explains, the public has only one person to communicate with, and as long as he and Pat function in private as 50–50 owners of the company, that's all he is interested in.

"He tells people that my job is to satisfy the clients, and his is to keep me working," laughs Pat.

Because their industry is so male dominated, Diane and Leonard Johnson of Central Pipe & Supply sometimes have to contend with getting their public, especially their suppliers, to accept the fact that Diane is co-owner of the company. They have had their biggest problems in other countries, particularly Japan, where women aren't welcome to go through the steel mills. But the Johnsons insist on going through a mill to see how the product is made and to assure themselves that it is a quality product before they recommend it to their customers. Leonard doesn't back down when it comes to getting permission for Diane to tour a mill with him.

"She may have to go to a different bathroom, but she is treated the same as Mr. Johnson," he says. Diane attends all the business meetings and, Leonard chuckles, "they really have a hard time dealing with how the hell to seat us."

They have been to Japan so many times now, he adds, that the Japanese know "you don't send some little office clerk to go take Diane shopping."

While men like Steve Bursten and Rocco Altobelli may have had to struggle more than others to become supportive husbands, it is much to their credit that they made the effort and succeeded. Their companies and their marriages have benefited as a result. The men who come by their supportive roles with more ease— Bill Criswell and Ed Langiotti, for example—radiate an inner confidence and security, frequently borne of earlier personal success. As Bill Criswell has admitted, he is not sure he could have shared power with his wife had he not been a success in business before. And Ed Langiotti states that his personal growth needs are not such right now that he is looking for position or status. He realized and maintained self-fulfillment in previous positions, and he has satisfied that need. Now, he says, "I can concentrate on other things." He can develop previously undeveloped skills that are of value to his and Pat's company. But in his view, having leadership of the company is not necessary to him.

Perhaps another dimension to the role of the supporting husband is suggested by Debbi and Randy Fields. Randy regards himself as somewhat old-fashioned when it comes to domestic roles, and to Debbi, being a wife and a mother are both very important. She frequently says, in fact, that being a mother is far harder the running Mrs. Fields Cookies. Because Debbi cares so much about the traditional roles, Randy sees her as a "superb role model for women." She is, in his eyes, the "new woman." First, he explains, there was woman as subordinate. Then there was women's liberation, with women "the same as men," wearing women's clothes but doing men's things. Now, there is a resolution in which "women can be women, can be mothers, can be wives, and be in the business world."

"Those," he says, "are not incompatible things."

Not, of course, as long as a husband will give support to all of that.

9

ENTREPRENEURS AS PARENTS

"Frequently, It's the Business Child Who Gets Mom's and Dad's Attention"

If parents decide to go into business together, that decision will affect their children.

If an entrepreneurial couple decides to have children, that decision will affect the business.

The business plays an important role in the lives of the children. At the very least, it is their bread and butter. But children, in turn, play an important role in the life of the business, whether or not they go to work in it. Nearly every day, their parents are trying to juggle the needs of the family and the enterprise. Some are able to do so; others find they are not so successful.

The presence of children raises many, many issues for the entrepreneurial couple. Should one of the parents withdraw from the business and stay with the children during their early years? If so, how will pulling out affect that parent's involvement with the business and with the spouse? Should children come first or should the business come first? How can parents make the business attractive to their children as a career? How can parents use the business to teach responsibility and other values to their children?

There is no single answer to any of these questions. Any answers depend on a multitude of variables, such as the age of the couple and their children; the type of business, as well as its age and size; the couple's value systems; and the children's individual needs and personalities.

However, couples do need to be aware of the intense relationship between their business and their children in order to come to decisions about how they will handle both.

While not all entrepreneurial couples would agree with her, psychologist Marta Vago says, "It is a safe bet to look at the entrepreneurial venture that a couple embarks on as a child. And chances are that child is going to be the favored child— and possibly the only child. If it is going to be an only child, that's fine, because that child is going to get all the attention and fussing and worrying that it deserves. If it's not going to be an only child, then whoever the real child is may have to get used to being a stepchild."

Frequently, she says, it is the business child that gets Mom's and Dad's real attention. "Parents are not going to leave their business to a nanny, but I think they are more likely to leave their biological offspring to one."

CONTENDING WITH THE CHANGES

Rachel Borish and Jeff Slater of Rachel's Brownies found that the decision to have a child can affect the business even before the baby is born. When pregnant with their second child, Borish was ill and bedridden most of the first trimester, and she describes it as one of the toughest periods she and Slater had to go through as business partners.

Her illness came at a time when the company was scheduled to move several miles away into larger facilities. Slater not only had a sick wife and an infant daughter to look after, he also had the day-to-day responsibility for the business, with the added strain of the move. And no partner to share these things with.

"I just felt like I was out there alone," he says. "I felt a great deal of stress. I couldn't bring any of the problems home to talk to Rachel about. I didn't want to burden her because she was feeling so lousy." The experience made him wonder how any entrepreneur can go into business alone. "It's just a tremendous emotional burden to have all the problems resting on your shoulders."

Couples who decide that the wife will stay home when they have children sometimes find they have a new set of problems. One wife said, "I *died* when I wasn't in the business." Not only did much of her self-image and self-esteem rely on the business, but, in large part, so did her marriage. "Without the business, I barely had a relationship with my husband. That is where our major interests lie."

Mitchell and Linda Berliner are the founders of Berliner Foods, a Gaithersburg, Maryland, frozen food distributorship that grew out of a gourmet food booth at a farmer's market. They had been in business 11 years before they started a family. When Linda went home to be a full-time mother, she and Mitch (the son of Jerome and Pauline Berliner) both had some adjustments to make. She missed the business; he missed her *in* the business. Their relationship itself underwent some changes when they were no longer working side by side every day.

Linda continued to be a partner in the business, along with Mitch's brother, Guy. She still did some paperwork and consulting for the company and was a part of the major decisions. But she found that she missed the daily involvement. She had always known what was going on before. Now, when Mitch came home at night, he didn't want to go over what happened during the day.

He could understand her frustration. "For 11 or 12 years," he says, "she was there for every little bit of gossip and every minute detail of the business." But that understanding didn't make him want to rehash the day with her. He had already lived through it once; he didn't want to do it twice.

While Linda and Mitch still talked about the major business issues, such as new products, Linda found other ways to fill the information gap on items of less significance. She kept abreast by calling people at the office—her brother-in-law, Guy, was a particularly good source of news. She could even glean information by listening to Mitch's end of the conversation on business calls that came to their home.

For his part, Mitch missed the contribution Linda made to the business, saying it took two people to replace her. While they have a competent staff, he says, "She would still be a tremendous asset if she were at the office."

Linda says that as time went by, her frustration diminished.

Still, she reflects, "It's difficult to leave the business in the office. We lived the business, and that was our baby before we had children."

THE TUG-OF-WAR BETWEEN CHILDREN AND BUSINESS

Even though running one's own business offers parents much greater flexibility, making it possible for them to be at home if they are needed or providing more opportunity for youngsters to be present at their parents' place of work, many parents— particularly mothers—feel torn between their children and their businesses. Despite her success and fame, and despite the fact that she is a grandmother in her sixties, Olga Erteszek talks of the guilt she felt, and still feels, over helping to build a business instead of staying home with her three daughters.

She often wished she could devote more time to the family, she says. The Erteszeks reared their daughters during a period when working mothers were rare. "Other mothers are home when the children come from school," the girls chided Olga. "You're never here."

"I reproached myself many times," Olga says. She feared that she was not doing the job that was given to her as a parent to do.

Jan, too, recalled that their daughters "always seemed to feel that it would have been better if their mother was not a working woman." He tried to comfort Olga with reminders that he and she were both the products of working couples. Their daughters would learn independence, he assured her. He also told her how important she was to the business.

Nevertheless, the memories of some of the things her daughters said still hurt. "They made me feel very, very unhappy, but I think that they came out very wonderful," says Olga, who adds that she has a "loving family."

The perception of both the conflict and the loving family is apparently accurate, at least in the eyes of one of the Erteszek children. In a company biography, Christina Erteszek Johnson, now an Olga designer, is quoted as saying: "When I was a little girl, like most children, I wanted my mother to be exactly like those of my friends. I longed for what I considered the perfect 'peanut butter and jelly' mother who would always be at home to care for me and my two sisters every hour of the day. While I may have been resentful that my mother was different, I realize now that I am the beneficiary of my mother's self-confident, career-oriented life style. My sisters and I always had freedom of choice. We were taught to function within the context of a loving family environment with clear ethical and moral definitions. We were all encouraged to find our own realistic, creative and responsible place in the over-all scheme of things. We were always allowed to develop our own inner individuality, to understand and enhance our perception of ourselves in as great a depth as possible."

It is a new generation and today's children see working mothers everywhere. Nevertheless, many of today's women entrepreneurs experience the same tug-of-war between the needs of their children and the needs of their businesses. Debbi Fields is more than 35 years younger than Olga Erteszek. Like Olga, she has three daughters. She is a national symbol of contemporary entrepreneurship. Is it possible she could feel guilty?

"You bet," she says. "If I come home and one of my daughters has scraped her knee, I feel like I should have been there."

She believes she is a good mother and says she and Randy would like to have more children—but only if they can "feel that we are giving them the kind of attention that they need."

To offset the times she can't be there for scraped knees, Debbi and Randy deliberately make a lot of time for their children. They try to be home by 5:30 or 6 in the evening. They have dinner with the girls and put them to bed. They don't leave the house until 8 A.M. on workdays, so they have some time with the children before they go to the office. The only time they will work on the weekends is when the girls are taking their naps.

They avoid business dinners because they don't want to lose that time with the children. If they must have dinner over business, they prefer to invite people to their home for something as casual as hot dogs or hamburgers.

The girls frequently come to their parents' workplace. Randy says that "two or three times a week, they are in the office eating lunch with us or playing on the floor."

"When we travel, they travel with us," he says. "They have slept in the finest restaurants in the world."

Like Debbi and Randy Fields, many couples insist that the family comes before the business. Others admit the distinction is not so clear. Diane Saliba of Richardson Home Builders is the daughter of an entrepreneurial couple; now she and her husband work together in the business that her parents started. Asked about the difficulty of rearing children when you are in business with your spouse, she says: "I know this problem both as a child and as a parent and believe me, it is very painful to be in either position if great care isn't taken to put family first ahead of business. So many times as a child, I remember trying to interrupt heated discussions between my parents about building houses to get some much-needed love and attention. Now I find Steve and I doing the exact same thing with our kids. The tensions get higher and higher until one or more is crying. (Sometimes I'm one of them.) It does damage to a child's self-esteem to feel that his parents are too busy to listen to him."

Some fathers feel guilt, too. Says Wesley Kranitz of WCK Associates: "You just can't seem to find enough time to spend with your children. You live and breathe the business." The retired Jerome Berliner says that he and Pauline often felt guilty about discussing the day's business at the dinner table. "I think that if we had to do it all over again, we would have allocated specific time slots to the children to the exclusion of business matters—no matter the urgency.''

Tari Vickery of KVTV Carpets admits that her daughter, Heather, ''knows that she comes after the business in our list of priorities. The business consumes our lives.'' However, Vickery, one of our questionnaire respondents, asked Heather, then nine, what the pluses and minuses are of having a mother and father in business together. ''She said the advantage to having us work together is that we have more money than most of her friends. She said the disadvantage is how little attention she gets.''

Even though Vickery says business comes first, some of what she writes suggests the opposite. Heather was born the month after their business was incorporated, and, Vickery says, ''The first year, we worked out of our home, so we were both with her most of the time. When we moved to an office, it was just the two of us, so we took her with us. Consequently, she has really grown up with the business and has always been a part of it. When we built new offices two years ago, we included a kitchen, dining room, and personal bath, along with a special room just for her (she calls it her 'office'). We have all three slept on the floor several nights because we were working so late. Finally, we got a sofa bed. Therefore, I feel that she understands the work that goes into owning a business, and she feels included rather than excluded.''

Like young Heather, entrepreneurial parents do recognize that there are advantages, as well as disadvantages, for their children.

Susan Stangland of Pepperwood International says, ''The children don't always understand why Mom can't be home more or why Dad has to travel so much or why family time is usually spent working at the factory on weekends. On the plus side, we're all in this together and the boys, hopefully, are gaining a more graphic understanding of how life is an integrated experience and not a departmentalized one.''

Ronald Fleming of the Townscape Institute says that having children in a business family "creates more of the old-fashioned frontier ethic of a family working together." He and his wife, Renata von Tscharner, are deeply involved in environmental issues; having their business in their home and having business guests to dinner means that they can readily share with their children the values they hold about the environment and urban beautification.

THE OVERWHELMING BUSINESS

When a business becomes all-consuming, the children resent it, according to consultant Tom Hubler, because they feel cheated. His partner, Steve Swartz, says, "We've had children say to us that not only is the business like another child in the family, but it's the favored child. It's the one you have to be careful not to criticize, not to offend."

Hubler cites a case where a son felt so deprived of parental attention that when he took over the family business, he went to the opposite extreme, indulging his children so that they would not have to go through what he went through. His response created a completely different set of problems with his children, because he failed to teach them the responsibilities necessitated by the business.

In another business, built by a couple with five sons, the children were involved in the enterprise from a very early age. "Their whole life as young kids was working in the business," says Hubler. When they grew up, the parents—particularly the father—desperately wanted one of the sons to take over, but they were not interested. They had had enough. The business had been so much a part of their lives that one of the sons said, "I've never had the experience of going home from work." He also regretted that he had never had the opportunity to really know his father outside the context of the business.

Even the youngest of children can feel resentful. Recalling how difficult it was for her and her ex-husband to keep business issues out of their home life, Barbara Aiello of Kids on the Block, an Alexandria, Virginia, company that makes educational puppets, says, "And once business problems are home, they're at the dinner table. Once they're at the dinner table, they're on the couch. Before you know it, they're in bed with you, too."

One time, their three-year-old daughter, Rosanna, became so upset with her parents' business talk that she said, "Puppets! Puppets! Enough puppets!"

Several years later, after her parents had divorced, Rosanna was asked by a researcher if she wished her parents would get married again. "No," she answered, "because all my parents ever did was fight about puppets."

ALLOWING FOR DIFFERENCES

Because children have such different personalities, the same set of parents and the same business can have quite different effects on different siblings. One child may be drawn happily into the family business. One might not. One might be able to make peace with the parents over childhood resentments; another might hold a grudge for a lifetime. What is important for parents is to be sensitive to the needs of each child as an individual and not expect that each will respond in the same way to the same set of circumstances.

In her autobiography, Estée Lauder says son Leonard "always had business on his mind." When, toward the end of the Korean War, he had to choose between serving two years in the Army as a clerk-typist or three and a half in the Navy as a supply officer, she says, "For him, there was no choice. As a naval supply officer of the *USS Leyte* he handled more money and supplies in one month than our business, at the time, handled in a year." She felt he was preparing himself in a myriad of ways, consciously and unconsciously, to be the chief executive officer of Estée Lauder.

Leonard's younger brother, Ronald, was a different story. He stayed in the company for 17 years, and his mother credits him with making the Clinique line profitable. But he was not in love with the business the way Leonard was, and in 1983, much to his mother's disappointment, he left the company to become deputy assistant secretary of defense for European and NATO policy. "In my heart of hearts," wrote Estée, "I'd still prefer him to be in the family business. It would be dishonest of me to say otherwise."

Some children find that if they do join the family business, there can be unexpected rewards. For Doris Mattus Hurley, it strengthened the bond with her parents, Reuben and Rose Mattus, who founded the famous Häagen-Dazs Ice Cream company. After her children were old enough, Hurley went to work as a sales representative for another company. When she was offered a promotion a year later, her father made a more attractive bid, and she accepted. Not long after, she convinced him she should launch the Häagen-Dazs Ice Cream stores, a franchise operation.

"As a child," she told *Nation's Business*, "you don't necessarily understand what is going on when you have parents who are completely dedicated to their business." Because she had an opportunity to become part of the business, she said, resentments she felt as a girl were dispelled, and she came to a greater understanding of the sacrifices her parents made in building the company. She admitted it can be emotionally difficult for family members to work together. But, she said, "our extraordinary feelings about the business and the product" overrode any other considerations. (Hurley has since left the company, now owned by Pillsbury.)

Even in families where the parents have a profound dedication to business, children can grow into adulthood without residual ill feeling. Despite the fact that business was always being conducted and discussed around the house, George Makrauer of Amko Plastics in Cincinnati says he never felt any resentment about it. "It was just the way we grew up."

His parents, Janet and Irvin Makrauer, shared their love of business with George and his sister, Zola Berning, involving them in it early. Before Amko was founded, they worked in their parents' first business in the summer and earned their way through college. But they weren't pressured. George was encouraged to test a music career if he so desired, and he tried law school for one year before he settled on working with his parents. Zola worked as a bank systems analyst before she joined Amko.

Janet Makrauer says that as much as she and Irvin loved the business, the children came first. She and her late husband apparently had extraordinary communication skills that enabled them to create both a successful business and a close family. As George recalls it (and his mother does not disagree), his parents never argued with each other. They had disagreements and discussions, sometimes heated ones, that others, such as employees, might view as quarrels.

"Once they've been there long enough, they realize that we're not quarreling, we're each fighting for our idea and for our approach to solving a problem," says Janet.

It was the same at home. It may be that the older Makrauers had learned the fine art of disagreeing without wounding each other. George said that when he was a child visiting the homes of friends, it would seem strange to him to hear one parent raise a voice against the other. He became aware of the strife that can go on in families through his friends or through television and films, but it was not something he ever saw at home. What he appears to remember most about childhood has been the love of business and the love of family.

What it comes down to, ultimately, say Hubler and Swartz, is a matter of balance. There are times when the children must come first. But there are times when the business must come first.

"The business *does* need attention," says Swartz. "During the entrepreneurial phase, it would be a serious disservice to the business to be imbalanced and focus entirely on the family." The business, he points out, "is not a hobby. It is supporting the family."

"The problem with entrepreneurial couples, as I see it," says Hubler, "is they get so engrossed in what they're doing on the business side that they have a tendency to overlook other aspects of their life."

10

COPING WITH FAILURE

"I Had to Lay Off My Husband"

In her autobiography, *Estée: A Success Story,* Estée Lauder re-
counts the period beginning in the late 1930s when she and
husband Joseph not only separated but were divorced. Despite
Joe's brilliance with numbers and organization, his own business
ventures were not doing well in a country beset by depression,
while Estée says she "was moving steadily forward" in her chosen
world of skin care. Joe was ambitious, but she was more ambitious. He liked a quiet life; she wanted activity. "I did not know
how to be Mrs. Joseph Lauder and Estée Lauder at the same
time." Tensions mounted.

"We were, in short, having problems that both of us were
too immature to deal with," writes Estée. "Feminism was almost
unheard of then. There were no guidelines to help a strong
woman live happily with a much loved but gentler man."

As such stories go, theirs had a happier ending than most.
After four years of divorce, Joe and Estée remarried in 1943,
"this time forever—but with a few changes. First of all, my primary identity would be Mrs. Joseph Lauder, not Estée Lauder.
Second of all, we decided that Joseph would give up his business
and come into mine, where we would be equal partners in every
sense of the word." And together, they went on to create the
Estée Lauder cosmetic and skin care products empire.

Entrepreneurs know they face the risk of failure in their businesses. It comes with the territory, and they accept it. Some
are simply so optimistic that they think they will beat the odds;
others are confident they can pick themselves up again, and
still others believe that failure can't hurt them too much. When
Courtney Garton and Margie Bryce borrowed $7,000 to start
Hats in the Belfry, Courtney says, they decided "the worst that
can happen is that we will lose every bit of it. But then we
will just go back to teaching." Since neither had ever had much
money, they didn't feel pressured about losing it.

Entrepreneurs also face the risk of failure in their marriages.
In *The Entrepreneurial Life,* venture capitalist A. David Silver
observes that the entrepreneur who invites a meaningful contri-

bution from the mate is rewarded with a "tenacious, enthusiastic cheerleader." More often, however, the opposite happens. "The spouse is frozen out of the entrepreneur's thoughts, actions, and conversation. He does not seek her advice, does not welcome it when it is given, and, in a moment of business stress, launches a verbal tirade of invectives at her for 'butting in.'" In time, he says, the marriage crashes. But the end of the marriage only strengthens the entrepreneurial drive. The divorced entrepreneur wants to show the ex-wife that he can make it without her. "Venture capitalists are high on divorced entrepreneurs," Silver confesses.

To my knowledge, no studies have been done to show whether the divorce rate among entrepreneurs or entrepreneurial couples is higher than among the rest of the population. And as we have seen, many couples say that being in business together strengthens their marriage and enhances their intimacy.

Nevertheless, like all entrepreneurs, entrepreneurial couples may fail in their ventures. Like other couples, they may fail in their marriages. Sometimes, they may lose both. Throughout the 1970s, a young couple in Detroit built their photography studio to a point where it was quite well known and was garnering a number of corporate jobs, including work from the auto industry. When economic disaster hit Detroit, however, it hit the couple's business, too. Neither the business nor the relationship could withstand the stress, and by 1981, both had been dissolved.

LOSING THE RELATIONSHIP

Adversity in business will certainly test a couple's personal relationship. However, sometimes problems that exist in the relationship itself threaten the business and, in the extreme, lead to its downfall. Sometimes, a business is saved and the marriage isn't. A business known as Fitness for All (not its real name) in a midwestern city was on the brink of failure in the early

1980s. The only way its founder and president, a woman we'll call Mary Ferguson, felt she could turn it around was by terminating her husband's position as vice president and business manager and bringing in a new business partner.

Fitness for All is a health and exercise center aimed at men and women who, for one reason or another, might shy away from other fitness spas. A hospital dietitian who once had aspirations as a dancer and who even performed in some little theater musicals when she was in her early 20s, Mary had the second of her two children when she was 35. To get back into shape, she began going to a neighborhood health club and found herself somewhat self-conscious and uncomfortable. The men and women around her all seemed to have such spectacular bodies that, she says, "It looked like you had to be in training at least a year before you even joined." What's more, most of the members were her age or younger. Rarely did she see any middle-aged people, or people with real "body image" problems, that is, people who were truly overweight. She began to think there might be a market for a health and fitness program for people who did not want to exercise side-by-side with the svelte and the beautiful, and she was right. Mary drew on her dietetics experience and her dance background to offer nutrition counseling and lead exercise classes designed for middle-aged or older people, with special sections for people with particular problems, such as obesity. At first, Mary used the facilities of a local school, but Fitness for All began to draw such a steady stream of clients that she rented space in a shopping center.

Mary's husband, Mike, a magazine artist whose career seemed to be faltering, became the company's business manager when it was started in the late 1970s, "primarily," Mary admits, "because I didn't want to do it." Actually, both of them were creative people, and neither had business skills. They were not a complementary team. As time went by, Mike's lack of business background and mistakes Mary felt he made began to be more and more of a sore point with her, and their differences in values and in goals for the business drove them further apart. Mary and some of her clients had appeared on television a few times and Mike began to dream of opportunities to do television in a big way. He also wanted to expand the company's activities to products, such as T-shirts, exercise clothing, and even souvenirs. Mary let him convince her that they should produce and market, on their own, a series of exercise audiotapes, and they began to produce a newsletter and to sell such items as exercise bags bearing the Fitness for All logo.

Unilaterally, however, Mary turned down an offer of an outside company that wanted her to do an exercise videotape for the over-50 market. As Mary describes it, Mike became "absolutely livid." Mary thought that more television and the opportunity to do videotapes would be desirable in the future, but for now, she told Mike, concentrating on marketing and on refining their existing program was essential. She felt that she had only begun to scratch the surface of developing sound diet and exercise regimens for the company's particular market and that they needed more time to perfect their programs. The more involved she became in the business, the more committed she found herself to making a real difference in the lives of her clients. She worried that if she and Mike moved too fast, they would sacrifice the quality of their services. Mike argued that they could do a better job of marketing if they used television and other media; he also envisioned franchising the concept.

Because Mary had initiated the business and was its chief spokesperson, Mike came to be seen as the backup person. He did not seem to mind this role, Mary recalls, but his parents gave him a hard time about it. Another problem was their inability to keep business out of their private life. "We didn't realize that we had to set a limit—a rule which said, 'We will not talk about Fitness for Life after 7 o'clock,'" says Mary.

Meanwhile, financial problems the company was experiencing grew worse. Fitness for Life had expanded to a second location, and the additional rent and staff caused a strain; in addition, the audiotapes and exercise bags were not selling well. "Finally," Mary says, "I was faced with the *implausible* decision of having to lay off my husband. It was during the end of the last recession. We were having tremendous cash flow problems and we were eliminating positions in the company, and I had to ask myself, 'If this position were staffed by anyone other than my own husband, would it continue?' And my answer was no."

She asked Mike to get a job so that they and their children would have some stability if the company failed. He refused, choosing instead to collect unemployment and come into the office and work without pay. She saw him as not wanting to support the family; he saw it as sacrificing himself for the company. Counseling did not help them resolve their problems, and they finally divorced.

Mary credits her new partner, a retired accountant, with rescuing the company. Fitness for All had grown to $650,000 in annual revenues and 20 employees by 1985, the same year Mary married again—this time to a man who is *not* in business with her.

As she looks back on the experience, she remarks on the lack of adequate professional "therapeutic" help for couples in business, and the lack of knowledge she and her ex-husband had about what being in business together would do to their relationship. She believes now, however, that the marriage was so full of problems that it would probably have failed anyhow. And despite the difficulties she had in getting Fitness for All launched, in true entrepreneurial style she is so enthusiastic about her business that she says, with a laugh, "I'd go through it all again."

Karen and Doug Greene, an idealistic young couple, had been married just about two years when, in 1978, they started a trade magazine called *Natural Foods Merchandiser,* aimed at coalescing the new industry based on more healthful eating. Eventually, they moved their business from California to New Hope, Pennsylvania, and renamed it New Hope Communications. It grew into conferences and into more publications, including *Delicious!,* a consumer food magazine, and *Expansion,* an economic development magazine that debuted in April 1986. In 1982, the Greenes somehow found time to have a son. New Hope Communications is now a $4.5-million-a-year company with 60 employees. Karen and Doug own the company equally. However, since 1983, they have been separated, and they are still trying to determine the next step in their personal relationship.

Karen, a very private person, graciously declined to be interviewed for this book. However, Doug, a charismatic, ebullient entrepreneur who has been praised by John Naisbitt and others for his forward management (employees, for example, are instructed not to do business with customers who are rude) talked openly about his relationship with Karen. "I've always said that she was the brains and I was the mouth," he says, adding that she has always been very introspective while he has liked being out in the public, talking. "A lot of times, the things that I'd be saying in the marketplace were her thoughts. And I was always hailed for being one of the spokespeople for the natural foods industry." Early on, Karen asked not to be included in the publicity. "She wanted to keep her life just like it was."

When Doug speaks of Karen, he speaks with great caring and respect and friendship. Because of her, he says, the business achieved in three years what might have taken seven if he had had to start it without her. However, they reached a point where he says their intuition told them both they needed to separate, physically, if not legally.

"As the business grew and grew and as all our responsibilities grew and grew," Doug says, "we just found ourselves not communicating in areas where we should have communicated." They did not recheck their assumptions about each other. For example, because of Karen's earlier request to be kept out of the limelight, he says, "it became Doug Greene's magazine, Doug Greene's show." People change, however, and while Doug was "still running" with the assumption that Karen did not want recognition, now he thinks that she did. It was a mistake on his part, he says. "I should have more aggressively included her in the recognition that we were getting."

They also failed to nurture their personal life as much as they needed to, Doug reflects. "We almost worked seven days a week for the first year nonstop." In retrospect, he says they could have—and should have—taken more time off together. But they had never talked ahead of time about how being in business might affect their marriage—partly because they hadn't really intended to go into business together. Doug, who had initiated the venture, needed an editor, and Karen came in "to help out for the first couple of weeks." She fell in love with the business and stayed.

Even after she and Doug separated, Karen continued to work in the company for two more years. Now she works at home, conducting the company's research and development activities.

Doug was with Karen in the delivery room when their son was born. "I thought, 'My god, I've never seen anything so close to starting a business in my life!' " he says. "You have those periods of contractions when you can't imagine that you can go on. And then you have some breathing room, then the contractions come back again. Those same cycles of birth are what you go through in starting a business."

A nurse once told Doug that, during labor, some couples fight and argue because they are so touchy and on edge.

"Through our labor, Karen and I, I don't think, have ever been closer," says Doug. "It was a magical experience, the most magical in my life."

They weathered childbirth together and now, in their own fashion, the Greenes are trying to see how their relationship can weather their business.

Asked what he would suggest to couples who are thinking of going into business together, Doug says that before they do it, they should spend a long weekend alone together to look at how sound their personal relationship is. "If it's a good, solid relationship, I would tell them to hasten with caution." Once the business is started, they should continue the dialogue, discussing how it is affecting their marriage. He also tells others to do what he feels he and Karen failed to do often enough: "Create time to go away and just snuggle each other and just connect as human beings. You get a great return on that investment."

THE CONSEQUENCES FOR BUSINESS

It's not all that unusual for a separated or divorced couple to continue to work together in the business. But Laventhol & Horwath's Ric Zigmond doesn't recommend it. He has seen businesses suffer under such circumstances because the man and woman try to get employees to take sides, which results in turnover. Furthermore, they don't communicate with each other or set a real direction for the company, "so business is sort of going sideways and dropping off."

But working together doesn't seem to have harmed the Greenes' business—it doubled in sales between 1984 and 1986. Another couple who continue to run their company together despite a divorce are doing it on a much larger scale. They are June M. Collier, president and chief executive officer, and Ben Collier, chairman of the board, of National Industries, Inc., a $130 million diversified manufacturing company in Montgomery, Alabama. With more than 2,500 employees, it is central Alabama's largest private employer.

Why did the Colliers, who were divorced in July 1985, choose to stay in the company together?

"I think it's one of those cases where they did it because there was no option," says company spokesman Jay Lewis. "People like you and me and folks who are less than captains of industry can afford to consider what *we* want to do and what *we* want to say and how *we* want to live. But when you get to the point where 2,500 people are dependent on you and you really hold their fate in your hand, then you're conscientious about that . . . as both the Colliers were."

When a couple splits up, employees and other stakeholders have to be informed. Mary Ferguson says that while she did not discuss details with employees, she did keep them apprised of such facts as when she moved out of the home she had shared with her husband and when the divorce was filed. Employees, in turn, were able to provide customers and others with some reassurances about the business. Jay Lewis recalls that when it became public knowledge that the Colliers were getting divorced, June Collier had to take time to calm employees' fears about job security.

When the Greenes separated, Karen went to Florida to visit friends and Doug went to a prescheduled company retreat. There, he told employees of the separation and says the result was "shock waves. People were speechless. And people got nervous. People got scared." He thinks they weren't afraid for their jobs, because they knew the company was growing rapidly and in a good cash position. He believes they feared change. "I think that, fundamentally, we're all scared of change," he says. Despite his own pain over the separation, Doug found himself in the position of having to comfort and help his employees.

Barbara Aiello, founder of Kids on the Block, discovered that, after her divorce, she had to rebuild relationships with a number of customers and other stakeholders. Her husband, for example, had started negotiating a contract to do a puppet tour for Encyclopaedia Britannica. After the divorce, Aiello, a former special education teacher, had to approach Encyclopaedia Britannica all over again, and she eventually came out with a contract to represent the company in educational programs in 40 shopping centers over an 18-month period. Rebuilding relationships as a woman, she says, was harder than it would have been if she were a man because she was viewed as the puppeteer, the teacher, the creative one, and the performer, while her husband was seen as "the mainstay of the company."

DIVIDING THE SPOILS

Looking back on her experience, Mary Ferguson wishes that some provisions had been made for dissolving their business relationship when she and her ex-husband had corporate papers drawn up. But when the partners are married to each other, she says, no one, not even lawyers, brings up such questions. Such provisions should be included as though the partners were not married to each other, she contends, "otherwise, there's no way to extricate yourself." She found that the lack of clarity about the business made the divorce proceedings more difficult. Reaching a settlement was complicated further by the fact that she and her ex-husband held their stock jointly, "another major mistake." You should own your stock separately, again just as you would if you were not married, she says. Over time, she had to pay her ex-husband $17,000 to buy him out.

Marta Vago and her partner did have a buy-out provision built into the business agreement for their psychotherapy training center, but it didn't help. When they separated, neither partner had enough money to buy out the other's share, so the business folded. Furthermore, Vago says, the agreement didn't cover enough bases. Who, for example, would get custody of the corporate name?

"We had a name that was worth gold," she says. "We were highly respected. We were known by the media. We were known all over the country by other professionals and professional organizations." If one of them had kept the name, that partner "would have benefited unfairly at the other's expense by the goodwill of the public visibility that we had built," says Vago. As it was, no one benefited. Their employees lost their jobs, the company name was gone, and Vago and her partner had to start all over again, separately.

Most couples, it seems, resist drawing up any agreement for their partnership, let alone making an arrangement for its dissolution. They seem to fear that asking for such an agreement is tantamount to expressing lack of trust in the spouse, or they are confident that their relationship will never end.

Even lawyers are resistant. "I suppose this sounds naive," says Sheri Criswell, "but I can't imagine sitting down and writing out a partnership agreement between the two of us, and I suppose that's the proper thing to do. But we've been married too long and known each other too well to start worrying about doing a partnership agreement."

TURNING LEMONS INTO LEMONADE

Not infrequently, a couple in business has to deal with the near loss or actual failure of the business itself or an important business venture. It is devastating. But not for long. Entrepreneurial couples move on quickly, using what they have learned from such experiences to build a stronger future for themselves and their businesses.

One of Penthouse International's ventures, *Viva*, a magazine for women, was just under five years old the day it folded.

"It was the worst day of my life. I'll never forget it," says Kathy Keeton, who, as editor, had the agonizing task of telling *Viva*'s staff that their magazine was shutting down. But Keeton says she's an optimist and not one to spend much time crying over setbacks. "I tend to say, 'Okay, that's a mistake,' and look forward to tomorrow."

Besides, she and partner Bob Guccione turned the *Viva* experience to their advantage when they started their highly successful science magazine. "The lessons that we learned on *Viva* were applied to *Omni*, and *Omni* was a textbook launch," says Keeton. "It was perfect in every way."

Their company is thriving now, but Decorating Den's Steve and Valerie Bursten remember all too well the spring of 1983 when, as a result of two years of recession, their 13-year-old enterprise nearly went under. Combined retail sales and sales of Decorating Den franchises had dropped from over $10 million annually to $8.4 million, with only a small profit, in 1982. In April 1983, the Burstens received an internal operating financial statement that told them the hard truth: Their personal holdings in the company were completely wiped out.

Within two weeks, they had to go into the annual meeting of their franchisees, put on a happy face, and, says Steve, "tell everyone how wonderful everything was." Somehow, they did it.

The Burstens decided they had two choices: to accept defeat or to fight back. They chose to fight. "The one thing I don't like is being poor," says Valerie.

They cut back employees to the point where Valerie and Steve were the only ones selling franchises. They cut travel and overhead expenses. They didn't have the money to hire a much-needed manager for their southeastern region, so Valerie took the job on herself. "I had to sell franchises over the phone, and that's when I started getting really good," she says.

By the end of the year, they had restored their losses, boosted sales to $9.2 million, and even increased corporate net worth by $15,000 to $170,000.

One evening in 1984, Valerie returned a call to Jim Bugg, of Chevy Case, Maryland, who had phoned earlier that day after reading about Decorating Den in a *Woman's Day* article. It turned out to be the magic phone call.

Bugg had been one of the powerhouses who transformed Century 21 into a large national real estate franchise system. He and his wife, Carol, an interior designer, had thought of starting their own decorating franchise. But after making inquiries about Decorating Den and talking with the Burstens, Bugg was convinced he could come out of retirement and do for them what he had done for Century 21. The Burstens were convinced, too. The following November, they took Bugg on as partner and named him president. (Carol Bugg has become Decorating Den's regional director in the Washington area.)

"Val and I were on a good comeback trail, but Jim has made the company a breakthrough, runaway success," says Steve, who continues as chairman. Using marketing strategies borrowed from Century 21, Bugg organized a regional system of selling franchises. The number of franchises doubled to more than 300 in 1985 and was expected to double again in 1986. Sales, projected at $12 million in 1985, jumped to $13.1 million, and the company's net worth climbed to nearly $500,000.

The Burstens reflect on the tough days when they had to sell at least one or two franchises a month just to keep Decorating Den from going out of business. They agree that that was when Valerie really learned the art of selling, inspiring people to spend their own money to fly to Indianapolis and talk with them about making a $20,000 investment in a business.

"Then," says Steve, "she made the biggest sale of all, because she invited a person who became the president of our company."

Avis Renshaw and Steven Cox of Herndon, Virginia, were not so fortunate. They lost their first business. They owned two once-successful produce markets stocked with fresh foods from a farm they rented. But several seasons of drought and a promised government loan that fell through did the business in, forcing the couple to close its doors in June 1981 and file a $750,000 bankruptcy. They had one child and another on the way.

Their mental state, recalls Renshaw, was one of shock and anger.

"For people who are used to working a whole lot, it was real strange not to be working," she says. "It was very depressing."

In true entrepreneurial style, however, they were soon back in business, baking 300 pies a week at home for area farm markets. Now, under the name of Mom's Apple Pie Company, they are turning out an average of 5,000 pies weekly (and aiming for 50,000) in an industrial park facility, with the aid of 15 employees. They have won additional clients, such as area restaurants, Safeway stores, and Bloomingdale's, and annual sales are nearly $750,000. And they have added a third child to their family.

However, having declared bankruptcy with the first business

has made it harder on the second one. To this day, it hampers the couple's credit, interfering, for example, with their ability to purchase equipment that would make their operation more efficient. Renshaw tells other couples facing a business failure to avoid bankruptcy if they possibly can, and to have faith. And if they're entrepreneurs, she adds, they'll probably have faith anyway.

Despite their loss, Cox and Renshaw never gave much thought to working for anybody else. Says Renshaw: "I think there was an innate feeling that we would start another business."

It's in the nature of entrepreneurs to turn negatives into positives and not to be undone by failure. The Burstens say that if Decorating Den had gone under, they—like Cox and Renshaw—would have started another business.

Doug Greene even looks for the positives in the unsettling experience of being separated from his wife. Because he and Karen have sought to handle the difficult period in a caring and loving way, trying to be generous with each other and to keep their friendship and respect for each other intact, Doug can say, as he said in the fall of 1985, "The thing I'm most proud of in my whole life is how we've gone through these last two years of being separated." Because failure is evidence that one has taken a risk and tried something new, the corporate culture at New Hope Communications calls for celebrating failure in business. Perhaps, in a similar respect, Doug suggests, failure in relationships ought also to be celebrated.

What sees many couples through the devastation of a business setback is their commitment to their relationship. Often their dedication to each other is played out as a dedication to the business itself, giving them the strength, as with the Burstens, to turn a situation around, or, as with Cox and Renshaw, the resilience to bounce back and start anew.

Tony and Susan Harnett of Bread & Circus are confident their marriage would only get stronger if their business failed. "Hard times always make you come to grips with who you are, and going through hard times together, for the right people, will always bring you closer," says Tony.

"Business is just one of the things that people do in life," he continues. It doesn't make sense to him to let your happiness depend on the business. And if the business fails, it doesn't mean that *you* fail. "You have gone through a valley. Just find another peak."

For the Harnetts, their marriage is their first priority. As Susan puts it, "There are plenty of businesses we could do, but I would have a hard time finding another Tony."

11
WHEN TROUBLE COMES

"He Looked Terrible and
Acted Worse"

Before Kids on the Block started manufacturing its own puppets, one supplier, angry because Barbara Aiello and her then-husband would not take him on as a partner, held more than 200 puppets hostage in a locked warehouse, delaying deliveries to some of Aiello's customers as much as a year. Aiello felt that not only was the business at stake, so was her reputation. Most of the orders for the puppets were prepaid; she had taken people's money and now she couldn't deliver.

If they lost the business over this incident, Aiello thought her husband, a musician, could go to New York and rebuild his musical career. But what would she do? As a result of Kids on the Block, Aiello had become well-known nationally in the special education field; she felt that failure to deliver the puppets would tarnish her name so much that she would never be able to return to teaching. Only a good lawyer and paying what Aiello calls "an exorbitant price" for the puppets enabled her to free her inventory.

Howard and Jeanette Shapiro of Howard-Shadim Electronics were once almost ready to give up because bad advice from a technical consultant had caused them to botch up work for one of their first major customers. It would cost them $25,000 to redo the work, and to make matters worse, they didn't know how to overcome the technical problems. It was so early in the life of their business that both were still working at other careers. And they had just sold their "dream home" and put the equity into their company. They were beginning to think maybe they should forget the business when a friend of the consultant offered to buy it. But, he said, he could not pay much because "it's not much of a company." That made the Shapiros furious. "Before we would sell the company to you," Howard told the would-be buyer, "I would smash the equipment and take our losses." Their anger became the catalyst that gave the Shapiros the energy they needed—and the will—to solve their problems and get their company going again, dropping the consultant and hiring more competent people.

As chilling as some business tales are, they pale in comparison with the personal crises some entrepreneurial couples have had to face. Couple-owned businesses are vulnerable to personal traumas in ways that other businesses are not. When there is trouble for one in such a partnership, the other bears not only a greater personal burden but added business responsibility as well. Or when one of the couple's children suffers a crisis, the impact will be felt in the business. Personal problems call for an extra reserve of strength and courage on the part of entrepreneurial couples, who must not only help the family keep its equilibrium but maintain that of the business as well.

SERIOUS ILLNESS

Jerry and Robert House were just beginning to expand their tiny Watonga, Oklahoma, restaurant into the catering business in the mid-1970s when they learned Jerry had throat cancer. He was given a 20 percent chance of survival.

For the next several months, five days a week Jerry and Roberta got up at 5 A.M. and drove the 75 miles from Watonga to Oklahoma City, where Jerry received cobalt treatments. They returned to Watonga in time to work the lunch shift.

Jerry's weight dropped from 189 to 129, and his neck turned black from the treatments. He kept working, but business at the drive-in fell off considerably.

"Cancer is like leprosy," says Jerry. "People don't eat with you when you have cancer." It was too depressing for the customers, Roberta explains. "He just looked terrible, and acted worse."

As Roberta recalls that period in her life, she says, "It was the roughest, most devastating experience that I've ever gone through. It was something that I was almost not able to handle emotionally." She had been told more about Jerry's illness than he had, and she found herself nearly overwhelmed by compassion and sympathy for him.

As a means of fighting back, Jerry underwent a personality change. He became verbally mean, Roberta recalls. "His attitude was cruel."

"All I needed was a whip," Jerry interjects.

Jerry's attitude was hard on both his employees and his family, but, says Roberta, "we all felt like that was his way of getting through it."

They were on financial tenterhooks, too. Not only did they lose business at the drive-in, but, before they knew Jerry was ill, they had sold another small business of theirs, a ski lodge in New Mexico, and plunged the proceeds into a building for the catering venture. Now they found themselves faced with medical expenses.

By the time they knew Jerry would recover, they had gone through all their savings. They had been financially secure with the drive-in before. Now it was almost like starting over.

CHILDREN IN CRISIS

In 1980, shortly after Dianne and Rocco Altobelli opened their fifth hair salon, their youngest son, Nino, then 12, lost an eye in a yard dart game accident. Dianne, who can be calm in the middle of the storm, saw both the family and the business through. (She breaks up *after* the crisis, when he gets stronger, says Rocco. That's one of the ways they complement each other.)

It was Dianne who told Nino that his eye would have to be removed. Rocco was so torn up he couldn't bring himself to go to the hospital that day. "I felt that it would be worse for Nino to see me than Dianne going in there and coolly talking to him about it," says Rocco. "It would probably give him a lot more confidence than to see me broken up." Dianne and the doctor talked with Nino about the reasons his eye needed to be removed and, she says, "he realized that this was something that had to be done so that he could progress with his life."

It was Dianne, also, who ran the business from Nino's hospital room for the next two weeks and then went back to the office. Rocco took three months off, not only to be with Nino but also because he just could not face going into the salons.

Dianne refers to Nino as an "Unsinkable Molly Brown" who has never let the loss of his eye keep him from doing the things he loves to do, from playing football and soccer to motorcycle riding and downhill skiing. But the experience had a profound effect on Rocco. He made a conscious decision to spend more time with his children. "I repositioned my values a lot," he says. Or as Dianne interprets it, business "is not number one" in Rocco's life anymore.

"I found out that I would have given it all up just like that to have him have that eye," Rocco agrees. He still is very involved in his work and still tries to do "the best job humanly possible." But, he admits, business is just not that important now. It's not the big driving force it once was for him.

It was early Sunday morning on October 23, 1983, and Ted R. Ehrenfried was driving from his home in Newport News, Virginia, to a karate tournament in Lancaster, Pennsylvania. It was a business trip. Two years before, he had lost his job as the marketing head of the U.S. operations of a West German construction equipment firm and, at the urging of Scott, the oldest of his three sons, he started a business manufacturing leg-muscle stretching machines that could be used by karate enthusiasts and other athletes. To finance the business, Ted and his wife, Doris, had raised nearly $100,000 by selling their house, two boats, and a car and renting an apartment to live in. Now they were seriously considering having Doris join the firm, Treco Products.

As Ted crossed the Bay Bridge Tunnel that spans the Chesapeake Bay, he heard the news on his car radio: the U.S. Marine barracks in Beirut had been blown up in a truck suicide bombing.

Brook, the Ehrenfrieds' second son, was in those barracks. Ted turned around and drove home.

Doris was visiting friends in Massachusetts and couldn't be located. She was not to learn of the bombing until that evening, when she and her friends heard the news on the television at the restaurant where they were having dinner.

Ted stayed with his youngest son, Barry, and Barry's wife. When he and Doris finally reached each other by phone in the evening, he asked her to come home. But she couldn't bring herself to return just then. "I knew that if *anybody* would survive, Brook would survive," she says. "Coming home only meant admission of death. So I just could not leave."

As he tried to sleep on the couch in Barry's apartment, Ted would wake up every time he heard a vehicle, even if it was a block away. He had let the Marines know where he was staying, and he knew their policy was to notify the next of kin, in person, of the death of a Marine. Each time he heard a car, he was sure the Marines were coming to tell him. For the same reason, says Doris, she stayed away from the windows of the home where she was staying in Massachusetts. She did not want to see the Marines drive up.

Instead, they walked into Ted's office the next morning, Monday. Their formality and choice of words were confusing. "Are you Ted Ehrenfried, the father of Lance Corporal Brook Ehrenfried?" one asked. When Ted said yes, the Marine said, "We are here to report on the status of your son, because he was in the Beirut barracks, and unfortunately we have to inform you that he was a casualty." In his distress, Ted could not remember what "casualty" meant. "Does that mean he's dead or alive?" he asked. Brook was alive, but in very critical condition.

For Ted and Doris, that was enough. They knew Brook was a fighter. They were sure that if he had come this far, he would make it the rest of the way. The next time they saw him was at the memorial services at Camp LeJeune for the 241 who died in the bombing.

From a business standpoint, the experience could not have come at a worse time. A $130,000 Small Business Administration-guaranteed loan, applied for nearly a year before, had virtually been spent before it was finally received. And drive mechanisms in more than 300 of the $295 "Powerstretch" devices that Treco had sold had failed. To protect the company's credibility, Ted had to hire extra people and pay overtime rates to recall and repair the defective machines.

Business problems, however, did not compare with what Brook had been through. After the blast, he had been given a 25 percent chance of survival. But about six weeks later, he was at Treco, answering the phone and doing other jobs that could be done despite a badly injured right hand and damage to thigh muscles.

The Ehrenfrieds are not sure what got them through those difficult days, but Doris agrees that it was therapeutic for the whole family when Brook came into the business to work for a while.

"We fudged through it," Ted says. Then he adds that they forgot themselves pretty quickly because they knew 241 other sons had not made it out alive. Having come so close to Brook's death, they understood how the other parents felt. And they knew how fortunate they were.

PRIVATE BETRAYAL

Infidelity on the part of one of the husbands in our interview group was a crisis that one of the couples had to work through. "I strayed," is how the husband put it. It happened during a period when the wife had pulled out of the company to look after the children. The business was going well. Her husband was getting a lot of attention; he traveled a lot, went to the right parties, and began to think he was hot stuff.

For a year after the affair came out in the open, the couple says they must have talked "nonstop." It was more than a year before the wife, who was very embarrassed by the feeling that everyone in town knew about it, could bring herself to talk about it with her parents or friends. Some of them asked her why she didn't get a divorce, but she says the thought never occurred to her. Once, however, when he had taken the children to the movies, she took all the husband's clothes that she felt represented the relationship with the other woman and burned them. The rest of the family came home earlier than she expected and caught her at it, but the children were too young to question their mother's strange behavior.

The wife says she came to realize that she had become very dependent on her husband. When he "betrayed" her, she decided she would have to become more independent again. "If you're ever able to make a positive situation out of a negative one, this was it, because it was a real turnaround for me," she says.

Years later, the children asked about the time Mom burned Dad's clothes, and the couple says they were very open in discussing what had happened in that difficult period in their marriage. They wanted their children to know that marriage is a relationship that needs to be worked at.

THE PUBLIC RECORD

Sometimes a crisis can become a very public matter, as in the case of the well-known Philadelphia fashion firm, Albert Nipon Inc., founded more than 20 years ago by Albert and Pearl Nipon. By 1984, according to a November 16, 1984, *Wall Street Journal* report, it was a $60 million company. The Nipons had been guests at the White House and their designs had been worn by Rosalynn Carter, Nancy Reagan, and Barbara Walters.

Three months later, however, Albert pleaded guilty to federal charges of tax evasion and conspiracy to defraud the United States. His $200,000 bribery of two Internal Revenue Service agents was said to be the largest single payoff ever uncovered in investigations of corruption inside the IRS, and it was estimated that he had cheated the government out of more than $800,000 in personal and corporate income tax. In May 1985, he was sentenced to three years in prison.

What might have been a quieter matter in a less well-known family became an important news story in Philadelphia and in the fashion press, and even made *Time* magazine. And by the end of 1985, the *Philadelphia Inquirer* was reporting hard times for the company, citing layoffs and poor sales.

Pearl Nipon understandably did not wish to discuss the matter for this book. The wounds were too fresh. "Albert and I have had a difficult experience this year," she said in October of 1985. She wanted to put it behind her.

As difficult as a crisis may be, the couples or individuals within the relationships or the companies themselves often display a remarkable resilience. They bounce back, often stronger than before. We had heard rumors that Pearl Nipon had gone into seclusion, but when we found her by telephone, she sounded feisty and sure and was back in the thick of business, ready to go to France on a fashion trip.

By 1985, Rocco and Dianne Altobelli had added a sixth salon to their chain and were planning additional sites; they had also been named Small Business Persons of the Year for their state by the Small Business Administration.

Jerry and Roberta House also won the same award for the state of Oklahoma. Not only had they gone ahead and built the catering service they had so hopefully started the decade before, but Jerry had been cancer-free for ten years.

The Ehrenfrieds' company was back from the brink of disaster, too. Despite the troubles of 1983, Treco Products had experienced good growth that year, its second in business, doing $170,000 in sales compared with $15,000 the year before. By early 1986, Ted Ehrenfried said he was expecting $6 million in annual sales. Brook had never regained full use of his right hand, but for muscle therapy for his legs, he worked with a

Treco Powerstretch. "Today," his dad says, "he doesn't even walk with a limp." Retired from the Marines on disability, Brook enrolled in college and began work on an accounting degree.

The couple who had to deal with infidelity have been married more than 25 years now, and have been working together again in their business for many years. "I love this lady," the husband says in a way that makes you know he means it. The admiration the wife expresses for her husband makes it clear she returns his feelings.

"We've put so many patches on our relationship that you can't even see the original fabric anymore," says the husband. "It's all patches. But they hold. They're a lot stronger than the original pieces of material. A patch on a patch makes a lot of strength."

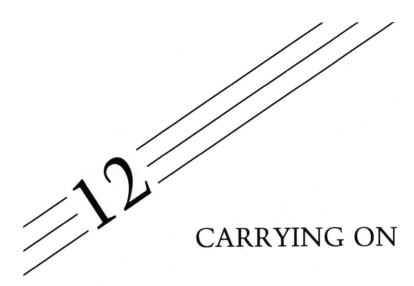

CARRYING ON

You Don't Live Forever

There comes a time in every entrepreneurial couple's life together when decisions must be made about the continuity of their business. They must consider not only their personal and family needs and goals but also the needs and health of the business, which may now be the source of livelihood for many employees and their families. Not infrequently, they discover that the skills that made them entrepreneurs—people with a tremendous talent for starting a company—are not the same skills they need for the ongoing management of a healthy company; in such cases, they may decide that it is best for the company to turn management over to professionals. Others find that their own advancing years and the lack of a family successor make selling their business the most desirable choice. Still others find they can carry the company on and see it make the transition to the next generation of family management.

Whatever their choices, entrepreneurial couples, like lone business owners, must face the fact that they will not live forever and that some provision must be made for the succession of leadership and ownership of their company. Each individual must not only prepare for his or her own death but also prepare, as much as it is possible, for the ultimate crisis—the death of a beloved partner.

When Irvin Makrauer died of lung cancer in 1983, Janet Makrauer was not at all sure she wanted to take over Amko Plastics. They had worked together since 1940—while Irvin pursued a career in another company, he and Janet ran a packaging business on the side. In 1966, in their early fifties, they launched Amko, which makes plastic shopping bags for such clients as Neiman-Marcus, 3M, and American Express and now does over $20 million in sales annually. Their son, George, then 22, started the company with them and eventually became their partner.

Janet credits her son with pulling her through those last three months of Irvin's life. She spent all day every day at the hospital. George would come by at eight in the morning with paperwork for her to do and would return at noon to retrieve the completed work. "When he was hiring important people, he'd send them over to the hospital to make sure that I was involved in the interview," says Janet. "He kept me going."

But George denies it was a ploy. "It had always been a three-way business and it was going to continue that way as long as we could."

Either George or Janet could have succeeded Irvin as president and chief executive officer of the company. After Irvin was gone, Janet says, "I didn't want this tremendous responsibility." But her board of directors and her son tried to convince her otherwise.

She tells what she calls her "Wizard of Oz" story: "It took me about a week or two to make up my mind, and I said, 'George, do you think I can do it?' And he said, 'Mom, you're like the Wizard of Oz. Heart, you have. Brains, you have. The courage, I'm not sure, but I will give it to you.' "

With that, Janet, at age 69, decided to go ahead. Two years later, she could still glow about the telephone call she received from George's wife, Taaron. "She said, 'Mom, I'm so glad you made the decision. It's your turn. George will have his turn.' " Janet thinks it was one of the most beautiful expressions of support and confidence a woman could receive from a daughter-in-law.

The Makrauers say the company was so well structured that it never missed a beat after Irvin's death. Growth continued strong, and Janet was named Ohio's Small Business Person of the Year in 1985. Somewhat to her astonishment, women in Cincinnati have singled her out as a role model for women in business, a development that surprises George not at all.

Grace Shafir was only 35 in 1984 when her husband, Jere Shafir, died at age 62 and she had to take over Kingshead Corporation, the scissors wholesaler in Hackensack, New Jersey. She did not have the same internal support that Janet Makrauer had and the demands on her at home were much greater—the youngest of her four daughters was only two months old.

Was she ready to run the company?

"Of course not," she answers with gentle humor. "But it had to be done. You just do the best you can."

She was already president of the company; Jere, as chairman and CEO, had begun to turn his energies to diversifying the business, giving particular attention to a scissors manufacturing operation they had started in 1981 in South Carolina. Despite the fact that he had been married before and had grown children, Jere had been smart enough to leave the company in the control of Grace, who was the one most able to manage it. She inherited 50 percent and the other 50 percent was put into trust for their daughters, with Grace and their attorney as co-trustees.

Jere's death thrust her into the big leagues fast, Grace recalls. "And here I was, up at bat, trying to use a toothpick."

She was prepared in the sales and marketing area because she had been handling most of these responsibilities already. The customers knew her better than they knew her husband. She made it a point to visit with major customers and appear at trade shows "so people could see me and see the company was still running."

What she wasn't prepared for was the fact that the General Services Administration canceled a $2.8 million contract with Kingshead immediately after she notified GSA of her husband's death. "They said we were late on deliveries," she says. But she thinks GSA canceled because her husband had died, not because of the deliveries. Kingshead had indeed been running late, but she had visited GSA officials six weeks before Jere's death and had worked out a new delivery schedule. Now, with the help of her congressman and yet another meeting with GSA officials, she convinced GSA to reinstate the contract.

She also found she wasn't prepared for some of the personnel and production problems she would have to face. After a "honeymoon" period of several months, two of her key employees became engaged in a power struggle with each other. Grace feels that, like many men, they could not adjust to the fact that a woman was in charge.

Matters deteriorated to the point where the two men would not speak to each other and the flow of communications in the company was jeopardized. At the suggestion of one of her advisers, she brought in a strong male to be chief operating officer, one who might be able to control the other two personalities. That didn't work either. She finally fired all three.

She now says that hiring the COO "was probably the dumbest thing I ever did. I have since come to the conclusion that the only person who can run the company is me."

Her problems were compounded by the fact that the factory in South Carolina had never done well. Jere had been about to close it, but Grace hung on to it, knowing that it had meant a great deal to her husband. "I tried to create a monument to him," she says. "Unfortunately, it just didn't work." Production, she concedes, is not her forte. If she had really been smart, she reflects, she would have closed it immediately.

Despite the problems, Grace has been able to do more than keep the company afloat. It has been growing at a rate of about 20 percent a year, and she has been moving it into children's crafts and other new areas that are compatible with its existing market for health and personal care implements.

She never considered selling the company. "If you sell the business in such a situation," she says, "it's always a sacrifice sale. I never entertained it because I had to be able to support my children."

Of course, it is not always a wife who has to carry on. Sometimes, the husband must do so, and it can be just as difficult for him. Several years ago, I was contacted by a public relations agent and asked to do a story on a company celebrating its silver anniversary. I agreed to do so, and a time was set for an interview with the owner; he was to call me at 3 P.M. on a Thursday early in March. The hour came and went without the phone call. When I reached the public relations agent, she was as puzzled as I was. The man's wife, his business partner, had died several months earlier, and we subsequently learned that he was still so grief stricken that he could not bring himself to do the interview—or any other interviews, for that matter. He was having a hard time carrying on without her, and he was thinking of selling the company they had started together.

TURNING CHILDREN INTO OWNERS AND MANAGERS

Family business consultants keep urging business owners to plan their succession by middle age but find that traditional male entrepreneurs are particularly reluctant to do so. Reminders that they are mortal often go unheeded, with the result that when death does come, there is no one ready to take over or there are ownership and power struggles that make television soap opera business families seem realistic after all.

It remains to be seen whether entrepreneurial couples can make the transition of a business to succeeding generations more easily than lone entrepreneurs. That will be for some future Ph.D. candidate to determine. And it is not our intention here to probe the complex problems of succession—some sources for further information are listed at the end of this book. Sooner or later, however, many entrepreneurial couples discover that theirs is no longer just a husband-and-wife business.

Katherine and Ron Harper say they were startled a few years ago when their attorney and accountant asked them why they didn't admit that theirs was a family business. The Harpers thought of it as a corporation, separate from the family. But their advisers pointed out that their five children were now grown up and several of them had been working in the company for some years. The Harpers realized that despite differences they had with their children about how the company should be run, the children, as Katherine puts it, "are really capable adults." Each year, they seemed to have more confidence in themselves, and Ron believes that one of the sons could probably step in his parents' shoes tomorrow, if he had to.

"They may prove to be the professionals who are going to take our places," says Ron.

In some of the oldest and biggest companies, the transition from the founding couple to the children is very visible, if not yet complete. Andrew Lewis has succeeded his father as chairman of Best Products, for example, and Robert Gore became the president of W. L. Gore & Associates, founded by his parents. While Estée Lauder has been chairman of Estée Lauder since her husband's death, son Leonard is firmly ensconced as president and chief executive officer.

Other couples are not as far along, yet it is clear that they intend to make an orderly transition. Actress Beverly Garland and her husband Fillmore Crank began early to take steps to attract their children into their hotel business and prepare them to take over. Crank was a widower with a teenage son, Fillmore, Jr., and daughter, Cathleen, when he and Garland married. They added two children of their own—a daughter, Carrington, now in her early twenties, and a son, James, in his late teens.

Fillmore, Jr., returned from Vietnam when the couple's Beverly Garland Hotel in North Hollywood was nearing completion, and Garland and Crank put him to work as manager.

When the family business expanded to a second hotel in Sacramento, young Fillmore oversaw its construction and soon became manager of the 207-room facility. Cathleen, who had been housekeeper of the North Hollywood hotel, took over as manager until she left to have a baby.

Crank is in his sixties and Garland is in her fifties and, like other entrepreneurs, they must plan a transition of ownership and wealth as well as management—or it will be done for them by the courts and heirs after they die.

One issue they are considering is fairness. Fillmore, Jr., in his late thirties, is the only member of the second generation deeply involved in the business and the one most clearly prepared to take over. To provide him with an incentive besides salary, Garland and Crank have begun to transfer interest in the company to him under the tax provision that permits each to give him up to $10,000 a year tax-free.

Other couples are taking similar steps. Beginning in 1986, Joseph and Donna King, both in their fifties, started turning Florida Azalea Specialists over to their three sons, all of whom work in the company full time. In the first year of the transition, they expected to give each son 5 percent of the company.

Jerry and Roberta House's End O' Main Restaurant and Catering Service grew so much that it easily absorbed their three children—all in their thirties—and one daughter-in-law. The Houses incorporated in 1984 and now they know they must get down to the harder work of planning a transition of ownership and management.

Generally, the most successful transitions are those where the children are *invited,* not coerced, into the parents' businesses. They feel they have a choice about what they can do and that joining the family enterprise is one of a number of options. Furthermore, once they are in the business, their parents give them real responsibility (with real opportunities to make mistakes) and a chance to take part in the decision making. Rarely, if ever, is the transition easy, even under the best of circumstances. In fact, family business specialists say that transition in a family business is one of the most difficult management tasks the owners can undertake.

When George Makrauer looks back two decades to the time when he started in business with his parents, he remembers the care that his father, Irvin, took to teach him the business and make him feel that he had a meaningful and well-defined role in it. The first year George was in the company, Irvin took him to some industry conventions and let him sit in on the meetings that Irvin had with other business leaders. George could see that his peers, the children of other business owners, were stuck in booths handing out literature and taking down the names of potential customers. "But the opportunity I had was to be with my father, sitting in on these meetings with presidents of chemical companies and ink companies and printing equipment companies and plastics machinery companies and really getting exposed to what makes a business operate," he says.

It was that way back at the office, too.

"Whenever we had important people calling on us for equipment or supplies or any new ideas that were going on in the industry," says Janet Makrauer, "my husband never just sat there and talked to them. He would call George in. He wanted him to learn from the ground floor." He would often call Janet in, too, so that she fully understood what was going on.

Sometimes George would want to try something that Irvin had already tried in the Makrauers' first company and found didn't work. If George really pressed, Irvin would let him go ahead. Janet would ask her husband why he had given in, and he would say, "I want George to make his mistakes while they're cheap mistakes." But Janet says her husband was always open minded. He knew that just because something had not worked before did not mean it would not work now.

As George developed, he became a full member of the team, with an equal vote. Like his parents, he had his own area of authority, and they deferred to him in his area. If, for example, a supplier wanted to show either parent something that dealt with catalogs or advertising, they would refer him to George because marketing and sales were his responsibility.

George's sister, Zola Berning, a systems analyst, joined the company a few years ago, and George and Janet are trying to follow Irvin's example in bringing her along in the business. George says he still misses having his father's advice or being able to share a success with him.

"The way he showed his love for us was by the way he got us involved in the business," says George.

THE SELLING OPTION

Turning a business over to the next generation is not always feasible or, in the couple's judgment, desirable. Olga and Jan Erteszek were in their sixties and knew they had to make some decisions about the continuity of The Olga Company. Their oldest daughter had worked in the firm for a while and then left to pursue a career in real estate; their second daughter is a nursing supervisor; and their youngest, Christina Johnson, joined The Olga Company at age 28 in 1978 as a junior designer after following a career as a special education teacher.

Despite the fact that they finally had a daughter in the company who looked like she would stay, the Erteszeks decided it was in the best interest of the company to sell it to Warnaco in 1984. Jan stayed on as chairman of the board until his death and Olga is still vice president, design. Jeffrey Paul, an executive hired in 1980 at age 34 and groomed by Jan, is president. Christina is now responsible for the "Olga's Christina" label, marketed as a more contemporary line aimed at "the woman of the 80s."

Some couples, however, find that it's better for them and the business if they sell it while they are still young. As we have seen, for example, Mel and Patricia Ziegler sold the Banana Republic in 1983 to The Gap, Inc., and stayed on to run it, freeing themselves of some of the administrative and financial demands that were beginning to usurp most of their time.

"I think the business got out of hand for us," says Mel. He and Patricia both prefer doing creative work, but the business was so successful and growing so fast that Mel says, "we found ourselves spending 90 percent of our time negotiating credit, borrowing money, hiring and firing, making computers work, and working with accountants." That wasn't how they wanted to live.

Furthermore, they needed to get into manufacturing instead of buying clothes on the surplus market. And they needed cash, lots of cash, in order to fulfill the company's potential for growth. They had reached a point where they needed more than a bank could provide. They either had to sell part of the company to venture capitalists, in which case they would still have the same operational headaches. Or they could sell the Banana Republic to a retailing company that could take over the business and financial side of their enterprise and, with the parent company's expertise and resources, make the Banana Republic grow the way the Zieglers had envisioned.

"There was just an overbearing need to break this deadlock of endless work and the frustration of never being able to deliver enough product fast enough or never being able to fill the orders, to get caught up, to hire enough people, to grow with the demand," says Patricia.

A mutual friend introduced the Zieglers to Donald G. Fisher, president of The Gap. It appeared to be a good fit for both companies, and the deal was made. Fisher asked the Zieglers to stay and they agreed, provided they kept creative control. With The Gap behind them, the Banana Republic began to fulfill the potential the Zieglers knew it had.

"The speed with which we're able to make these dreams become a reality is so great it's thrilling," says Patricia. "All of a sudden, you see your visions across America, just the way you imagined them. That's very fulfilling." On the other hand, she admits, the business side of building the Banana Republic in its earlier days, "including all the dirty work," was fulfilling, too. "And I can't say I wouldn't want to do it again."

The Zieglers say the arrangement has worked out well in money-making terms and that has "cemented" the creative autonomy they sought. No one is looking over their shoulder to tell them what they can or cannot do creatively, they say. From the inception of the Banana Republic, they have traveled the world to come up with ideas, and in the spring of 1986, they came out with a "Soviet Safari" catalog. No one from The Gap said they couldn't do it. "We're probably the first retailer in the history of the United States to go to the Soviet Union to produce a catalog," says Mel.

Mitch Berliner calls the decision that he, Linda, and his brother, Guy, made to sell Berliner Foods to Dreyer's Grand Ice Cream in December 1985 "the best thing that ever happened to this company." The Berliners needed a company like Dreyer's, an aggressive Oakland-based company with every intent of going national, in order to expand into the ice cream market the way they wanted to and for the financial resources that Dreyer's could offer. Dreyer's needed the Berliners because of the trade relations they had already developed in Baltimore, Washington, and Virginia.

Now a wholly owned subsidiary of Dreyer's, Berliner Foods continues to operate under the Berliner name. Under the agreement, Mitch and Guy will run the subsidiary for a minimum of five years, but the move permanently "retired" Linda, who had pulled out from daily involvement earlier to rear her and Mitch's two young children. Dreyer's also assumed the Berliner financial obligations, "so we could concentrate on sales and just growing the company," says Mitch. By April 1986, Berliner Foods had already jumped to 75 employees from the 55 of the previous fall. Both parties stand to make a lot more money than they could without each other, Mitch contends. They are not merely satisfied with the new arrangement, he says. "We are thrilled. There's no other adjective."

Selling can be bittersweet, however. When Lorraine Mecca and Geza Csige left Micro D in July 1985, Mecca was quoted by *Savvy* magazine as saying that leaving the company at the end of five years had been her plan. The company had been experiencing losses, however, and the *Wall Street Journal* reported Mecca as saying that the election of Linwood A. Lacy as chairman "consummates our efforts to transfer the management of the company into the hands of a professional management team."

"I believe they felt their entrepreneurial style was such that there was a need for more professional management," says Lacy. "It really does take a different kind of person to start a company than it does to manage it at a larger size. I think also that it was a tremendously intense experience and they wanted time away from it. They are not workaholics by disposition, but if there is a goal or a task, they'll work the hours it takes to get it done. And so, as the task was done, they had a chance to spend time on other things."

By the summer of 1986 Mecca and Csige were living in Austin, Texas, at least temporarily. Their feelings about leaving Micro D, says Mecca, "range daily from being on Cloud Nine to kicking ourselves. We continually discuss what we could have done or should have done and yet there are other times when we're just so glad to have the money and be planning our next venture."

When Micro D went public in 1983, Mecca says, "we put in a layer of vice presidents at the request of the venture capitalist and the underwriters to make it look like a more professionally managed company." The result was predictable. Micro D became more of a traditional hierarchy; it reflected the founders less and the managers they hired more. Mecca and Csige agreed that it needed more professional management, but they felt less in touch with it and "less like it was ours," says Mecca. "It became less enjoyable."

Mecca says she and her husband are "definitely entrepreneurs," but she thinks they learned so much from their experience with Micro D that with their next venture, they can become ongoing managers as well. They expect to stay in technology, and this time, they may not have to worry about meeting the request of some venture capitalist. When Mecca finally sold her 51 percent interest in January 1986, press reports say she took home about $6.7 million, considerably more than the $25,000 she had to launch Micro D.

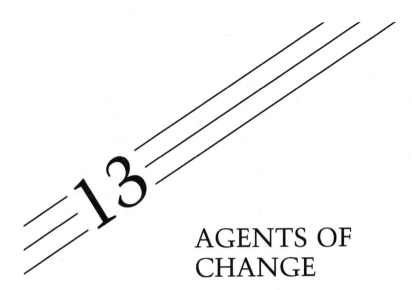

AGENTS OF
CHANGE

The Path to New Business and
Personal Life Styles

To be an egalitarian entrepreneurial couple is, in and of itself, to be an agent of social change. The men and women who form entrepreneurial partnerships are advancing many of the changes initiated by the women's movement, in their homes and in their workplaces.

The women in these partnerships find an opportunity to achieve, to develop themselves, and to be rewarded for their contributions in measures far greater than generally found in our society. The men find they have wives who understand them better than would be the case if they were go-it-alone entrepreneurs, and they experience some relief of the burden of running a business when they can share the problems with a valued partner.

In many cases, both sexes report more intimacy and bonding with each other than they believe they would have experienced had they followed separate paths in their work life. Many also speak of the reward of family closeness, a result of the flexibility that owning their own business offers. While they work long hours and hard ones, men and women alike can often move work schedules around in order to meet the needs of children. Frequently, Mommy's and Daddy's business is a stopping-off place for the children, who may be going to or from school or who simply need some looking after. Jean Flaxenburg of French Creek Sheep & Wool was a tad late for my interview with her and husband Eric in their barn-office because she had taken a few minutes at their house up the lane to fix some soup for a sick child. Like the Flaxenburgs, many entrepreneurial couples seem to see far more of their children than career parents who work for other employers.

The entrepreneurial couple's lifestyle is a new model for the rest of society. Valerie Bursten of Decorating Den suggests that the women's movement and the growth of franchising are making it possible for many Americans to recapture the values of farm families, enabling them to combine work and family life. Steve adds: "That's exactly the feeling I see with many of our franchises. It's like the farm closeness of the family pulling together; there's just something of great strength there."

Nevertheless, the entrepreneurial couple is, in important ways, different from the traditional farm family, where the male is the farmer and the female is the farm wife. No matter how vital her contribution to that economic unit is—and it *is* vital—the woman in that model is seen as the helper, not the doer. Increasingly in husband-and-wife enterprises, both are doers *and* helpers. And not infrequently, the wife is the doer and the husband is the helper. When the wife is in the position of business leadership, a couple is really blazing a difficult trail, going against a rigid norm that stipulates that the man must be smarter, must be at the forefront, and must make more money. If a couple carries this arrangement off successfully, they make a contribution by demonstrating that men and women can play whatever roles suit them best and still be warm and loving mates, even when the male is in the supporting role.

Raymond J. Steiner of Saugerties, New York, is vice president of CSS Publications, Inc., founded by his wife, Cornelia Seckel. Their main product is *Art Times,* a monthly that covers the art scene in upstate New York and Manhattan. Although he is 13 years her senior, Raymond, the company's writer, editor, and bookkeeper, describes Cornelia as the driving force of the business and the boss; she functions as the publisher and advertising manager. He refers to himself as a househusband, responsible for keeping the home in order, and says: "I feel very fortunate to have found a personal partner who has been willing to become my business partner in my writing. I know of no better way for a writer to have his work published—I am given visibility while allowed to have a say in how that visibility is accomplished."

Many writers have uneasy relationships with their publishers, he points out. "I at least know mine intimately and can trust her to have my sensibilities at heart. When I feel she doesn't, I at least know she will hear me out and take my input into consideration. Further, few writers have such encouragement both spiritually and financially; playing househusband seems little inconvenience for the support I receive."

RESHAPING THE BUSINESS WORLD

In addition to providing us with new models for marriages and families, entrepreneurial couples are changing the shape of business itself. Like women executives who work for someone else, the female partner of an entrepreneurial team is serving as a role model for women, paving the way for acceptance of women at the upper levels of corporations and creating opportunities for other women. Only she is probably doing it faster, not only because she has the power but also because the respect that her mate shows her in the business environment sets an example for everyone else in the company.

A point is made when visitors walk into the elegant high-tech lobby of Micro D, for example, and discover the portraits of the founders on the reception area wall. Here are not visages of grim-faced, pompous males, but the pictures of a young woman and a young man: Lorraine Mecca and Geza Csige. It makes a point, too, when you are leafing through a twenty-fifth anniversary publication of W. L. Gore & Associates, and the faces of two founders smile out at you: Vieve and Bill Gore.

Bill Gore, by the way, credited his wife with involving women in Gore, and Vieve herself says, "We have got some terrific women." She believes it is important to show women the opportunities that are available in the organization and to demonstrate to them that they don't have to worry about being held back. She takes a special interest in encouraging women like herself who have come into the business world after rearing children.

The husband-and-wife team also makes an important statement to the wider world of business. In many cases, it is the
female partner who is determining who should get a contract
or a large order or otherwise making significant corporate decisions. In doing so, she is gaining visibility for the clout that
women are gaining and she is helping to build up credibility
for women in business.

Nowhere in the business press, for example, is there a hint
that Marion and Herbert Sandler are anything but equals in
running Golden West Financial Corporation. The *San Francisco
Chronicle* has referred to them as the " 'dynamic duo' management team" and quotes Allan G. Bortel, an S&L analyst with
Shearson Lehman Brothers Inc., as praising the company for its
impressive growth and saying, "I don't know any harder-working
management. They live and breathe the company. There's no
comparable story in the financial services industry." In its August
19, 1985, issue, *The Wall Street Transcript* named the Sandlers
the best chief executives of the year in the savings and loan
industry.

Another couple, Olga and Jan Erteszek, of The Olga Company,
were awarded the California Industrialist of the Year Award in
1985. It was the first time a woman had received that honor.
And the first time for a couple. Another first came in May 1986,
when Robert and Ruth Kehl of Dubuque, Iowa, became the first
couple to be named national Small Business Persons of the Year
by the U.S. Small Business Administration. (Ruth Kehl, with
this award, became the first woman to achieve this nation-wide
recognition.) The Kehls founded Roberts River Rides, a Mississippi riverboat cruise company credited with revitalizing the
economy of northeast Iowa by creating a boom in the tourist
industry.

As we have seen from the example of Diane and Leonard
Johnson, the entrepreneurial couple can even make an impact
on the way business is done in foreign countries by insisting

that the businesswoman be accorded the same respect as the businessman. Couples like Liz Claiborne Ortenburg and Arthur Ortenburg and Patricia and Mel Ziegler and others who travel the world frequently on business must also be changing the perceptions of the role of women.

BUSINESS INNOVATORS

An entrepreneurial couple's influence for change extends far beyond the promotion of equality of the sexes, however. Working together, synergistic teams of men and women have been innovators, creating new products, new services, and new management systems, and shaping industries.

When Sydney and Frances Lewis founded Best Products in 1957, basing their operation on the idea of saving the consumer money, discount retailing was in its infancy. Catalog showrooms, somewhat a rarity, were usually specialty stores, limited to toys or jewelry rather than offering the broad range of goods that the Lewises offered.

Following their initial success, growth was modest but steady. When son Andrew joined the firm in 1969, there were five showrooms and annual sales had reached $20 million. The infusion of energy and enthusiasm that Andy brought with him was a big factor in the Lewises becoming the first to take a catalog showroom company public, which they did in 1970. They were also among the first, according to former Best senior vice president Linwood (Chip) Lacy, to recognize the importance of suburban locations. Their foresight enabled them to build the company, by construction and acquisition, to more than 200 showrooms and $2.5 billion in annual sales.

In another innovation, the Lewises, who love art and have acquired a renowned collection, commissioned SITE, a New York design firm, to do something special for a number of the boxy-looking Best showrooms. SITE created unusual and sometimes bizarre facades—the whole front wall of one seems to tilt; on another, the brick front appears to peel away. The designs have won national attention for the company.

When the Gores went into business, they wanted not only to create new products based on the polymer polytetrafluoroethylene, better known as Teflon, but also to demonstrate an entirely new way of managing a company. They achieved both goals with astounding success. Their waterproof Gore-Tex fabrics have become famous among backpackers, mountain climbers, and other outdoors enthusiasts. More than a million people worldwide have received Gore-Tex replacement blood vessels, used to combat cardiovascular disease. And Gore-Tex fiber is used for the outer protective layer of space suits. The company also makes coatings and filtration and electronic products. "They are really just great products," says Vieve. "They are all things that our society needs."

Their "lattice" organization has also won wide recognition and is a model for executives looking for effective, nonauthoritarian approaches to management. It is based on the notion that people work better and more creatively in small groups or task forces, where they know everybody and can perform interactively and cooperatively. Workers are called "associates," not employees. No one is "boss." Leadership emerges naturally. ("I can tell a leader every time," Bill once told *Industry Week* magazine. "If he has followers, he's a leader. It's the only criterion I've ever found.") Under the Gore system, you ask for people's help; you don't tell them what to do. If one associate can't help you, you find one who can. Associates find their own way to make a contribution. No single person has the power to fire anyone; firing and compensation are group decisions. Describing the system, Bill chuckled and said he could give orders, but nobody would take them.

The lattice system, said Bill, is based on four principles—that everybody will:

□ Sincerely strive to be fair with each other, suppliers, customers, and all persons with whom he or she carries out transactions.

□ Allow, help, and encourage associates to grow in knowledge, skill, scope of responsibility, and range of activities.

□ Make their *own* commitments—and keep them.

□ Consult with associates before taking actions that might cause serious damage to the enterprise.

The Gores found that the maximum effective group is around 150, and as their company grows, new plants are built to accommodate new associates rather than putting an expanding staff into a larger and larger facility. Plants worldwide number about 40, and in 1985, the company had about 4,500 associates and was increasing at a rate of 25 percent a year.

Listed in *The 100 Best Companies to Work for in America*, The Olga Company, too, has become known for its management as well as for its products. Again, workers here are called "associates," and in speeches and articles, Jan Erteszek stated that he and Olga made a commitment to "becoming a 'pilot plant' that would test the validity of Judeo-Christian teachings in the conduct of business."

"Our (my wife Olga and myself) main objective," he wrote in a 1983 issue of *New Management*, the magazine of the University of Southern California Graduate School of Business Administration, "was not just to find a new way of conducting a more successful economic activity. We sought, rather, to create a new 'socio-economic model,' one relevant to the highly interdependent social and economic life of the 20th Century."

In the interview for this book, Jan said that he and Olga came to look at business as more than an economic effort. As the member of the team most involved with hiring, he found that people who work for others are often unfulfilled because they spend 40–45 hours or more a week doing something that is meaningless to them, and "life starts after business hours." The Erteszeks felt that their company had to do more than just meet immediate economic needs.

"Business is maybe the prime community of our times," said Jan. "At one time, you had the neighbor, you had the church and the village. But now, really, most people spend most of their waking hours in some working endeavor." A company is, he said, "the main place of human intercourse."

In 1954, the Erteszeks initiated a profit-sharing plan. "At that time, profit-sharing plans were very rare and almost nonexistent in the apparel business," observed Jan. The Olga plan is noted for its generosity—25 percent of the profits *before* taxes go into it.

The company, however, fosters reciprocal rights and obligations. In periodic "creative meetings," associates are expected to offer their own ideas on how to improve their jobs and what they would like to see the company doing. The company agreed to a request of a group of sewing-machine operators to offer classes in basic English for associates who had immigrated to the United States. The hour-long classes have been conducted at the end of the workday, with half the hour on company time and half on the workers' personal time. Olga also follows a policy of planning for full employment and has avoided significant layoffs. But although the associates share in the good times, they are expected to share in the bad times as well. During the recession in 1982, Olga cut back to four-day weeks to avoid a 20-percent layoff, with the state helping to make up the loss of the fifth day's pay under a special "workshare" program.

"The Olga Company has become an unusual place where people *live*," emphasized Jan. Former employees come back to visit or keep in touch for years, according to Olga, because the company was a home to them.

When the Erteszeks decided to sell the company, they sought a buyer that would continue their socioeconomic concepts and settled on Warnaco as the most likely to do so. The sales contract included an agreement on Warnaco's part that it would maintain the profit-sharing plan for four years. But Jan felt Warnaco would continue profit-sharing even after the four years are up.

"It has become such a part and parcel of the soul of the company, the culture of the company; it would seem to me that it would be difficult to unscramble the eggs," he said. "Plus, I don't think it would be to the benefit of the company. This profit-sharing was not done as a token of our largesse. It had significant economic impact on absenteeism, on quality, on concern, on management—all those kinds of things that are not clearly, quantitatively measurable on the bottom line."

MAKING A DIFFERENCE

Even couples who own much smaller companies find they can make an impact. Two of them have shaped entire industries.

When Doug and Karen Greene, the founders of New Hope Communications, set out to create a natural foods trade journal, the goal was not just to put out a magazine. "We were helping America reinvent its food distribution system and its understanding of what food means in the role of the human being," says Doug. The company soon grew to include two large natural food trade conferences a year, one in Anaheim and one in Washington, D.C., and it has had an influence not only in coalescing the owners of health food stores but also in making natural foods more available through such channels as supermarkets.

Another couple, Jon and Christel DeHaan of Indianapolis, were elemental in the growth of the vacation time-sharing industry in this country. Under time-sharing, a purchaser buys the right to a given apartment or condominium for a certain time period each year. In most cases, the owner is actually buying real estate, taking title to his one or two weeks a year. Time-sharing began to make an appearance in this country in the early 1970s. In the beginning, promoters were fond of pushing the idea as an investment that could be sold later for a profit, a somewhat dubious idea since there was no history to verify it.

The DeHaans saw that buying a time share could offer a family a hedge against vacation inflation in a time of soaring hotel prices. But they also knew that many people just didn't want to take their vacation in the same place at the same time every year— a factor that impeded time-share sales.

They introduced the concept of "vacation exchange" and founded Resort Condominiums International (RCI) as a service to enable a time-share owner to swap his week for another in a comparable resort at a comparable time somewhere else, even in another country. They spent much of their early years educating builders and developers about time sharing and vacation exchange, stimulating a trend toward the development of resorts specifically designed for time sharing. And they worked to combat some of the questionable practices that made potential buyers wary.

The DeHaans' exchange concept revolutionized the time-share industry, according to a spokesman for the National TimeShare Council in Washington, D.C., enabling it to grow from a $50 million industry in 1974 to a $1.5 billion industry in 1983. By helping the industry, the DeHaans helped themselves. In 1985, their annual revenues exceeded $30 million, and where in 1977 they processed 1,500 vacation exchanges, they were expecting to process 230,000 in 1986.

Entrepreneurial couples like to make an impact. Jack and Ruth Pentes of Pentes Design in Charlotte, North Carolina, are proud of the fact that the "soft" play equipment their company designs for theme parks, fast food restaurants, and other clients is calling attention to the need for safer play equipment for children. Barbara Aiello and her ex-husband, in founding Kids on the Block in Alexandria, Virginia, set in motion an educational business that could make life easier for handicapped children around the world.

Even in their personal lives, entrepreneurial couples are often committed to making a difference. Frances and Sydney Lewis have helped to build a new $6 million wing of the Virginia Museum of Fine Arts and are donating their own fabulous art collection to it. After starting out in California, Debbi and Randy Fields moved their Mrs. Fields headquarters to the tiny ski resort of Park City, Utah. Not only was it beautiful and a good place to raise children, they reasoned; they also felt they wanted to live in a place where they could make some impact on the community. They have also made a major commitment to the eradication of cystic fibrosis, through corporate sponsorship of the Cystic Fibrosis Foundation and by giving their own time.

Debbi says that when her life is over, she would rather be remembered for helping find a cure for cystic fibrosis than for how many stores she had.

You can't make a difference by acquiring money, says Randy, and "creating a bunch of rich kids is not a very valid social end." In other words, it's what you do with the money that counts. In the final analysis, Randy sums up, "Money belongs to society."

14

DO YOU HAVE
WHAT IT TAKES?

How to Test Yourself

Being in business together is not for everyone. Entrepreneurial couples themselves are often quick to point that out. Nevertheless, most of the entrepreneurs who participated in this book are more positive than negative about the life they have chosen. Of the 60 individuals who responded to the questionnaire, 50 answered an unequivocal yes to the question: "If you had it to do over again, would you go into business with your spouse or the person you live with?" Some said they would do it sooner. "Definitely!" was Tari Vickery's response. "It has forced us to grow, and we have grown together, rather than apart. We have an intuitive understanding of each other's dreams, needs, and desires that I don't think we would have in separate lines of work." Wesley and Rosanne Kranitz made their point by observing that they had indeed gone into business together again, despite the failure of their first enterprise.

Of the 60 respondents, three did not answer that particular question, and three gave ambiguous answers that leaned more toward yes than no. Four said they would not do it again. One was the West Coast woman whose husband got into drugs and other temptations of the nightclub business. Another was a wife in a small start-up business who said, "It puts too much of a strain on our personal relationship when things don't go right."

Surprisingly, Jerome and Pauline Berliner, the retired couple who ran their successful export management business for 27 years, and who have been married for well over 40 years, said no, they would not do it again. They describe themselves as both being strong willed, with often differing opinions. "The possibilities of creating havoc with a marriage are too evident," says Jerome. The feisty Pauline says she could have run the business by herself but would have been smart enough to surround herself "with the proper personnel." In a letter accompanying his questionnaire, Jerome writes that he and Pauline had agreed to fill out their surveys without consulting each other. "Only after completing our answers did we compare them. And that led to an outburst of laughter." They discovered that many of their answers bore striking similarities. "It was obvious that after 43 years of marriage, our 'independent' opinions began to converge along the same paths."

A "DANGEROUS THING"

The couples who agreed to be interviewed were not asked the same question, but nearly all expressed a high degree of satisfaction with being part of an entrepreneurial couple. However, even though he and Patricia have combined business and marriage with apparently astounding success, Mel Ziegler of the Banana Republic says, "I would never recommend going into business with your spouse. I think it's perhaps the single most dangerous thing that a human being can do to himself or to herself. It's pitted with possibilities of failure. Although the rewards are staggering—if it works—I don't think anybody who has a healthy, happy relationship with his wife should put that at risk for the rewards and benefits of a business relationship." The challenges to a marriage notwithstanding, Patricia's view is that being an entrepreneurial couple has given her and her husband much more to share—and to celebrate or be depressed about together—than if they had not joined forces in business. "There's an excitement, there's a communication that I think wouldn't be a part of your life if you're just going two different ways with two different careers."

Despite his own very strong reservations about encouraging other couples to go into business together, Mel says he and Patricia have worked out the problems of being business partners. And, he says, I don't think we've built our last business. I think we're going to do more together."

Chris and Winnie Dickerman warn that one of the disadvantages is that you lose some of your identity, individuality, and independence as you try to fit yourself into a business unit that may be greater than the sum of its parts. Chris says you have to ask yourself, "How independent and dynamic a personality do I have? Can I do this?"

Not only do you have to have trust and belief in your partner, the Dickermans say; you also have to be willing to support your partner when he or she makes mistakes. When you are in business together, Winnie points out, "You see a lot of weaknesses in the other person. He's seen me at my very worst, which can be absolutely abominable, but he's not going to dislike me. And I have enough trust in him that I'm not worried about defending myself. I have a right to screw things up and look bad."

"We do phenomenally stupid things," she continues. "Sometimes we compound them together, and we make things a lot worse." But they talk such problems out and share them, with one saying, for example, "Boy, did I screw this up bad. I'm really sorry," and the other responding, "Don't worry about it. We'll fix it."

Psychologist Marta Vago says that men and women are drawn together because of common interests and common goals—which in this day and age are very likely to be found in business ideas. Often, they make the mistake of thinking that because they share a love for a business idea, they are in love with each other. "Before they have a chance to truly develop a solid and full personal relationship, they get carried away and go into business together. The business relationship becomes a lot more solid and a lot more full and rich than the personal relationship ever had a chance to be."

She believes that it is important that a couple start out as a couple first, taking the time to build a foundation of mutual trust, respect, and intimacy and going through some rough times together. They must have what she identifies as a "true understanding, appreciation, and acceptance of the other person." Then if they go into business together and the business fails, she says, the couple can say, "Well, it was just a business! It's not you. It's not us." Now they have two choices. They can say, "We're a terrific couple and we can't do business together." Or they can say, "We're a terrific couple and this *particular* business was not appropriate for us. Maybe another one will be better.''

THE ENTREPRENEURIAL COUPLE'S CHECKLIST

How can a couple know if they stand a good chance of combining a business and personal relationship successfully? There are no guarantees, but the following checklist should be helpful. Keep in mind that a self-quiz or checklist can only be a guide and not an infallible predictor—either of success or failure. Joseph R. Mancuso, president of the Center for Entrepreneurial Management in New York, has devised a self-test for would-be entrepreneurs, and he once told me that his own brother scored low on the test. However, the score made him so mad he went out and started his own business! Likewise, if a number of couples in this book had measured themselves against this checklist before they went into business, they might have discovered some alarming shortcomings. Through hard work and commitment— to the health of their relationships as well as the health of their businesses—they did what they set out to do, in many cases improving their marriages and producing thriving businesses at the same time.

You and your mate should be able to answer yes to most or all of the following questions. The starred questions are the ones that, in my observation, are the most critical, and if you cannot answer yes to these questions, a decision to go into business together deserves much more deliberation. While the other questions may be less critical, if you do answer no, then you should be able to answer yes to another question: "Is this an area we can work on and improve to the point where someday we can say yes?" Lack of commitment to working on problem areas may signal a lack of commitment necessary to make the business or the partnership a success.

The questions below reflect issues that have been touched

on throughout this book and they are, by design, questions that pertain more to the relationship than to an individual's ability to be a successful entrepreneur. Books that deal with the latter abound. These questions are intended to help you determine whether you and your mate can make a good business team and keep your personal relationship strong at the same time.

*1. _____ Does your relationship have a solid foundation? Has it been tested sufficiently so that you know how you function as a couple under stress?

*2. _____ Do you totally trust each other?

*3. _____ Do you totally respect each other? Are you able to give each other's ideas and opinions a full hearing and to admit it, without resentment, when the other is right or has a better idea?

*4. _____ Do you know yourself and your mate well?

*5. _____ Do you work well together on projects you have undertaken together?

*6. _____ Do you have fun when you work together?

7. _____ Can you maintain a sense of humor even when things go wrong?

8. _____ Do you have complementary skills and talents, with one strong where the other is weak and vice versa? If your skills are not complementary, can you admit the deficiencies and work together to resolve them (e.g., take courses, hire consultants)?

*9. _____ Can you have disagreements with each other without taking things personally or attacking the other personally?

10. _____ Can you criticize—that is, give feedback to—each other in a constructive, nondamaging way? Can you accept criticism from each other?

11. _____ When your mate makes a mistake, can you accept it as just a human error, without loss of respect for him or her?

12. _____ Do you avoid blaming the other person when things go wrong?

13. _____ Can you avoid playing "If it weren't for me" or "If it weren't for you" games? ("If it weren't for me, this business would have gone down the drain a long time ago." "If it weren't for you, we could have gotten that contract.")

*14. _____ Do you work toward win–win solutions and decisions instead of one being the winner and one being the loser?

15. _____ Do you enjoy your partner's successes?

16. _____ Are you good collaborators? Can you join forces with your mate to compete against the outside world instead of competing with each other?

17. _____ If the nature of your business would throw the limelight on your partner, can you view that in a positive way and not be envious?

18. _____ If the nature of your business throws the limelight on you, can you share credit with your partner, putting him or her forward when it is appropriate?

*19. _____ Do you have good ongoing communication between you? Do you talk problems out when they arise instead of letting them fester?

*20. _____ Can you share power and decision making comfortably with your partner? And can you agree on how power should be shared and decisions made in your business?

*21. _____ Are you both totally committed to the business? Do you have a "shared vision" of what the company should be like?

*22. _____ Are you both totally committed to the relationship?

*23. _____ Do you understand your own motivations and your partner's motivations for going into business? Are your motivations compatible? (If one's is solely to make money and the other's is solely to have artistic or creative freedom, it may not work.)

24. _____ Are you both willing to pitch in and do your share of tasks you don't like as well as tasks you do like?

25. _____ Can you make a division between business and personal time that is acceptable to both of you? (Many couples need a distinct separation between the two; others rarely separate them and enjoy the continued blending of business with their personal life.)

26. _____ Are your needs for work and personal time compatible? (For example, if one is a workaholic and the other is not, are you comfortable with that? Can the workaholic work without resenting that the partner knocks off for personal time? After a reasonable day's work, can the nonworkaholic do something else without feeling guilty or resentful of the other?)

27. _____ Have you discussed your respective management styles? Can you live with and respect each other's styles?

28. _____ Can you leave business problems at the business and domestic problems at home?

29. _____ Can you agree on a division of responsibility—that is, how you will carve up turf and who will be the "boss" of what?

30. _____ Can you give each other room to grow and change and develop new skills, even if it means growing beyond the turf you start out with?

31. _____ Can you agree on what titles you will have and on what the material rewards will be for each (salary, profits, equity, perks)?

32. _____ Do you cope with hard times and failure in constructive and mutually supportive ways?

33. _____ Can you work out a division of domestic responsibilities and child care that is fair and that you are both comfortable with?

34. _____ If you do not yet have children, have you discussed the effect that having children will have not only on your personal relationship but also on your business?

35. _____ In a business, would you be able to recognize your partner's contribution as being equal to and as valuable as your own? For example, if you were the creative person and your spouse was the administrator or business manager, would you be able to see his or her role as deserving of respect as yours?

36. _____ Can you defer comfortably to your partner in his or her area of expertise? Does your partner defer to you in yours?

37. _____ When decisions must be made or opportunities arise, can you both take an attitude of "Will this benefit the business?" as opposed to "Will this benefit me?"

38. _____ Are you willing to commit a business plan to paper?

*39. _____ Do you enjoy spending a lot of time together?

40. _____ If one of you is more experienced than the other, do you have the willingness and patience to give your partner time to catch up? Will you still be able to treat your partner as an equal?

TRUST YOUR INTUITION

People often know intuitively whether they will make a good business team, Vago says. Sometimes they ignore the inner voice that tells them that, because of the personalities involved, a business relationship would not work for them. They ignore it either because they don't want to hurt their mate or because the business idea is so good they want to make it work. This is not to say that personal differences and problems cannot be resolved. "But," says Vago, "they really need to respect their intuitive judgment about their mate."

This calls for honesty, she says—"honesty with oneself and honesty, sometimes brutal honesty, with the other person." She cites one wife who declined to leave her job and join her photographer husband in his business. The woman knew it would be good for the business if she joined him. However, she also knew that he had personality traits that brought out the worst in her—he was forgetful and not at all concerned about details. She knew she would end up nagging him and that, even though he needed the nagging, he would come to resent it—and her. "Our marriage means more to me than that," she told Vago. "He's just going to have to find someone who is willing to nag him. After all, he's going to be paying that person."

DEFINING THE FUNDAMENTALS

Husbands and wives can learn something about preparing for a business from business partners who are not personal partners.

Writing in the May 1984 issue of *Nation's Business*, David H. Bennet of Dynamic Systems, Inc., a Reston, Virginia, engineering and management consulting company, describes the process he and his three co-founders went through before actually going into business together. Even though the four men had all known each other from eighteen months to eight years before they began to talk about forming a corporation, a key to their eventual success was that they took still more time to know each other well. "We already knew we had good rapport," says Bennet. "We also had a high regard for one another's professionalism: the ability to communicate, to accept responsibility, to get things done and to have open disagreement and still respect one another.

"Even so, we took another year, meeting as often as once a week, before we actually incorporated our business. We used this 'courting' period to be absolutely sure we all had a similar vision of what we wanted our company to be—that is, what kind of corporate culture we wanted to create." They decided they wanted DSI to be known for its integrity, its fast response, and its competence.

Like Tom Hubler and Steve Swartz, Bennet also advises would-be business partners to establish, ahead of time, the ground rules under which they will operate. "We spent a significant amount of time talking about how we would make decisions. Determining how we would handle basic issues was easy—we agreed immediately, for example, that we would do nothing illegal. But what about the gray areas? For example, how strongly did we value our independence over our cash flow?"

Not long after DSI was founded, a private firm offered it $25,000 to evaluate a system developed by the firm and used by the federal government. Bennet and his partners soon learned that the client wanted to have the last say in the report—that is, to make changes if it did not agree with DSI's findings. Still the report was to be published under DSI's name.

DSI was still very small and $25,000 was a lot of money. But if the client was to have the final word, the DSI partners knew their study would no longer be independent. They wanted to maintain the integrity of their company and they turned the contract down.

"Had we not talked about such a possibility the year before we started the company," says Bennet, "there could have been some strong differences of opinion and some very fundamental problems for our partnership.

"As it was, we were united in what our company stood for. And when the test came, we passed it. We were not just *talking* about integrity; we were willing to back our decision by turning down money."

Couples who can face issues like the one described by Bennet by coming to agreement ahead of time on what they want their business to be and defining fundamentals give themselves a head start. Every business brings with it the unknown. The more you agree on the basics before you start your business, the more you reduce the risk of conflict between you and your spouse afterward and the more you prepare yourselves to cope with the unexpected.

A couple might also consider the life span of their proposed business, or how long being in a particular enterprise might work for them.

"Businesses have their seven-year itch, too," says Vago. She and her partner "worked like a charm together for two to three years and then everything started to go blooey. By the fifth year, I was ready to kill him and by the seventh year, I simply had to get out. Almost anything can work if it's exciting enough and lucrative enough and absorbs people's energies enough; almost anything can work for two or three years. But what about 10 years from now?"

Perhaps you are not meant to be in a certain type of business for more than five years, she suggests. Some businesses are limited and don't provide stimulation beyond three to five years; after that, a couple may want to hire professional management or sell it and move on to other projects. Or the couple might anticipate what measures they can take so that they are not boxed in, year after year, in the same activities in their business. Each partner will have a need to grow and to operate at his or her highest level of competency. That could mean developing a new aspect of the business, such as adding a new service or product. Or the partners could even switch roles. Such steps can stimulate the couple's creativity and provide them with the opportunity to exercise new skills in their personal and professional development, according to Vago. "Not only will they be happy people but the business will benefit. Then the business can become a wellspring of satisfaction and nourishment for a very long time to come."

THE LAST WORD

Entrepreneurial couples themselves should have the final opportunity to offer the wisdom of their experience. In both the interviews and the questionnaires, the couples were asked what advice they would give to other couples who are considering going into business together. Here are some of their thoughts.

*   *   *

Valerie Bursten, Decorating Den: "I would tell them to be kind to each other. Respect and support each other. If you go into something with kindness and not expect *you* to become the winner, you just work better that way and you emerge as stronger people."

*   *   *

Steven Bursten, Decorating Den: "I would say, number one, ask yourself why you want to do it, and have some real hard discussion about why it's important and think through your motives. What's in it for you? What do you want to be in the long run? Once you figure out that it's really right, then the next thing is to be patient and kind, just like Valerie said, because there are going to be so many things that go wrong through the years. There are going to be so many mistakes."

* * *

Jan Erteszek, The Olga Company: "The first prerequisite would be that they have to respect each other or they're going to end up in an explosion." (Olga interrupted with, "That would be the *only* advice I'd give them.") Then they have to have preferably different talents so that they don't step on each other's territory. . . . The third thing they have to do, they have to be optimistic. They have to have faith and somehow live with disappointment, without being crushed." As entrepreneurs, he continued, they have to think in terms of being unique, because, as a start-up, they cannot compete on the basis of size; they have to do it on the basis of uniqueness. "And I say one more thing that pertains to all marriages anyway—that the marriage, particularly in business, is not a relationship of equality but a relationship of charity." Does that mean it's not a 50–50 proposition but that you each have to give 100 percent? "That's correct," Jan replied, and Olga added, "Right."

* * *

Elisabeth Aymett, Cecil's Messenger Service: "Talk a lot. Think about it three times over. If you have any doubts about yourself, or each other, don't do it. If you have to have a secure income, don't do it. Make sure of what you're getting into and that you can handle it. And when you get mad at each other (and you will), talk it out, resolve it, and *let it go.*"

* * *

Norma Goldberger, Akron Women's Clinic: "Decide the decision making process first. Use counselors whenever an improvement in the relationship is desired. Make a decision to be committed to each other no matter what and to limit criticism and blame no matter how it turns out in the end."

*　*　*

Robert Harnish, Cortina Inn: "Be ready to share the work load at home. For couples working together or both working separately, the old husband/wife roles change dramatically. On the job be dignified and caring and occasionally loving; it's a wonderful example for the staff. Sarcasm and jealousy have no place here. It poisons the relationship and the staff's attitude."

*　*　*

Eric Flaxenburg, French Creek Sheep & Wool Company: "I think the personalities have to be right. Just because you're married doesn't mean that the personalities are right for that kind of a joint endeavor. . . . You've got to like each other and you've got to respect each other. And if you can do that in a business partnership, your marriage should be more successful. It should really cement the marriage."

*　*　*

Leonard Johnson, Central Pipe & Supply Company: "I don't think it is any different for a husband and wife than it is for any other people who become partners. If you become equal partners, you better both bring equal contributions to the table. If you don't, then it shouldn't be equal. Just because you are married doesn't have a damn thing to do with running a business."

*　*　*

Chris Dickerman, C & W Seafood: "Couples that are going to think about going into business together have to make an extremely critical evaluation of the quality of their marriage, and the key word is honesty. It's honesty. Can you tolerate being in that person's physical space for extended periods of time?"

* * *

I. N. "Skip" Schatz, Virginia Adjustable-Bed Manufacturing Co.: "They should make sure their marriage is sound before they do it; they should make sure their relationship works. I've seen people have babies to try to hold marriages together; it obviously doesn't work. Going into business to try and keep a relationship together is not going to work either. If your relationship isn't sound to begin with, the extra strain of the business, I think, will drive it apart."

* * *

Warren Kaplan, Action Packets, Inc.: "Think of the benefits: planning vacations together; planning business trips together; eating out together; the excitement of an office love affair; the benefit of *not* feeling guilty by staying late or having sex in the afternoon; building a trust and a relationship together; sharing a business success."

* * *

Ginger Oppenheimer, Tim Boyer Ginger Oppenheimer Photojournalists: "Talk things out. Make sure you are clear with one another. Make your individual short- and long-term goals known to each other and discuss your business goals. TALK. TALK. TALK. Communication is a golden key. Don't let things build up; be honest and open. Devote time to each other; make the other person feel special. Make your personal lives of ultra-importance."

* * *

Margie Bryce, Hats in the Belfry: "I think it is important to look at your values. We didn't do this, but looking back on it, both Courtney and I came from the same kind of a background in terms of working class values. . . . [We were both taught] that if somebody pays you a dime to do something, you give them 20 cents worth of work.'' (She adds that she and her husband both bring that "hard-work attitude" to their business.)

* * *

Gail Husbands, H&H Research, Inc.: "It's the old pioneer spirit of 'two against the world.' That's how it seems at times, especially when you start out. Your family and friends may consider you crazy, stupid, or eccentric (or all of the above). You have to be determined enough that you will not be affected by others who would drag you down."

* * *

Sam W. Warren, retired publisher, The Northern Sun, Jackson, Mississippi: "There should be be a clear understanding as to who is overall boss (perhaps backed up by division of ownership), a clear division of responsibility and authority. It probably would help if one is an extravert (as is my wife) and one is an introvert (or ambivert), which I consider myself.

"And certainly it helps if one member is all understanding, sweet, and forgiving. Thank heavens for my wife, Marlene."

It is clear from the couples we have visited on these pages that there is no one model for success. And while the road is tough, it is rewarding. Courtney Garton of Hats in the Belfry says he thinks that being in business with his wife "is the most intimate kind of sharing that you can have in a relationship."

If you choose this adventurous road and find, some days, that it is particularly bumpy or you have taken a wrong turn and need to find your way again, keep in mind the optimistic words of photojournalist Tim Boyer, who says if he had a chance to do it all over again, he'd go into business with his wife even sooner. "Because this is gonna work and we'll be in fat city soon."

RESOURCES

Finding Help

Couples in growing businesses who are seeking counseling and other resources to help them build and maintain successful marriages and businesses may have trouble finding the right assistance. Since such couples are pathfinders, support services to meet their special needs are still rare. Some counselors who have gained national prominence as professionals with the background and skill to work with couples in business are listed here. They come from a variety of disciplines—including psychology, organizational development, business consulting, marriage and family therapy, business therapy, education, and law. You may learn, by word of mouth, of capable professionals in your own community. In seeking help, be sure to get references. Find out if the consultant has a good understanding of both relational issues and business issues. If you are not comfortable with one consultant, find someone else.

Because couple-owned businesses are a form of family business, or often become full-fledged family-held firms, some resources for family businesses are also listed. Some of the centers, such as those at universities, are nonprofit. Others, such as the Center for Family Business in Cleveland, are businesses. They may offer a variety of services, including seminars, research, consulting, and publications.

Consider also the possibility of contacting your trade association for assistance—or, if you run a franchise, your parent company. Some trade associations are beginning to conduct seminars and other programs on family business; others, perhaps, could be persuaded to sponsor programs especially for couples.

Also listed below are books and articles that offer insight into entrepreneurial couples and family businesses.

CONSULTANTS

RICHARD BECKHARD
Richard Beckhard Associates
320 Riverside Drive
New York, NY 10025
(212) 666-2222

DAVID BORK
Coda Corporation
7236 Ridge Road
Frederick, MD 21701
(301) 473-5200

MARDY GROTHE
Performance Improvement
Associates
75 Wells Road
Lincoln, MA 01773
(617) 259-8770

BARBARA S. HOLLANDER
Barbara S. Hollander Associates
1174 Harvard Road
Pittsburgh, PA 15205
(412) 922-8499

THOMAS M. HUBLER and STEPHEN B. SWARTZ
Hubler/Swartz and Associates, Inc.
701 Fourth Avenue South
Suite 810
Minneapolis, MN 55415
(612) 332-7920

MATILDE SALGANICOFF
Family Business Consultancy
556 North 23rd Street
Philadelphia, PA 19130
(215) 751-0396

MARTA VAGO
1421 Santa Monica Boulevard
Santa Monica, CA 90404
(213) 394-8602

KATHLEEN WISEMAN
1101 17th Street NW
Washington, DC 20006
(202) 659-2222

FAMILY BUSINESS CENTERS AND ORGANIZATIONS

CENTER FOR FAMILY BUSINESS
5862 Mayfield Road
P.O. Box 24286
Cleveland, OH 44124
(216) 442-0800

CENTER FOR PRIVATE ENTERPRISE
Loyola University of Chicago
820 North Michigan Avenue
Chicago, IL 60611
(312) 670-2892

NATIONAL FAMILY BUSINESS
COUNCIL
60 Revere Drive
Suite 500
Northbook, IL 60062
(312) 480-9574

THE WHARTON SCHOOL
Office of Executive Education
University of Pennsylvania
200 Vance Hall

Philadelphia, PA 19103
(215) 898-4470

YALE PROGRAM FOR THE STUDY
OF FAMILY FIRMS
Yale School of Organization
and Management
Box 1A
New Haven, CT 06520
(203) 436-2428

BOOKS AND ARTICLES

Alcorn, Pat B. *Success and Survival in the Family-Owned Business.* New York: McGraw-Hill, 1982.

Bach, George R., and Wyden, Peter. *The Intimate Enemy: How to Fight Fair in Love and Marriage.* New York: William Morrow, 1968.

Bennet, David H. "Making a Partnership Work." *Nation's Business,* May 1984, pp. 66–67.

Bork, David. *Family Business, Risky Business.* New York: AMACOM, 1986.

Danco, Léon A. *Beyond Survival: A Guide for the Business Owner and His Family.* Cleveland: Center for Family Business, 1982.

Danco, Léon A. *Inside the Family Business.* Englewood Cliffs, NJ: Prentice-Hall, 1982.

Danco, Léon A., and Jonovic, Donald J. *Outside Directors in the Family Owned Business.* Cleveland: Center for Family Business, 1981.

Israel, Lee. *Estée Lauder: Beyond the Magic.* New York: Macmillan, 1985.

Lauder, Estée. *Estée: A Success Story.* New York: Random House, 1985.

Miller, Sherod, Wackman, Daniel, Nunnally, Elam, and Saline, Carol. *Straight Talk: A New Way to Get Closer to Others by Saying What You Really Mean.* New York: Rawson, 1981, 1982.

Nelton, Sharon. "Making Sure Your Business Outlasts You." *Nation's Business,* January 1986, pp. 32–38.

Nelton, Sharon. "Strategies for Family Firms." *Nation's Business,* June 1986, pp. 20–28.

Rosenblatt, Paul C., de Mik, Leni, Anderson, Roxanne Marie, and Johnson, Patricia A. *The Family in Business.* San Francisco: Jossey-Bass, 1985.

Sommer, Elyse, and Sommer, Mike. *The Two-Boss Business: The Joys and Pitfalls of Working and Living Together—And Still Remaining Friends.* New York: Butterick, 1980.

Stern, Milton H. *Inside the Family-Held Business: A Practical Guide for Entrepreneurs and Their Advisors.* New York: Law & Business/Harcourt Brace Jovanovich, 1986.

Wojahn, Ellen. "Divorce Entrepreneurial Style." *Inc.*, March 1986, pp. 55–64.

INDEX